Feminism and the Politics of Literary Reputation

Feminism and the Politics of Literary Reputation

The Example of Erica Jong

CHARLOTTE TEMPLIN

 UNIVERSITY PRESS OF KANSAS

Published by the University Press of Kansas (Lawrence, Kansas 66049), which was organized by the Kansas Board of Regents and is operated and funded by Emporia State University, Fort Hays State University, Kansas State University, Pittsburg State University, the University of Kansas, and Wichita State University

Library of Congress Cataloging-in-Publication Data

Templin, Charlotte.
   Feminism and the politics of literary reputation : the example of
Erica Jong / Charlotte Templin.
     p. cm.
   Includes bibliographical references and index.
   ISBN 0-7006-0708-0 (cloth)
    1. Jong, Erica—Criticism and interpretation—History.
   2. Feminism and literature—United States—History—20th century.
   3. Politics and literature—United States—History—20th century.
   4. Women and literature—United States—History—20th century.
   5. Criticism—United States—History—20th century. 6. Authorship—
Sex differences. 7. Canon (Literature). I. Title.
PS3560.056Z89 1995
818'.5409—dc20   94-23529

British Library Cataloguing in Publication Data is available.

Printed in the United States of America

10 9 8 7 6 5 4 3 2 1

The paper used in this publication meets the minimum requirements of the American National Standard for Permanence of Paper for Printed Library Materials Z39.48–1984.

Contents

PREFACE / ix

ACKNOWLEDGMENTS / xi

1 Can It Be Good Literature If It's Funny, Sexy, and Written by a Woman? / 1

2 Evaluative Communities in the Reception of *Fear of Flying* / 26

3 *How to Save Your Own Life:* Mass Culture, Gender, and Cultural Authority / 65

4 *Fanny:* The Anatomy of a Literary Success / 103

5 Jong in a Postfeminist Age: The Last Three Novels / 129

6 Jong among the Academics / 167

Conclusion: Literary Reputation in the Real World / 182

NOTES / 189

BIBLIOGRAPHY / 205

INDEX / 221

*For my mother
and my sisters*

Preface

My work is related to a significant body of work in English studies that focuses attention on the reader as subject rather than solely on the literary work as object, and sees that work as constituted by the reader. "'Tis the good reader that makes the good book," says Ralph Waldo Emerson, acknowledging the important role of the reader but invoking a nineteenth-century epistemology: the good book has determinate value but must be read carefully and sympathetically to be understood or appreciated. Twentieth-century theory revises this view and makes possible the kind of analysis found in this book. I will omit the list of those who have taught us that truth is made and not found and mention only my debt to Barbara Herrnstein Smith, who has turned our attention from interpretation to evaluation. She has greatly influenced the conception of this study.

The readers I focus on are institutional readers—those who have been in a position to establish a cultural agenda and whose personal responses as readers have been invested with institutional authority. Those readers are, for the most part, book reviewers (and the editors behind them) but also other cultural authorities, including critics and academics. In arguing that literary reputation cannot be understood apart from local and specific historical interests, my work is a part of the project of recent years to examine reputation as a contingent phenomenon, emergent from social relations and related to particular historical and institutional contexts. The example of Erica Jong provides an unusual opportunity for examining the literary reputation of a woman writer in the widest possible context. Jong's subject was a magnet for drawing explicit discussion of social and cultural themes into the reviews. The *succès de scandale* of her first novel also insured that her reputation would be formed in the context of media image and information.

I first became attracted to this theoretical approach because I saw in it a way to understand the evaluations and reputations of women writers. After many years of discussions and arguments with friends, colleagues, and students about whether various works by women authors were ''good''—good enough to be compared with works by male masters, good enough to merit inclusion in course syllabi—I welcomed the opportunity for demystification offered by the new way of looking at value, evaluation, and reputation. But analyzing literary value as I have done does not in any way diminish the worth or importance of literature; in fact, my analysis demonstrates the supreme ''value'' of literature in people's lives.

My approach dictated that I learn as much about Jong's institutional readers as possible. Some of these, such as John Updike and Alfred Kazin, are public figures, while others were impossible to track down, and I could know them only through their reviews. I tried to get inside their skins, so to speak, to imagine how each experienced the novel. The most important factor in reaching an understanding of each reader was the information s/he gave me in the review itself. The reviewers revealed, sometimes explicitly and sometimes implicitly, their values, their ideological biases, and sometimes even their life experiences. I also tried to find other sources—books, articles, other reviews—to frame their reviews and establish a historical and cultural context for the reviewers' evaluations. The biographical data in my footnotes come from standard reference sources or personal inquiries. My inquiries were not always successful, and biographical information on some reviewers is incomplete or missing entirely. Of course I was able to establish the reviewers' identities, in the full sense of the word, only imperfectly. I apologize to any reviewer I have misunderstood, but I can't possibly know everything that enters into a reviewer's response, just as I can't always fully account for my own. I tried to include all reviews substantive enough to give me something to work with in making an analysis, but I realize that there are reviews I have not found.

Acknowledgments

I am grateful to the many people who made completion of this work possible. I want to thank my colleagues Alice Friman and Bruce Gentry for many years of help and encouragement and especially for reading my manuscript to each other in their car during an extended auto trip. I also appreciate the support of many other colleagues at the University of Indianapolis. Special thanks to my students, who have done much to stimulate my thinking and who have demonstrated in various ways that literary reputation is socially constructed.

I want to thank Barbara Herrnstein Smith, who directed the NEH Summer Seminar on Value and Evaluation at the University of Pennsylvania in 1985 in which this project was conceived. Thanks also to the members of the seminar and to the National Endowment for the Humanities.

This project could not have been completed without the help of librarians at the following institutions: the University of Indianapolis, Indiana University, the University of Pennsylvania, and the British Library, especially the Newspaper Division. Special thanks to Christine Guyonneau of the University of Indianapolis Library and to Frances Wilhoit of the Journalism Library at Indiana University.

I thank Erica Jong for responding generously to my requests for information and especially for granting three interviews. I was greatly encouraged by her interest in the subject of the woman writer and literary reputation, both historical and contemporary. Daphne Patai provided valuable suggestions and greatly needed encouragement during a crucial period.

Cheri Burton and Shirley Charles provided essential secretarial help. I am grateful to the University of Indianapolis for a sabbatical leave during the first half of 1986, which gave me the opportunity to do the basic research for the study, and for a summer research grant in 1989.

Thanks also to Myrna Goldenberg, Annette Zilversmit, Gary Spencer, Peggy Marshall, Susan Fischer, and Dorothy Deering, and to the anonymous readers of the manuscript, who made many helpful suggestions. A portion of Chapter 3 appeared in the *Centennial Review*, and I gratefully acknowledge permission to reprint.

1 / Can It Be Good Literature If It's Funny, Sexy, and Written by a Woman?

As this book will abundantly illustrate, the reception of Erica Jong's work has been noteworthy for a recurrent *ad feminam* strain in reviews and articles.[1] Jong is not alone in having been judged as a woman rather than as a writer, however. Ever since women have been involved in the creation of art, and certainly since the Restoration and the eighteenth century, when English women began to write for money, the writing woman has been a target for abuse of the most virulent kind. From the beginning, critical judgments of women's art have been colored by society's notions of what is proper for a woman—or by society's conception of the ''proper woman.'' Attacks on the character of women writers appeared as soon as the writers—Aphra Behn and her contemporaries, who wrote plays, fiction, and poetry—themselves.

As Janet Todd explains in *The Sign of Angelica: Women, Writing and Fiction, 1660-1800*, a writing woman was from the beginning seen as guilty of a specifically sexual impropriety: ''Verbal antics were confounded with sexual and the pen became a female instrument of lubricity'' (33). According to Todd, when women entered the profession of literature, they were portrayed as Amazons, whores, or witches, the three great types of offensive—because autonomous—female characters in Restoration satire. Wit, associated with erotic impropriety, was in itself suspect, and woe to the woman, like Aphra Behn, who made sexual impropriety the subject of her work. ''Sexual impropriety in literature indicated it in life'' (41) in the eyes of the men of the Restoration, who projected onto women their obsession with sex and the guilt and fear evoked by their own sexuality.

Joanna Russ, who in *How to Suppress Women's Writing* catalogues all the ways in which writing by women is denigrated, would place the criticisms leveled at Behn in the seventeenth century—and Jong in the twentieth—in the category "pollution of agency." The first line of attack against a woman who writes is to deny that she in fact wrote the work in question, says Russ. (Her husband, brother, father wrote it.) But if it can't be denied that she did write it, one can always argue that she shouldn't have:

> An alternative to denying female agency in art is to pollute the agency—that is, to promulgate the idea that women make themselves ridiculous by creating art, or that writing or painting is immodest (just as displaying oneself on the stage is immodest) and hence impossible for any decent woman, or that creating art shows a woman up as abnormal, neurotic, unpleasant and hence unlovable. (25)

Judging by the criticisms leveled against Jong's predecessors, "coarseness" has been rampant among writing females for a long time. Anne Brontë's *The Tenant of Wildfell Hall* is criticized for "coarseness and brutality," and Elizabeth Barrett Browning is said to be "often . . . more coarsely masculine than any other woman writer" (quoted in Russ 27). *Jane Eyre*, comments Elaine Showalter, summarizing contemporary reviews, is "a masterpiece if written by a man, shocking or disgusting if written by a woman" (quoted in Russ 27). In the twentieth century, Anne Sexton is castigated for a poem called "Menstruation at Forty." In a review of *Live or Die*, Louis Simpson charges Sexton with impropriety so extreme as to be intolerable: "Her previous books were interesting, but now mere self-dramatization has grown a habit. A poem titled 'Menstruation at Forty' was the straw that broke this camel's back" (Middlebrook 264).

Russ speculates that the modern characterization "confessional," applied to women in a derogatory way, is in its essence a charge of pollution of agency. Following Julia Penelope's analysis of the category "confessional," Russ notes that "such writing is *shameful* and *too personal* (the writer should not have felt or done such things in the first place, and if she had to do such things or feel that way, she certainly should not have told anyone about it)" (29). Although men (John Donne, Gerard Manley Hopkins) are allowed the expression of strong feelings and extreme states of mind, such expression is improper for women, with the most outrage evoked by the expression of two things: overt sexuality and anger. The requirement that women be chaste, which Virginia Woolf made much of in *A Room of One's Own*, is still with us. What Russ calls "pollution of agency via unchastity" (105) is the characterization made of Jong in a nutshell. Jong's critics participate in a centuries-long tradition in asserting that "coarse" writing (by what one must assume is a coarse woman) is not literature.

At one point in her study, Russ does mention Jong and quotes approvingly Jong's comment on the use by male critics of the term confessional: "It's become a putdown term for women, a sexist label for women's poetry" (29). But Russ herself indulges in a mild denigration of Jong. She asserts that writing that was formerly rebuked for impropriety is now called unacceptable because of its confessional nature, or in other words, "pollution of agency has only shifted its ground" (29). Russ then explains how it is that works such as Jong's *Fear of Flying* and Lisa Alther's *Kinflicks* have won approval:

> *Fear of Flying* and *Kinflicks* are tolerated because they are sexually (and economically) dishonest, women "talking dirty" in a way that's acceptably cute, just as Lois Gould's *Such Good Friends* is acceptably masochistic, like Joan Didion's passive, depressed heroines whose unhappiness is praised by the author as a sign of special, feminine sensitivity. (29)

I confess I find it depressing to read a putdown of four female authors (all of whom at this point have acquired some degree of recognition) in a book that undertakes to defend women writers against unjustified criticisms. The adjective "cute" (and the word suggests immediately the ploy of damning with faint praise) was applied to Jong in at least one instance, cited immediately below, but "acceptably cute" by no means describes the reaction of Jong's reviewers to her work. Reviewers have heaped upon her criticisms as cruel and insulting as anything Russ records in her book as having been meted out to other women.

One of the most appalling (but by no means unique) reviews Jong received (and it is a review of Jong rather than her work) is a review by D. Keith Mano in the *National Review* of her second novel, *How to Save Your Own Life*. Its undertone of violence—even sexual violence—is reminiscent of the old practice of putting uppity or rebellious women in their places through sexual intimidation. Attempting to redefine female sexuality, as Jong did, is perhaps the ultimate rebellion—and is punished accordingly.

Mano's review begins with a reference to Jong's Jewishness:

> I'm treed; it irks me no end. I have to—have to—ravage Erica Jong's new book. Irksome, because this is just what Erica wanted all along: the barracuda treatment. I mean, a man and a Gentile blitzing her: oh pogromsville and joy. . . . She'll relish this flop the way Al Goldstein secretly relishes going to Leavenworth for public lewdness. Discipline is love; American society has been too permissive. Erica, I love you. *How to Save Your Own Life* is Christawful. An aphid could have written it. (498)

Later in the review Mano expresses sympathy for the "hapless Chinese husband" of a figure he calls "Erica-Isadora-Candida," in reference to author and the fictional protagonists, and comments, "If I were Mr. Jong I would have decked her long ago, or gotten out a Tong contract" (498). *Fear of Flying* was "cute as baton-twirlers" Mano says, but the new work is "sump gush" (498). In almost every comment, Mano makes reference to Jong's gender: "Erica writes, Lord, just like a *woman*. And that's my very best pejorative" (498); "this time, as the self-proclaimed 'amanuensis to the Zeitgeist,' she has managed to make being a Ms. a big mistake" (498); and "Literature is risk. Erica didn't accept the risk: unsurprisingly, she has no balls" (498). Mano doesn't like Jong's subject matter: her treatment of the institution of marriage and her assertive sexuality ("Erica turned herself into a sideshow geek. Look, there's the woman who has to masturbate three times per day"). There are several points of interest in this review: the idea that Jong will like being attacked, the violence of the language, the repudiations of an active female sexuality, and the references to male anatomy (Jong has presumably tried to be male).

As my discussion of Jong's reviews will demonstrate, Jong's sin is not being a proper woman. The one period in which criticism of her softened was when she became a mother, which happened during the writing of her third novel, *Fanny*. Not only was *Fanny* well received, but journalistic articles about her at this time portrayed a new Jong: the happy mother and suburban matron. There were a number of reasons that *Fanny* was a success, but the fact that Jong was viewed as behaving in acceptably feminine fashion at the time cannot be totally discounted as an explanation for the more benign attitude toward her. Margaret Atwood, who has often been the subject of outspoken criticism in Canada, and was so especially in the early years of her career, has commented that attitudes toward her turned around completely when her daughter was born:

> People's attitudes toward me changed remarkably in many cases once I became a MOTHER. You wouldn't believe it. It's not that I'm a different person. I'm exactly the same as I always was, pretty well, give or take a little evolutionary change along the way. But it's not as though becoming a mother suddenly renders you this warm, cozy, cookie-handing-out individual, if you weren't before. (65)

Russ also includes anecdotes detailing advice given to young female writers to make not books, but babies. When Ellen Glasgow showed her manuscript to a publisher, he said

> he wanted no more writing from women, especially from women young enough to have babies. . . . "The best advice I can give you . . . is to stop writing and go back to the South and have some babies. . . . The greatest woman is not the woman who has written the finest books but . . . the woman who has had the finest babies." (quoted in Russ 11–12)

In our day, it is no longer politically correct to tell women writers to go home and have babies, but the change in the attitudes of critics that writers report after they have had babies testifies that the old values are still with us. Unfortunately, however, the she-did-the-right-thing-and-had-a-baby effect wears off. The fact that Jong had a daughter didn't significantly alter her ultimate literary reputation. She mentions Molly, her thirteen-year-old daughter, in *The Devil at Large: Erica Jong on Henry Miller*, commenting that the fear of AIDS has replaced the fear of pregnancy for her daughter's generation. But being the mother of a teenage daughter didn't prevent some reviewers, such as Walter Kendrick of the *New York Times Book Review*, from making outspoken personal criticisms of Jong.

In America attacks on women writers became epidemic in the nineteenth century when male writers felt threatened by a rising tide of female authors. Two writers who endured attacks remarkably similar to Jong's are Sara Payson Willis (or Fanny Fern) and Kate Chopin. Willis walked out of a disastrous marriage, and, thrown on her own resources, employed her pen to support herself and two daughters. In *Ruth Hall* she portrayed an independent heroine whose life story resembled her own, and she used her gifts of satire to indict marriage as an institution and the cruelty and hypocrisy of society. When Fanny Fern (as she came to refer to herself) was pronounced "not sufficiently endowed with female delicacy" (quoted in Warren x), she was deeply hurt: "And how I *did* cry if an editor reviewed *me* personally, instead of my book, in his book notices. How I used to wish I were Tom Hyer, or Jack Sayers, or some high and mighty muscular pugilist, to make mincemeat of the coward, who wouldn't have dared to 'hit one of his own size' in that sneaking fashion" (quoted in Warren xviii). Fanny Fern wrote a regular newspaper column and was the most sought-after newspaper writer of her day. Like Jong, she acquired both celebrity and wealth from her writings. But her novel, published in 1854, dropped from sight for a century, receiving respectful attention only when it was rediscovered by feminists in the 1980s.

Kate Chopin's *The Awakening*, a novel dealing with a woman's search for sexual and personal freedom, is now regarded as highly successful aesthetically. But when it appeared in 1899, it was condemned by reviewers as "morbid," "essentially vulgar," and "gilded dirt" (cited in Showalter, *Sister's Choice* 65). Chopin's novel claimed new territory in the exploration of women's sexuality, and as a result the novel was banned in St. Louis and criticized across the nation. The novel has now been accorded the distinction of being included in its entirety in several major teaching anthologies, after having been rediscovered by male critics from France and Norway (in the 1950s) and subsequently championed by feminist critics.

It could be said that Jong's work combines characteristics of *Ruth Hall* and *The Awakening* by uniting a satirical portrait of a male-dominated society and increased candor about female sexuality. Attitudes from the nineteenth century are still with us, but the trajectory of

Jong's reputation suggests that in one way there has been a change for the worse: the powerful influence of the media (both print and electronic) in the twentieth century has had an important effect on Jong's reputation, constructing a negative image of her so powerful that it took on a life of its own.

However, critical and theoretical advances now suggest new ways to theorize literary value and reputation and make the present moment a good time to focus on the reputations of women writers. With theory that is attentive to the social contexts of literature, we are better prepared to understand the vagaries of literary reception and to suggest a new framework for understanding the reception of popular and/or controversial work by women writers.

Some recent studies of major writers, which make use of poststructural theory, problematize the notion of literary reputation. These studies discard the traditional idea that literary reputation comes about when a work of genius, triumphant in a process called "the test of time," makes its inevitable way toward recognition, like cream rising to the top of bottle of milk. Under the old paradigm, "great" works are naturalized as bearers of intrinsic merit. Their relation to history is largely obscured as is their embeddedness in social relations and institutional power, and thus they are not seen as owing their status to a process of selection. The new studies—of figures such as George Orwell, Thomas Hardy, Sappho, William Faulkner, and Willa Cather—put literary works back into the historical process. In *Creating Faulkner's Reputation*, Lawrence H. Schwartz reveals a complex web of personal and institutional influence in what he describes as the reinvention of Faulkner. Although he had been narrowly viewed as a regionalist, Faulkner was refashioned as an existential modernist in 1945–1950 in order to serve the needs of Cold War intellectuals for an American writer of the stature of European modernists. On the other hand, Cather suffered a loss of reputation in the World War I years, according to Sharon O'Brien, when critics who had previously praised her castigated her writing as lacking manliness and strength.

Dependent on institutional and socio-cultural context, literary reputation is constructed in history and can be studied and analyzed. Those works that are the monuments of our culture, such as *Hamlet, War and Peace*, and that perennial favorite among the undeniably "great," the works of Homer, seem to have a uniqueness and self-sufficiency that places their value beyond question. But they all entered the literary universe as new books do today, unknown and unsung, candidates for immortality or, more likely, for the dust heap or the publisher's shredder.

In her important study of value, *Contingencies of Value: Alternative Perspectives for Critical Theory*, Barbara Herrnstein Smith describes the "dynamics of endurance" through which such works maintain their exalted status. Ultimately they create the cultural values that give them their worth: "The canonical work begins increasingly not merely to *survive within* but to *shape and create* the culture in which its value is produced and transmitted and, for that very reason, to perpetuate the conditions of its own flourishing. Nothing endures like endurance" (50). Loyalty to long-time favorite works of literature can work miracles of sympathetic re-creation of value, as George Eliot knew long ago: "The text, whether of prophet or poet, expands for whatever we can put into it, and even his bad grammar is sublime" (37), she writes in *Middlemarch*. Any work that has reached the pinnacle where endurance perpetuates endurance has gone through a complicated history of evaluation. Its value has been created and maintained through innumerable acts of evaluation by publishers, literary critics, and all those who quote, cite, praise, or purchase the work or perform any other type of evaluative activity, but preeminently by its academic users, who are institutionally placed to give the work a series of nudges toward immortality by assigning it in courses, writing about it, and including it in anthologies and on reading lists.[2]

If reputation is dependent on institutional influences and socio-cultural fit, it follows that value itself is contingent. Works have different value for different people, and the matter of whose evaluation becomes a "public" assessment is a function of power relations. Historically, women have had little influence on the institutions that confer reputation: the publishing industry, the press, the academy. For many years, women simply were not permitted the role of "institutional readers," those whose personal voices are magnified by their institutional affiliations. But in recent years women have joined the ranks of institutional readers, with the result that the reception histories of some writers, largely women, have been affected in very interesting ways.

Along with "reputation" and "value," "meaning" has been problematized as well. In the new paradigm, individual texts and literary history are seen as having no meaning apart from interpretations created within historical contexts. I do not have the space here to trace the full history of this paradigm shift, but it can be summarized as the claim that truth is made and not found. In *Is There a Text in This Class?* Stanley Fish asserts, "all objects are made and not found, and . . . they are made by interpretive strategies we set in motion" (331).

The important point is that one cannot look to the text per se—its formal elements—as the sole source of meaning. As Cary Nelson writes, "We cannot jettison our cultural and disciplinary assumptions and psychological needs to perceive some level of sheer unmediated textual materiality. If we could do so, the text 'in itself,' to echo Jacques Derrida, would be nothing more than black marks on a white page. An uninterpreted text would have no meaning at all" (5). The creation of meaning is a social process, and texts are the sites around which the social act of creating meaning takes place. Texts are unstable and open until meanings are attributed to them in a social process governed by contemporary needs. Jong's portrayal of the new woman of feminism—a woman who experienced herself as subject, with both sexual and intellectual dimensions—became a site around which the struggle over women's nature and role, and indeed women's value, was enacted.

Importantly, the process of determining meaning is intimately connected with the process of determining literary value. The social act of interpreting Jong's novels intersects with the attribution of value. Thus the value of Jong's works is intricately related to how some other questions, fundamentally social in nature, are answered, such as "What is a proper sexual role for women?" or "How should a female author or narrator talk about sex?"

We are on the cusp of a paradigm shift, and it is not surprising that traditionalists feel threatened by those who promote new ways of doing literary history. In the view of the old-style literary historians, canon formation comes about through the actions of the canonized themselves. In an article about the political nature of the challenges to the canon, editor William Phillips of the *Partisan Review* writes:

The so-called canon has never been decided by popular vote, or by academics, or by political pressures. Figures in various fields have been perpetuated by various figures. Thus Plato and Aristotle and

Descartes, for example, have formed the basis of subsequent developments in philosophy. So too, writers like Homer, Shakespeare,
John Donne, and George Eliot, and so on up to the present, have
been made part of the literary tradition by subsequent writers. (176)

Hugh Kenner gives a similar explanation, stating that the modernist
canon was made "in part by readers like me; in part . . . by later writers
choosing and inventing ancestors" but "chiefly . . . by the canonized
themselves, who were apt to be aware of a collective enterprize, and repeatedly acknowledged one another" (quoted in Newcomb 7). From
the perspective of the revisionist literary historian, Phillips and Kenner
are simply acknowledging the "dynamics of endurance" discussed earlier. Their accounts leave out the cultural and institutional dynamics
that made individual works visible in the first place. Since the accounts beg the crucial questions of how and why choices are made,
they fail to explain the dynamics of canon formation. That creative artists choose canons in some universe of pure art, removed from social
and cultural conditions, is a highly dubious proposition.

   Creative writers often do play a role in establishing the reputations of
other writers, however, as we see in the example of the influence of
John Updike and Henry Miller on Jong's reputation. Recognized writers
have tremendous cultural authority and can, as book reviewers or in
other ways, single out a new writer for a special kind of attention. But,
like other agents in the reputation-making process, they must work
within institutional structures, and their recommendations are articu-
lated from within historical and cultural conditions. Current works of
revisionist literary history may recognize the important contributions
of writers of reputation to the success of other writers, but they also
deal with a host of other influences—book reviewers, literary critics,
university professors, journals, foundations, the film industry, and even
libraries housing writers' papers (or the librarians that control them).

   The contemporary literary scene offers an unparalleled opportunity
to study the social, cultural, and institutional forces that influence,
and indeed determine, reputation. In an article in the *South Atlantic
Review* John Timberman Newcomb supports the idea that evaluations
that produce canons take place "not in the minds of a few great individuals but in a wide variety of concrete institutions" (9). Newcomb,
who reminds us that there are many canons, asserts that we should

treat canons as ''descriptions of multiple, often opposed evaluative operations of various overlapping groups of actors over a defined span of time'' (11). By turning our attention to the contemporary scene, we can focus closely on the groups of agents engaged in various and conflicting evaluative activities and draw conclusions both about how evaluations are made and what effect they have over time. In the case of Jong, for example, we can trace close to twenty years of evaluation, beginning with the publication of *Fear of Flying* in 1973.

For the student of literary reputation, the story of Jong's reception and evaluation offers riches beyond the dreams of scholarly avarice. Jong began her literary career as a poet but burst on the scene as a novelist in 1973 with *Fear of Flying*, a book that simultaneously made publishing history and became a document in the women's movement. To be sure, Jong's career was remarkable in terms of sales and critical notice, but it was extraordinary in terms of the media attention it received, attention of such magnitude and intensity that it transformed her literary career into public spectacle. Jong's reception provides data for analysis of all the issues involving positioning by reviewers, acceptance by academics, and the influence of institutional and social factors in creating literary reputation, but it offers something more. It opens a window on two significant topics: the role of an important social and cultural movement—the feminist movement—in influencing literary reputation, and the role of popular media—print and electronic—in creating and projecting images that can decisively affect literary reputation. A study of Erica Jong's reputation is also a study of the cultural history of the late twentieth century. It teaches us a great deal about how feminism affected the consciousnesses of a group of women who welcomed it enthusiastically and how it affected other women and men who responded with fear and anger. It also brings into focus the subject of celebrity and shows us the American cultural need for the famous: our need to raise them up as we project our desires on them and then, in an inevitable next step, to cast them down to assuage our failures. We can explore, through Jong's example, the interesting ways in which this cultural history figures in literary reputation.

Because Jong's novels are utilized so frequently to explore readers' feelings about feminism or to provide a public forum for the discussion of feminism, one must conclude that the response to her novels is inseparable from the social reception and construction of feminism.

Jong's work was seen as highly eligible to represent feminism because of the nature of her protagonist and her candid treatment of female sexuality. Isadora, the sexy, witty protagonist of three of Jong's novels was taken, by both admirers and detractors, as representative of the ''new woman'' of feminism. Jong's explicit treatment of sexuality prompted many to accord Jong the role of feminism's whipping boy (or girl) but also won the approval of those who welcomed the entry of the woman novelist—especially the woman dealing with female sexuality—into the domain of sexual fiction. Her first novel, *Fear of Flying*, became loaded with such cultural weight that an association with feminism—specifically with the feminism of sexual politics—would follow Jong throughout her career.

The fact that Jong came to be represented by a media image may be the most important single influence on her reputation. Jong's mediatization and her subsequent—and related—identification with low culture makes the story of Jong's reputation a particularly instructive one for our time. My examination of the evaluation of Erica Jong's novels is based mainly on book reviews, along with treatment of her work in critical essays and books and references to her work by scholars and cultural figures and mass media spokespersons (though, in terms of reputation, statements by the latter have force largely as they affect the former). Through this analysis, I am able to give a general account of literary value and a description of the early stages of the process of reputation formation. I have chosen a series of moments to tap into the evaluative universe enveloping Jong, and in this way I have simplified Jong's evaluative history enough to be able to give an account. The evaluative process is continuous and constantly shifting, and each evaluator changes from moment to moment as he or she acts and then is acted upon. Examining the reviews of each novel allows us to identify significant moments in Jong's evaluative history—the only way such history can be written. (The literary historian must stay the flux for a moment to tell the story.) All the evaluators I cite are institutional readers. Among these authorities the largest group by far are reviewers. Others are academics, who treat Jong's work in a scholarly context. There are, of course, also academics among Jong's reviewers, but I have not found, as Carey Kaplan and Ellen Cronan Rose did in the case of Doris Lessing (see Chapter 5 of *The Canon and the Common Reader*), examples of the same persons reviewing Jong's books and later writing about them in scholarly works. Others commenting on Jong are journalists—the literary journalists among the reviewers and also journalists who write feature stories. The reviewers are all cultural spokespersons, even cultural authorities, because they speak for institutions (including the media). Literary reputations are made in the real world in which institutional imperatives in one entity affect the decisions and viewpoints in other institutions in a complex interactive process.

The reviewing process, coming, of course, right after publication, is an important stage in the valuational history of works of literature. There are, however, few studies of book reviewing. Under the old paradigms of literary history, book reviewing was not regarded as very important. To those who accept an objectivist, essentialist notion of literature, a book review of a subsequently canonized work is simply a curiosity, in Northrup Frye's words, "leisure class gossip" (18), a possible source of amusement or contempt for those who failed to recognize the work's "true value" or, at best, a way to identify the true critics of the past. Similarly, a review of a new work is of limited significance since the "test of time" is all. In contrast, revisionist literary historians must take the book review very seriously as the first stage in the creation of value and as an indication of how an author will be read by subsequent readers.

One useful examination of the role of book reviewing is Richard Ohmann's study of the formation of a canon in American fiction in 1960–1975. Ohmann identifies the factors accounting for a literary success as hardback sales (an upper-middle-class influence), best-sellerdom, and, a significant factor in advancing the novel to the precanonical stage, favorable attention from reviewers in a number of leading intellectual journals. The last stage is promotion by the academic community—assigning the work in courses and writing about the work in academic journals.

Ohmann lists eight journals that have special influence in forming cultural judgments: the *New York Review of Books*, the *New York Times Book Review*, the *New Yorker*, *Commentary*, *Saturday Review*, the *Partisan Review*, the *New Republic*, and *Harper's*. In a survey of leading intellectuals, these journals were cited most often for their influence. Ohmann's findings indicate that a novel "had to win at least the divided approval of these arbiters in order to remain in the universe of literary discourse, once past the notoriety of best-sellerdom" (205):

Of these journals the *New York Times Book Review* is especially important in the early stages in bringing a work to the attention of the audience that gives the work its first visibility.

Ohmann reports that the *New York Times Book Review* has several times the readership of any comparable literary periodical. Among these readers are

> most bookstore managers, deciding what to stock, and librarians, deciding what to buy, not to mention the well-to-do, well-educated east-coasters who led in establishing hardback best-sellers. The single most important boost a novel could get was a prominent review in the Sunday *New York Times*—better a favorable one than an unfavorable one, but better an unfavorable one than none at all. (202)

Not surprisingly, Ohmann tells us, the large publishing firms make great efforts to interest the *Times* in their new publications. Ohmann also found a correlation between review space in the *Times* accorded a publishing house and advertising space purchased by that house. The *Times* also has an intellectual readership. According to a study done by Julie Hoover and Charles Kadushin, cited by Ohmann, 75 percent of elite intellectuals (including, of course, college professors) read the *New York Times Book Review* regularly.

Even though its readership is smaller, the *New York Review of Books* is particularly influential among intellectuals. Ohmann reports that according to the Hoover-Kadushin study, the *New York Review of Books* was more important to the intellectual elite than any other journal, mentioned twice as often by the intellectuals surveyed as the next contender, the *New Republic*.

Of these eight influential journals mentioned by Ohmann, reviews of Jong's novels have appeared in seven (all but the *Partisan Review*). Jong's first three novels were each reviewed in at least five of the eight. The fourth novel, *Parachutes & Kisses*, was reviewed in two and the fifth, *Serenissima*, and the most recent, *Any Woman's Blues*, in one. The *New York Times Book Review* has been particularly attentive, reviewing every novel, once with a rave review (*Fanny*) and always with the respect of attention, if not unmixed praise. That this publication has continued to review every novel is probably owing to the interest in

Jong on the part of its readership, a more general readership (the upper-middle-class readers whom Ohmann identifies as the first gatekeepers in the process of determining literary value) than that of the more narrowly intellectual journals. At least one highly favorable review has also appeared in three journals: the New Yorker, Saturday Review, and the New Republic. The journal Ohmann singles out for special attention, the New York Review of Books, has given Jong largely unfavorable reviews, with extremely negative responses to How to Save Your Own Life and Fanny. On the whole the attention given to Jong's work by these eight journals should be called the "divided approval" that Ohmann speaks of as necessary to advance a work to the next evaluative stage. And indeed, in the 1983 article Ohmann includes Jong among the forty-eight authors whose work, by his measures, had advanced to the precanonical stage.

Jong's books have also been reviewed in alternative press publications such as Spare Rib, a British feminist magazine, and the American journal, New Directions for Women. With the publication of Fear of Flying, Jong became a popular novelist and a media celebrity, and her subsequent novels attracted the attention of commercial publications such as People and Playboy.

Besides Ohmann's work, the only significant examination of book reviewing available is a study done in Britain by Women in Publishing (Margaret Cooter et al.) entitled Reviewing the Reviews: A Woman's Place on the Book Page. This study illustrates the stake of marginalized groups in the reviewing process. By counting and measuring book review space and interviewing authors and literary editors, the researchers found a bias against women in book reviewing. They pay attention to such matters as column inches given to women, placement of reviews on the page, gender of reviewers, and genres considered appropriate for women (preeminently fiction) as determined by which female-authored books were chosen for review. That men are the favored sex on the book review pages is troubling to the authors of this study, who see important connections between reviewing and long-term recognition.

The study of book reviewing allows us to see in operation the social dynamics that create value. As I examine and compare the judgments of a single work made by different reviewers, it is difficult for me to believe that value can be anything but contingent—not intrinsic, but dependent on multiple variables. An examination of book reviewing reveals that value is indeed radically contingent, as Barbara Herrnstein Smith and others argue, that it is a function of the individual perspectives brought to bear on the works by readers.

My study depends heavily on book reviews (along with media reports and articles), the more so because Erica Jong has not been the subject of as many scholarly articles as some other contemporary authors. Moreover, I postulate that the relative paucity of scholarly articles is related to the abundance and the nature of the reviews. Because of her association with female sexuality and female agency—or because of the conjoining of these two associations—Jong became typed early on in her career. She was well known, even a celebrity, and her books could hardly be ignored. But the notoriety she received also made her less eligible for scholarly study, as I explain more fully in Chapter 6. Reviews of Jong's works are therefore doubly important in analyzing her reputation. In the case of a writer who has received a very different reception, such as Margaret Atwood, articles would be more important than (or at least as important as) reviews, I suspect. Jong's example may serve as a rebuttal of the notion that reviews are trivial.

The extreme variety of evaluations in Jong's reviews raises questions about the nature of literary value. The student of these reviews might ask how a definitive judgment of the novels is to be reached, given the tremendous variety of opinions emanating from sources with equal claims to authority in literary evaluation. Take, for example, several reviews of Jong's third novel, *Fanny*. For most review readers, I believe, American academic Alan Friedman, writing for the *New York Times Book Review*, is as eminent an authority as British critic and writer Clive James, writing in the *New York Review of Books*. However, Friedman's review is highly favorable and James's review pronounces the book to be an utter failure. Similarly, playwright James Goldman, writing for the *Chicago Tribune*, deserves our attention equally with columnist and novelist Judith Martin, writing in the *Washington Post*. But Goldman finds nothing to praise in the novel while Martin finds it delightful. These examples are particularly interesting because, since critics in each pair would be regarded as having equal authority, a dispute about who is right could not be settled by pointing to one or the other as "unqualified." (See a discussion of these reviews in Chapter 4.) The traditional notion of literary value is that literary quality is an inherent property of texts, and that, over time, a true judgment of the work can be reached by the critical community, which, by training and temperament, is equipped to judge literature on its intrinsic merits. In this view, the appeal of a work is in its timelessness, universality, and transcendence. According to this view, at least since the time of the New Critics, a work of art has no social utility—the aesthetic realm is separate from such mundane concerns.

In the recent escalation of the critical wars, which accompanied the appearance on the academic scene of women, blacks, and other minorities, "false" critics are often accused of being not just inept or lacking in discrimination, but consciously biased. This view has been stated recently by Peter Shaw in the *American Scholar*. Shaw, a former vice president of the National Association of Scholars, has become an important spokesman for the conservative camp. In an article highly critical of feminist criticism, Shaw first repeats the familiar claim that the aesthetic is a separate realm: "What has been forgotten is that the value of the literary critical enterprise does not lie in its ability to perform any direct services to society. On the contrary, for the most part criticism operates within an enclosure, and in this space, the highest value is aesthetic" (511). He goes on to affirm that in the realm of literature, the aesthetic represents the equivalent of morality: "Literary criticism may never achieve a perfect account, but in attempting to reach one, it imitates moral action. The absence of such an attempt is what makes it appear to us that something is amiss when a critic consciously adopts a bias—just as we are disturbed by cheating at cards" (511).

The bad critic consciously adopts a bias, but the good critic is objective, Shaw insists. The attaching of claims about morality to purely formalist thinking deserves some comment here. Remarkable for the quasi-religious overtones, Shaw's statement bespeaks the blindness of those whose interest is served by insisting that literature can be separated from a socio-political context. Like all formalist thinking, Shaw's analysis is conservative. It confirms the status of a privileged group that has an investment in the traditional forms and in the notion that literature is a self-contained universe. It has the effect of a holding action directed against those forces that would introduce a transformative understanding of literature and literary history.

An examination of the social dynamics of evaluation in operation suggests a very different account of the creation of value from that assumed by Shaw and his school. In book reviewing, as in other examples of evaluative gatekeeping, judgments about quality are made by people, and their individual tastes, needs, interests, and purposes create the perspective that determines the judgments they make. To understand a reviewer's judgment, we need to look at the conditions under which a reviewer, like any reader, encounters a work of literature. Each reviewer, situated in a particular nexus of experiential, ideological, and institutional relationships, makes a response to a novel of the type we call political.

Among the poststructuralist critics, Barbara Herrnstein Smith has turned her attention expressly to matters of evaluation. Her account is useful in dealing with the diverse and conflicting responses found in book reviewing, one of the earliest stages of literary evaluation—which is concomitantly an act of social and institutional gatekeeping. Smith's theory proposes that in order to resolve questions of literary evaluation, we must turn our attention from the work to the reader and find, in the variety and multiplicity of judgments, a function of the identities and values of readers. For Smith, the most fundamental characteristics of literary value are mutability and diversity. The value of any entity, including the literary text, is "the product of the dynamics of an economic system: specifically, the personal economy constituted by the subject's needs, interests, and resources—biological, psychological, material, experiential, and so forth" (30–31). A subject experiences any object in a particular set of circumstances with certain "needs," "interests," and "purposes" (32). Smith asserts that to insist that the aesthetic realm is separate from the utilitarian, to define aesthetic value by distinguishing it from all other forms of utility, is to "define it out of existence; for when all such particular utilities, interests, and other particular sources of value have been subtracted, nothing remains" (33). Thus one could have no opinion at all if one could drop all beliefs, tastes, and interests because one would have nothing left to have an opinion with. The question in evaluating a literary work becomes not "How good is it?" but "How well does it serve the needs and interests of the reader?"

Two critics who have engaged questions of literary value in studies of the uses of literature are Jane Tompkins and Janice Radway. In *Sensational Designs: The Cultural Work of American Fiction, 1790–1860* Tompkins explains that readers see different texts, but not because they look at texts from different points of view. *"Looking,"* says Tompkins, "is not an activity that is performed outside of political struggles and institutional structures, but arises *from* them" (23). Tompkins asserts that the value of works of literature lies in their ability to "[provide] society with a means of thinking about itself," thus "doing work, expressing and shaping the social context that produced them" (200).

Radway too rejects the notion that readers are "passive, purely receptive individuals who can only consume the meanings embodied within cultural texts" (6). In *Reading the Romance: Women, Patriarchy, and Popular Romance*, Radway shows how romance readers' "readings" are a function of their interpretive strategies and the goals that are determined by their life situations. They look to their romance reading to "assuage unstated fears and simultaneously provide them with the emotional sustenance they require" (16).

Thus my purpose is not to determine the correct judgment of Jong's novels (since I believe there is no such thing) nor to present my own. I do however have an interest in this project that is political in the sense I have been using the word. I am interested in investigating how writing by women authors is judged and in demystifying certain notions about literary quality. At the same time I willingly admit that I admire Jong's writing. My response to Jong's work is similar to that of the feminists discussed in Chapter 2. But in part my attitude has to do with an empathy with women writers in general. I confess that I am capable of feeling personally grieved and angered by attacks on women writers I admire, and I have also experienced a glow of pleasure when coming across generous praise of women writers. I am inside one of the evaluative communities I have identified as comprising Jong's audience, but so is every other reader of Jong. It is axiomatic in the approach I take that one cannot get *outside* experience and values and find a position of objectivity, in the old sense of the word. My interest in women writers such as Jong is a function of who I am, and so is my chosen methodology. It goes without saying that a person in some other camp would have made a very different analysis, one that would be preferred by a certain group of readers.

Jong's reviewers, all of whom have their individual personal and political identities, describe and evaluate the novels from the vantage point of their personal enmities and friendships, the social and institutional structures that they inhabit and that their publications represent, their ideological biases, and the political struggles they see themselves and their society engaged in. The fact that every text is mediated by the political circumstances of the reader is demonstrated very clearly in Jong's reviews. As their political circumstances determine the nature of the text that is made visible to them, readers experience very different novels and make vastly different evaluations. In other words, the values and attitudes—the political matters such as ideology, literary taste, and social and institutional loyalties—brought to bear on the text create or constitute the novels that become visible to the reviewers. Some see novels they praise for their artistic effects while others see failures—incoherent novels, novels with no point, collections of clichés, works that are merely pornographic.

In making a judgment that a novel is a success or failure in aesthetic terms, readers react strongly to the content of the novels. Readers who relate positively to a given novel in terms of such things as ideological affinity, shared life experience, and common literary tastes describe the novel as a coherent artistic entity and judge it to be a success. Novels that are praised are also variably constituted, with different readers seeing different designs. Similarly, the interrelated factors that together make up the way of apprehending the novel also cause the foregrounding of certain features—often the sexual explicitness—of works that are experienced as unsuccessful. The magnitude of the response to Jong's sexual explicitness suggests that there are certain assumptions operative in the culture about who can write openly about sex. Evidently many people think this doesn't include women. Women writers have often commented on the restrictions placed on them in this regard.

Although most readers do ultimately describe a successful novel in terms of its form, there is no such thing as a purely formal reading. Stanley Fish has explained in the essay "How to Recognize a Poem When You See One" that "acts of recognition, rather than being triggered by formal characteristics, are their source" (326). He explains, "It is not that the presence of poetic qualities compels a certain kind of attention but that the paying of certain kind of attention results in the emergence of poetic qualities" (326). My research shows that these enabling acts of recognition are greatly dependent on ideological and experiential affinities rather than simply on having learned a set of strategies for literary interpretation and knowing in what circumstances to apply them. So called "aesthetic" appreciation is the *last* stage, not the first, or, more comprehensively, we don't even know what aesthetic is except in particular social worlds with particular values.

The responses to Jong's novels are also related to the particular historical moment of each novel's appearance. During the period of nearly twenty years, from 1973 to 1990, in which they appeared, some novels were prominently visible and others were less visible, depending on cultural conditions at the time. *Fear of Flying* received a great deal of attention when it was published in 1973. Feminism was an important topic of public dialogue then, and the novel became a site of political struggle. Some conservatives saw in Jong an embodiment of a threatening new force, and some feminists found in Jong expression of their new vision of themselves. By the time Jong published her next novel, *How to Save Your Own Life*, she had become a celebrity. Her perception as a cultural symbol mediated the response to her new novel. She was viewed as an emblem of a cultural decline, but the response to the novel was also related to the cultural perception of feminism. Her acclaim by women readers, her status as a feminist spokesperson, and the huge sales of her novels evoked fears. High culture reviewers perceived a threat to their cultural authority from Jong and from a new force in society which she represented. Feminism was also important in the responses to *Fanny* when it was released in 1980. With *Fanny*, we start to see males writing reviews that respond positively to the feminist content of the novel. We also see feminist reviews appearing more often in the mainline journals, not just the alternative or liberal press. By the time Jong published *Parachutes & Kisses*, a reaction against the feminism of the early seventies was very much in evidence, and the response to the novel was affected by the postfeminist culture of the mid-eighties. *Serenissima*, although a quite different type of novel from *Parachutes & Kisses*, also failed to attract the vocal and impassioned responses of the earlier works. Jong's most recent novel, *Any Woman's Blues*, has been very negatively reviewed, but even more telling is the fact that it has received so few reviews and attracted so little attention of any kind. Thus, in 1989, Rita Felski can dismiss Jong's work as failing "to reveal any serious questioning of the existing basis of male-female relations or any sustained refusal of the values of a male-dominated society" and thus not "oppositional in any meaningful sense" (14–15).

We see in the story of the reception of Jong's novels an illustration of the fact that the reputation of a novel can undergo change after its initial evaluation upon publication. Although *Fear of Flying* got few good reviews at the time of its publication, by the time of the publication of Jong's second novel, *How to Save Your Own Life, Fear* had come to be regarded as a literary achievement. Many of the reviewers who intensely dislike Jong's second novel look back fondly on *Fear of Flying*. Indeed, this revised view of *Fear* seems to have stuck; the novel has continued to be cited by many reviewers down through the years as innovative and clever, successful both in form and content.

If a work is kept before the public eye, its reputation often improves, a phenomenon many writers have noticed in regard to their own work. In a letter to the *New York Times Book Review*, Andrea Dworkin complains about the review given to her recent books, which she says does not even accurately address their content, and at the same time notes that her earlier books, which got no recognition when they were published, are now called brilliant.[3] Virgil Thomson, a twentieth-century American composer, makes a similar comment about the shift in the reception of his work, pointing out that his opera *Lord Byron* got very mixed reviews initially, but, fourteen years later, reviews of a recent production had become very good. In an Associated Press story by Mary Campbell, Thomson reminisces that when he and Aaron Copland gave concerts together, they at first got "terrible reviews," but, "all of a sudden, we got better ones" (8E).[4]

How can we account for the phenomenon of upward shift? One reason might be popularity among a large group of readers, but probably a more important reason would be continued attention on the part of opinion leaders. Ohmann suggests that canon formation takes place "in the interaction between large audiences and gate-keeper intellectuals" (207). The history of Jong's reputation in the early years illustrates the importance of endorsement by prestigious opinion leaders, in Jong's case John Updike and Henry Miller. The creation of value in literary works follows the same dynamics as the creation of value in other cultural objects, as we see in the example of violinist Anne-Sophie Mutter's rise to prominence. Being championed by conductor Herbert von Karajan did for Anne-Sophie Mutter what being praised by John Updike did for Jong. Mutter reports that although she played only a few concerts before she was noticed by Herbert von Karajan, her career was dramatically affected after von Karajan invited her to play in Salzburg:

"I didn't have to play with bad orchestras or audition or go through competitions" (E6).

In charting literary reputation we must also consider how an author or artist is situated in relation to the literary (or cultural) establishment. Surely the fact that some types of books are likely to get better reviews than others is related to the existence of a cultural establishment. There is a similarity of outlook among many reviewers who represent publications, institutions, and social groups with cultural power.

One index of the closed nature of the cultural establishment is the educational profile of the reviewer. As my footnotes in subsequent chapters indicate, almost all the reviewers have attended prestigious universities. The most common educational qualification for the British reviewer is an Oxford degree. According to Herbert Gans in *Popular Culture and High Culture*, the school attended is the best predictor of cultural choices (71). British reviewers also seem to move easily among several leading publications, e.g., *TLS* (*Times Literary Supplement*), the *New Statesman*, the *Observer*. One does get the sense, after reading the British reviews, that a small club is doing the reviewing for the entire kingdom. Although one would expect a more democratic array of reviewers in America, an examination of American reviewers reveals that if one scratches a reviewer, one typically finds a Harvard, Columbia, or Wellesley graduate. Many reviewers are academics and thus plugged in to the institutional structure in several places. Others are writers, often novelists. Certainly gender is a factor in the writer's relation to a literary establishment. We can note also that reviewers will have acquired preferences for certain literary styles as a result of their training in the homogeneous world of the elite university. The fact that Jong writes confessional novels in the comic mode is already enough to trigger certain biases in many reviewers. We may conclude with Ohmann that "the values and beliefs of a small group of people play a disproportionate role in deciding what novels would be widely read in the United States" (201). Ohmann also notes that the creation of literary reputations has to do with political struggles: "the gradual firming up of concepts like, say, postwar American fiction is always a contest for cultural hegemony, even if in our society it is often muted—carried on behind the scenes or in the seemingly neutral marketplace" (200).

Some recent scholarly work extends the efforts of Ohmann and earlier analysts of cultural power in our hierarchical society. In "Defenders of the Faith and the New Class" Andrew Ross addresses the role of intellectuals in supporting the hierarchies of taste that accompany and undergird hierarchies of social and cultural power. Speaking as an intellectual himself, he writes, "the often esoteric knowledge we impart is a form of symbolic capital that is readily converted into social capital in the new technocratic power structures" (104). He calls upon fellow intellectuals and professors to undertake a

> classroom critique of taste that draws upon forms of popular and minority-marginal culture in ways that explode the "objective" canons of aesthetic taste rather than simply reinforcing or expanding them by appropriating, as a new colony of legitimate attention, cultural terrain that was hitherto off-limits—an exotic source of fresh texts to be submitted to yet another round of clever formalist "readings." (104)

The reader will see that my project can be connected with the reforms that Ross calls for here. An analysis of the evaluations of Jong's novels reveals the problematical character of the "popular" in the light of its mediation by intellectuals and calls into question the old ways of talking about literary value.

My analysis, like that of Ross and other postmodern commentators on the postmodern, is made possible by the appearance of some new constituencies in the public arena, constituencies that have made that arena truly "public" for the first time. Their presence has demonstrated the contingent nature of value, a phenomenon not so evident when the cultural establishment was more homogeneous. With some doors opened to women and minorities, there is now more diversity in the cultural establishment. Perhaps the newcomers are not yet part of the cultural establishment, since their viewpoints have little influence in society as a whole. (I don't think one could call the writers for *Spare Rib* part of the cultural establishment, for example.) In any case, formerly subordinate groups are gaining some share of social and cultural power. It is only since the early seventies that we have heard from feminists in the book review pages.

Given the vagaries of literary reputation, it is beyond my powers to predict Jong's place in history. I hope, instead, to show that the evaluations given to the novels are related to the identities, the social roles, and the political struggles of the evaluators and that Jong's reputation is being determined by the institutional role of these evaluators acting in the social and cultural context of the late twentieth century. Erica Jong is a useful example for the study of the constitution of literary value and the construction of literary reputation. In the presence of Erica Jong, people are prompted to stand up and reveal who they are.

Literary reputations rise out of societal conflict and struggle (of which the book review is one important site). Struggles over literary reputations are not only about what is good literature but necessarily also about what ideas and interests will prevail in society. Responses to Jong's novels raise issues at the center of recent discussion about literary value: "Can a popular work be good literature?" "Can a woman writing about female sexuality be a literary genius? Or a good writer? (Or a good woman?)" "Does the public persona of a writer influence evaluation of his or her work?" and "Who shall decide what is good literature?"

2 / Evaluative Communities in the Reception of Fear of Flying

Isadora, Jong's protagonist, like Jong a novelist and often regarded as her alter ego, refers in *How to Save Your Own Life* to the explosive effect of her first novel by commenting that she had unknowingly acted as "amanuensis to the Zeitgeist" (12). The phrase is a bit of hyperbole that Jong has since described as a joke (interview, *Maclean's* 6), but Jong's first novel, *Fear of Flying*, did touch a nerve in the culture, as we see by the burst of energy released by its publication. The extraordinary story of its publication and early reception is a unique chapter in reputation history. The passionate response of its first readers, including the typesetters who refused to set it in type (Franckling, *Radical Novelist* IIE), the publisher's employees who stole galleys from the publishing houses, and the readers who passed it from hand to hand before it had become known through reviews or advertising (Jong, "Introduction: *Fear of Flying* Fifteen Years Later" xiii) is epitomized in the reviews. The passion it excited—sometimes the exhilaration of self-recognition, sometimes disgust, fear, and loathing (and sometimes a milder response somewhere in between)—is evident in the number, the variety, and the emotional nature of the reviews. Many reviewers, whether they loved the novel or detested it, found a use for the novel. For those who liked it, it was useful as a way of understanding and ordering reality and, for some feminists, the impetus for an exuberant flight of self-affirmation. For those who disliked it, it was useful for clarifying some aspects of modern culture and as a vehicle for exploring, or expressing, their own views.

Fear of Flying tells the story of Isadora Wing, poet, who goes to Vienna to attend a psychoanalytic congress with her psychiatrist husband. While there she meets a British Laingian analyst, Adrian

Goodlove, who seems to be the embodiment of her sexual fantasies. She accompanies him on a jaunt across Europe. In actuality, he is often impotent, and he has a prearranged date to meet his wife and children in France. The novel also recounts Isadora's mental journey back in time as she revisits scenes from her past—her first sexual experiences, her lovers, and her marriages. Left alone in Paris, she takes stock of her life and goes back to her husband, who is now in London. The novel ends with Isadora in a bathtub in her husband's hotel room, awaiting a reconciliation but determined not to grovel.

The story of *Fear of Flying* begins before the publication of the novel in November of 1973.[1] Erica Jong had already published two books of poetry, *Fruits & Vegetables* (1971) and *Half-Lives* (1973), and had written an unpublished first novel she calls "a Nabokovian *jeu d'esprit*" ("Introduction: *Fear of Flying* Fifteen Years Later" xi). Jong showed this manuscript to her editor at Holt, who, according to Jong, "asked why I was impersonating a male madman when in my poems I was busily inventing a new way for women to write about their lives" (xi). The editor turned down the manuscript, making the suggestion that Jong speak in her own voice. In doing so he clearly earned his pay. Other editors may have spotted best-sellers, one of the functions of a good editor, according to Ohmann; but Jong's editor (inadvertently) inspired or commissioned one.

But best-sellerdom was by no means a foregone conclusion at the time of the novel's publication. When Jong wrote the novel she was a young poet, a graduate student at Columbia teaching poetry at the 92nd Street Y. Not surprisingly, the novel was first seen by the publishing industry as a literary novel about a Barnard girl who wanted to be a poet. The publisher, who acquired the novel for a relatively modest $25,000 and did not see it as a potential best-seller, did not promote it in the ways that make the prediction of a blockbuster a self-fulfilling prophecy.

According to Jong's account, the book would have been published in an edition so modest as to be invisible, except that Elaine Koster, a woman editor at New American Library, read it and said, "This is the story of my life!" In the deal for the paperback rights that Koster negotiated with Holt, she insisted on Holt's printing a hardcover edition of thirty-thousand copies, instead of the six thousand or so that might have been printed otherwise, and she also printed a hundred extra copies of the galley—the advance reading copy—which have since become collector's items. Even before publication, the book acquired a kind of publisher's in-group celebrity, disappearing from people's desks. In this way it established itself as a hot book—one people steal in galleys.

The book got an early review in the *New York Times* by Christopher Lehmann-Haupt (all the reviews referred to here are discussed below), but it is unlikely that this lukewarm, tentative assessment had much impact on sales. A review in the *New York Times Book Review* followed, by a young poet that Jong asserts had once made a pass at her at a poetry reading and been rebuffed. This review, mildly critical of the novel and located on page forty of the magazine, is also undistinguished. The novel got little praise from the early reviewers; indeed, harsh criticism was more common, as the reader will see in the analysis of the reviews below. But in the meantime, the book was acquiring an underground celebrity, passed from hand to hand and enthusiastically recommended by its first readers. Jong reports that ''there was a great deal of excitement about the book in New York publishing circles among people who were dog-earing it, passing it along saying, 'This is really something new; you've got to read it.' The official response was luke-warm, but the underground response was hot'' (telephone interview, April 13, 1991).

A little later (December 17, 1973) John Updike published a review in the *New Yorker* that, because of the impact of the review, has since become known as something of an event in reviewing history. Updike's high praise of *Fear*, subsequently cited many times in connection with the novel, played an important role in the novel's early success and thus contributed in important ways to the novel's eventual literary reputation. Soon the novel had sold out, but in the meantime, Jong's editor at Holt had been fired, and there was no one in charge to reprint the book. About four months later, with a new editor at Holt, the book was reprinted and sales continued fairly steadily. Jong reports that the book ''kept hitting the bottom of the best-seller lists for months and months and months. At that time the *New York Times* list only went to number ten, and it would get on at number eleven or barely cling on at number ten, and then go out of stock; they never printed enough. It was a horror story of publishing. For the first year, I was developing an ulcer about all this because there was nothing I could do to influence it'' (telephone interview, April 13, 1991).

In the spring Jong received a fan letter from Henry Miller, who expressed his admiration of the novel and offered his help in promoting it. He published an appreciation on the op-ed page of the *New York Times*, and the *Times* asked Jong to write a complementary tribute to Miller. The two pieces appeared side by side on September 7, 1974 ("Two Writers in Praise of Rabelais and Each Other"). Miller also performed another extraordinary service for Jong: he sent the book to his publishers abroad, an action that laid the groundwork for Jong's worldwide reputation.[2] The notice given to the book by Updike and Miller played a role in the success of the paperback and was of vital importance for the novel's literary reputation. But it was too late to help the hardcover edition.

In November of 1974 New American Library (NAL) published the paperback, and, in Jong's words, "the book that everybody had heard of but nobody could get" (telephone interview, April 13, 1991) was available to the mass market. Jong reports that NAL promoted the book aggressively, touting the reviews by Updike and Miller: "By then they knew that the book had a kind of life to it, despite the mixed opening reviews, and I had behind me Elaine Koster, a woman of my generation, who felt the book was the story of her life" (telephone interview, April 13, 1991). The book sold three million copies in the first year without the benefit of the electronic media, who were not interested in Jong until the book became number one on the best-seller list (about January of 1975). Jong made several personal appearances to promote the novel, but there was no book tour because the publishers could not book Jong on enough shows to make a tour worthwhile. Sales continued rapidly, with word of mouth the main means of advertising. Eventually more than twelve million copies[3] were sold around the world.

The cultural moment of *Fear of Flying* is dominated by important changes in the subjectivities and the social behavior of women. Jong comments on this moment in the introduction to the fifteenth-anniversary reprinting of *Fear of Flying*: "Something new was beginning to happen. Women were starting to write about their lives as if their lives were as important as men's. This took great courage. It meant going against all the parental and cultural admonitions of the time. I wrote *Fear of Flying* with my heart in my throat, terrified by my own candor" (xi).

The prominent position of feminism on the cultural agenda when

Fear of Flying appeared is indicated by its high media profile. News stories appearing before the novel was released in late 1973 reveal the conflictive and combative character of the public dialogue about feminism and suggest in very concrete terms the struggle over ideologies and values that underlay the formation of the novel's literary reputation. Battle over the same issues that inform the novel was joined in arenas as diverse as the Cambridge Union, the scene of a debate on women's liberation by Germaine Greer and William F. Buckley, Jr., and the tennis court, venue of a match between Bobby Riggs and Billie Jean King. Other skirmishes that were part of the larger conflict included University of Michigan students burning gynecology textbooks in protest against their sexism, and National Organization for Women (NOW) members demonstrating in the gallery of the American Stock Exchange in protest against male domination of Wall Street. A major source of conflict in 1973 was the Equal Rights Amendment; six years remained in the countdown toward its approval.

Negotiation of power goes on continually through social processes, but at those moments when the stakes are especially high, negotiation begins to resemble combat. Since negotiation of literary reputations is inseparable from the larger process of power jockeying, the moments when negotiation turns to combat are especially revealing for those who wish to understand how literary reputations are constructed. The publication of Erica Jong's first novel is one such moment.

The debating union and the tennis court, like the book review pages, are sites of conflict over values and beliefs and of struggles based on self-interest. Jong's novel was evaluated within a larger social conflict, and the reception process became part of that conflict, which was particularly intense because it dealt with the emotional issue of woman's place. It appeared that women's public roles might undergo dramatic change and bring about a concomitant change in institutions based on women's subordination, preeminently marriage and the family, but beyond those, almost every institution in society.

The reception of Jong's first novel illustrates how the feminist movement of the 1970s—like the earlier movement for women's suffrage—became an ideological lightning rod, the focus for a multitude of fears about changes in the status quo in a time of great social upheaval. It is an extraordinary thing that for well over a hundred years fears about social change in a rapidly developing industrial society have been focused on women, and the women's movement has been blamed for the myriad social changes that characterized this period in history.[4] Perhaps paradoxically, Jong's novels—and in particular her first novel—became beneficiaries of the notoriety of the woman's movement of the 1970s and early 1980s. The attacks on Jong's novel, which was seen as a symbol by the two camps, respectively, of negative and positive social changes, gave it extraordinary visibility.

The question of women's roles had two faces—public and private—and we cannot forget that a very intimate and personal upheaval underlay the public conflict. Public and private selves are indivisible, and the men and women who reviewed Jong's novel were very personally implicated in the issues raised by the novel, especially the issue of female sexuality. The social conflict I have been describing had a bearing on sexual identity, and for male reviewers, on their relationship to women in their own lives. Men, who had been in control of the discourse on sex, might well have felt threatened by a new discourse that stripped away illusions perpetuated by men about themselves. The response of women reviewers also involved beliefs about sexuality and the relation of sexuality to larger questions of identity. The newspaper files for 1973 give a hint of the private face of the struggle in a *New York Times* news story about a NOW-sponsored women's sexuality conference.[5] Women were rethinking their sexuality, or at least going public with their concerns and feelings, thus creating for many men, and also for women, a situation fraught with anxiety.

My analysis of the reviews stresses ideology, literary tastes engendered by training and culture, and gender perspectives, but I must add one other variable: the personal interests and emotional biases of the reviewers, including personal relationships between the reviewer and the author. Reviewers of novels generally fall into three categories: the more literary journalists, academics, and other novelists, the latter group including a very large percentage of the total number of reviewers. A novelist who, like the novelist under review, submits his or her work for public approval is hardly a disinterested and objective judge of the work of another novelist with whom he or she is necessarily in competition. Though a novelist-reviewer may try to be objective, he or she is influenced by not only literary taste, ideology, and other factors that affect any reviewer, but also in some cases by more personal emotions, even envy, anger, or feelings of neglect. Is it surprising that a reviewer whose novels have had little success or an editor-novelist whose novels have gone virtually unnoticed would have personal feelings that affect what he or she writes about a fellow novelist?

Sometimes, writers know each other: since they attend the same parties and move in the same social circles, all the tensions mentioned above may be aggravated by personal frictions. It would not be unusual for a writer who has asked Jong for a blurb for his novel—and been refused for any one of a number of reasons—to bear a grudge that would influence his review of a Jong novel at a later date. Jong reports that reviews of her novels have been written by such persons and also by old enemies and rejected suitors. Jong identified the *New York Times Book Review* as a publication that has, on more than one occasion, printed reviews of her novels written by people with long-standing dislike for her and by some who had made sexual overtures to her and been rebuffed (telephone interview, April 13, 1991). (The *Times* has also given Jong some very good press—a page-one review of *Fanny* in the *New York Times Book Review*, for example.) Although I would not by any means argue that personal biases are the most significant factor in determining the reputation of a book, they should not be totally discounted. The New York literary scene, of which Jong is a part, is particularly inbred. One would not expect the same thing to hold true of those who live and write in, say, Mississippi or California.

Personal relationships affecting reviewers' judgments is not only a phenomenon of modern times. In an analysis of Hawthorne's literary reputation, Jane Tompkins has stressed the role of personal relationships in his early reception. In *Sensational Designs: The Cultural Work of American Fiction, 1790–1860*, Tompkins discusses a review of Hawthorne's *Twice-told Tales*, written by Henry Wadsworth Longfellow, which Tompkins believes played the "most decisive role in establishing Hawthorne's literary reputation" (9). Tompkins explains the personal connection between the two writers that underlay the positive review:

> [Longfellow] had been a classmate of Hawthorne's at Bowdoin College; they shared a common background and a common vocation. In the months preceding the publication of *Twice-told Tales* (which Hawthorne sent to Longfellow as soon as it appeared), Hawthorne had written Longfellow a series of letters suggesting

that they collaborate on a volume of children's stories. Shortly before the review in question came out, he had written to Longfellow speaking of his reclusive existence, nocturnal habits, and unavailing efforts to "get back" into "the main current of life." While none of these circumstances could guarantee that Longfellow would admire Hawthorne's collection of stories, they constituted a situation in which a negative response would have been embarrassing and difficult. (9)

We note the bonds between Hawthorne and Longfellow based on common background and mutual goals and interests. Let us also note their common gender. We can assume that they, like men today, felt an obligation to treat other men in their "club" with honor. Women writers have noted that many male reviewers do not feel the same obligation to give women equally respectful or honorable treatment; instead male reviewers feel free to use a form of attack against women—often including comments on a female author's appearance—that they do not employ against other men. In *Reviewing the Reviews*, Women in Publishing (Margaret Cooter et al.) report on an experiment conducted by the Writers Guild that called attention to the treatment of women writers by male reviewers:

At a meeting of the Writers Guild, [Andrea] Dworkin and colleagues selected "extraordinarily insulting" reviews of the works of eminent feminist writers, such as Kate Millet and Adrienne Rich. *But*, when reading these aloud to the audience, they replaced the names of the women with the names of eminent male writers. The audience was stunned by the derogatory tone of the reviews and refused to believe they had actually been written—until it was proved otherwise. (83)

Jong reports that it is not unknown for a male reviewer who has written a very negative, even insulting, review to ask her at a later date for a prepublication blurb for his own novel—in one instance reminding Jong that they had known each other in their university days. It seems that some men are not aware that their behavior may be resented. The "club" ethic that dictates honorable treatment of males does not extend to women.

I must also address the subject of anti-Semitism. Jong occupies a number of subject positions (she is a woman, a writer, a mother, and many other things), as it is now fashionable to say, and the fact that she's a Jew cannot be ignored. Direct expression of anti-Semitism is of course not socially acceptable in journals and magazines. References to Jong's Jewishness pop up quite frequently, however, and occasionally these references do have a whiff of anti-Semitism about them. Because Jong's Jewishness was alluded to so often, we can be sure it was a factor in her reception. Sometimes reviewers refer to the fact that there are numerous novels by and about Jews or Jewish women. Perhaps such references are not entirely innocent; one never hears the phrase, "Here's another novel by a gentile, or a Protestant." Daphne Patai's term for the heightened visibility that makes members of a minority group particularly noticeable and casts them as representatives of the group is "surplus visibility." Surplus visibility "is related to the invisibility of minorities, oddly enough—at least their invisibility in circles of power, as significant figures, as beings with positive values associated with them. This very invisibility seems to instantly lead to its opposite when a member of these groups *is* noticed." A member of a minority is always viewed, not as an individual, but as a member of that group. The theory of surplus visibility explains why "we do not notice WASP names among cheating stockbrokers, while Jewish names stand out, or why we notice noisy blacks, nagging women, and so on. Whatever the offense, it is at once generalized to the group and helps define negative ideas about that group" (unpublished essay). Members of minority groups typically share in these responses themselves, having an instinctive desire to blend into the dominant group. Patai concludes, "Surplus visibility assures that when 'one of them' is visible at all, 'all of them' are seen as taking over! When someone speaks this way, they are merely *naming* otherness."[6]

An unsigned article entitled "Methinks the Lady Protests Too Much" in the (London) *Daily Mail* contains explicit comments about the visibility of women writers and specifically Jewish women writers. This article, which might be considered a brief review of *Fear* and another new novel (by a young Irish woman), begins as follows:

The new novels, as usual, are by women—the last class with the leisure to write them. Never before have women torn into print with such loud cries: "*Listen* to me—I'm a *woman* and it's awful."

Listen, for instance, to the first novel of another very bright, New York Jewish girl, Erica Jong, called *Fear of Flying* [a quotation from the novel follows]. (7)

But there are more troublesome references to Jong's Jewishness in the reviews than those that fall under the heading of surplus visibility, as D. Keith Mano's review of *How to Save Your Own Life* (cited in Chapter 1) illustrates. There is also an anti-Semitic strain in the denigration of the persona in the Jong novel—which in many cases is fairly explicitly a denigration of Jong herself—through the characterization of the persona as a type of "Jewish American Princess": a spoiled, self-centered, pleasure-seeking woman, rich but tasteless, and more physical than intellectual. In an article in *Humor: International Journal of Humor Research*, Gary Spencer reports a very negative characterization of the Jewish American Princess (JAP) on college campuses: "[a] loud, aggressive, whining, self-absorbed, spoiled, materialistic, shallow, gaudy, clannish, nouveau riche bitch" (334). Spencer, who surveyed student opinions, believes that the term "bitch" added at the end has the effect of masking the anti-Semitism, disguising it as mere sexism, which most students find socially acceptable.

One thing the JAP is *not* associated with is intelligence. She is a figure totally defined by her materiality. It makes no difference to the students what her IQ is; she's still a JAP. Spencer's list of adjectives is reminiscent of the descriptions of Jong's persona or personae—and often of Jong herself—by a number of reviewers. It is very possible that the scorn heaped on the attempt of the persona to align herself with intelligence, culture, and a literary tradition can be connected with the cultural stereotype.[7]

There is also the problem of the sexual woman as writer. The response to young, female, sexually attractive writers—as Jong was when she wrote her novels—by male reviewers, editors, and so on, is relevant to literary reception. Women writers with sexual charisma may get a lot of attention initially, encouraged by their status as sexually "available" women, but literary history suggests that it is hard for men (and some women) to think "sexual woman" and "great writer" at the same time. Interestingly, with male writers the opposite effect is often evident. Sexual attractiveness, for women, is not associated with competence in the field of writing or in other fields, while it can increase the perception of competence for men. Having just read through the public record on Jong, I am very conscious of the numerous photographs of a very attractive woman that accompany news articles, feature stories and reviews. (The male library employee who recently made a number of copies from microfilm for me asked me if Jong was as beautiful as her pictures.) Readers of Jong's works have gotten the message that she is an attractive woman, but have they simultaneously made an assumption that she therefore cannot be a great or important writer? The epithet "dumb blond" encapsulates the prejudice that brains and sexuality are somehow incompatible in the female, and this pejorative has been explicitly applied to Jong. (See the review by Joshua Gilder in Chapter 4.) Can it be good literature if it's funny, sexy, and written by a *sexy* woman?[8]

Let us turn now to a consideration of the evaluative communities in the reception to *Fear of Flying*. The responses to Jong's novel indicate that there are no universal standards for interpreting or evaluating cultural objects; rather there are multiple and discrete communities of interpreter-evaluators with greatly divergent assumptions and standards. However, the finding that value is contingent does not suggest that unbridled subjectivity is the alternative to universality. Instead of a multiplicity of individual responses, we find a clustering of responses around experiential and ideological perspectives. An evaluative community is a group of agents who, to an important (though not necessarily absolute) degree, share determinate meanings of a cultural object and value the object similarly.

Reading—that is, interpreting and evaluating—is a discursive practice defined by Bronwyn Davies and Rom Harré as "all the ways in which people actively produce social and psychological realities" (45). In "Positioning: The Discursive Production of Selves" Davies and Harré argue that "the constitutive force of each discursive practice lies in its choice of subject positions. . . . Once having taken up a particular subject position as one's own, a person inevitably sees the world from that vantage point of that position and in terms of the particular images, metaphors, story lines and concepts which are made relevant within the particular discursive practice in which they are positioned"

(46). In other words, we make sense of our lives through certain "story lines" and "concepts," placing ourselves in subject positions in certain stories and adopting certain concepts or ways of viewing reality. A perspective is created from the way we are positioned that entails an emotional commitment and adoption of a moral system (47).[9] Those who read a given novel, discuss it with others, and/or review it, position themselves in certain ways. The feminist community is a particularly interesting example, especially in relation to *Fear of Flying*, because Jong's novel and other works of fiction and nonfiction became the objects that enabled certain readers to assume new subject positions. All the evaluative communities speak from positions of strongly held views.

The evaluative communities of reviewers of *Fear of Flying* (which presumably represent larger communities of the novel's readers) are distinct and, for the most part, well populated (a situation very welcome to the scholar who is therefore spared the task of extrapolating communities from a meager number of reviews). One large group is composed of critics of contemporary culture—cultural conservatives, male and female, who can identify politically with either the left or the right. They are highly critical of the novel. There are also male reviewers who relate positively to the novel for various reasons and see the novel as an imaginative triumph. Among the novel's most enthusiastic admirers are feminists, a category that includes all the women who praised the novel. It is important to note, however, that there are often differences among the members of these groups (or evaluative subcommunities). For example, among the feminists, some criticize Jong for being too preoccupied with women's relationships to men and failing to deal satisfactorily with women's relationships to each other. The responses of the feminist reviewers to this and subsequent Jong novels reveal some of the tensions within feminism and provide further examples of the conflictive social relations out of which reputations arise.

Although the clustering of responses suggests conclusions, it is important to guard against oversimplification. My analysis features feminism as a kind of axis on which responses to the novel turn, but there are other factors that determine evaluators' responses as well.

Let us take the matter of literary tastes, for example. Much has been said about the fact that Jong writes confessional novels. To some, such as the feminist community that came together over shared experience and engaged in consciousness raising, such a mode was welcome. Others, including many of the British reviewers discussed in this study, had little regard for the confessional mode.

Jong's choice of the comic mode is also significant. Comedy has never gotten much respect, and some artists have concealed their authorship of comic works. The composer Saint-Saëns, for example, didn't want it known that he had written *The Carnival of the Animals*. Other writers known for comedy have tried to enhance their reputations by authoring more serious works. Even Voltaire thought lightly of *Candide*, according to Stephen Weissman, who notes that he never mentioned it in his autobiographical writings. Edna St. Vincent Millay wrote comedy under the pseudonym Nancy Boyd, and Marietta Holley pleaded with her publisher to be allowed to write more stories in a serious vein instead of more of the comic "Samantha" novels. Alan Gribben says of Holley's contemporary Mark Twain that he is "the only writer we have recognized as an author of immortal prose after having branded him a 'humorist' " (24). To an heir of western civilization, comedy is too frivolous, too concerned with the despised body, to merit as much respect as more serious modes. An interesting feature of Jong's reception, then, is a fondness for comedy on the part of many of those who like Jong. Other readers share the cultural prejudice against comedy.

A number of reviewers who damn the novel roundly see it as a sign of the times—evidence of the poverty of values and vulgarity of modern life. Evaluating the novel in the context of a pessimistic view of history, these reviewers, critics of contemporary culture, deplore the influence of forces—self-expression, fragmentation, loss of traditional values— that they view as detrimental to society and see the novel as aiding those forces. Often such reviewers describe the novel as feminist, frequently calling the novel ideological and hence flawed. They see the novel as representative of a monolithic feminist movement that is wrong-headed and harmful to society. Interestingly, these critics can come from either the right or the left. For these reviewers Jong is useful as an example of disvalue. Her example is held up as an example of what is wrong with fiction today.

The dismay of the conservative reviewers of Jong's first novel is in large part a response to the women's liberation movement (as it was then called) that had begun in the 1960s. Victoria Geng describes two branches of the movement: "the reformers, daughters of [Betty]

Friedan [author of *The Feminine Mystique*], and the radicals, daughters of [Simone] de Beauvoir [author of *The Second Sex*]'' (52). The reformers founded the National Organization for Women in 1966. The radical feminist movement began in late 1967 when women (white women) began to see ''the disjuncture between the Movement's rhetoric of equality and their own subordination within it'' (Echols 21). Radical feminism was an important force within the women's movement in its early years (it came in conflict with cultural feminism about 1973 and was superseded by cultural feminism after 1975). Insisting on the primacy of gender as the basis for their oppression, radical feminists insisted that women were a sex-class, whose position of inferiority in the public sphere was bound up with their position of subordination in the family (Echols 3). Unlike the later cultural feminists, who emphasized women's differences from men, radical feminists emphasized similarities between men and women and pursued the political goal of equality. Thus one radical feminist, Kathie Sarachild, described the early women's groups as anticapitalist, antiracist and also anti–male-supremacist. For these women elimination of gender oppression was an extension of the goals of the left. Sarachild held the view that it was ''primarily in terms of the family system that we are oppressed *as women*'' (Echols 78). Radical feminist books that shocked the public in the early 1970s were Shulamith Firestone's *The Dialectic of Sex*, an outspoken critique of all aspects of patriarchal culture, and Kate Millett's *Sexual Politics*, which delineated woman's role as chattel.

Feminism, especially the feminism of the early seventies, was more, however, than just another example of the social disintegration that critics identified with the social movements of the sixties. The women's liberation movement of the early seventies was concerned with social equality, to be sure, but it also focused on sexual relationships between men and women. Feminists later became uneasy with the connection between feminism and sexual revolution, but in the early seventies, women's liberation and sexual liberation were closely linked. The fact that the burgeoning revolution had invaded the bedroom and had implications for the most intimate relationships between men and women is on the minds of the male and also the female reviewers discussed here.

In *Re-Making Love: The Feminization of Sex*, Barbara Ehrenreich, Elizabeth Hess, and Gloria Jacobs state the thesis that the so-called sexual revolution of the sixties was a *women's* sexual revolution: "If either sex has gone through a change in sexual attitudes and behavior that deserves to be called revolutionary, it is women, and not men at all" (2). Men had always sought numerous sexual encounters, in and outside marriage; that women should feel free to do the same was something new. Women also wanted to change the quality of the sexual relationship: "At the same time, the social meaning of sex changed too: from a condensed drama of female passivity and surrender to an interaction between potentially equal persons" (5). Furthermore, women had been "barred from the discourse on sex. They had nothing to say and no reason to be told anything, and whatever they felt was the product of male effort" (48). In the early seventies women began to participate in the discourse on sex, and the early years of the feminist movement produced watershed documents by Anne Koedt, Barbara Seaman, Alix Shulman, and others.[10] Women's participation in the talk about sex undermined physicians' authority on sexual matters, and the new authorities began to explore new sexual options, including oral sex (80–81). The new discourse on sex also entered the novel, a prime example being *Fear of Flying*.[11] The early feminists rewrote female sexual identity, and Jong's work, celebrating female sexual energy and in search of female autonomy, became a convenient focus for a backlash. Social history and the history of ideas suggest that there is hardly a more emotion-laden subject than female sexuality. The importance to her reputation of Jong's role as spokeswoman on behalf of the women's crusade for the freedom to "speak her own body, assume her own subjecthood" (Suleiman, *Female Body* 7) cannot be overestimated.

It is not surprising that men felt that an autonomous female sexuality threatened male potency and authority. But some women also felt threatened, as we see in the example of the conservative women who reviewed *Fear of Flying*. The first group of reviewers I will discuss are women who belong to a category that might be called cultural (if not always political) conservatives. Their views are similar to the male cultural conservatives I discuss below, but they place more stress on what they call solipsism in the novel, rejecting the author's perception of reality, while the men respond more markedly to the sexual explicitness. The women say, in effect, "Reality is not like this," while the men, reacting to the female author and the female protagonist, say instead,

"This book is disgusting." Both the women and men see the book as an artistic failure, incoherent and lacking in complexity of any kind. My method involves both analysis of the reviewers and construction of a social and cultural context; in providing cultural context for the reviews, I also provide a personal context for the reviewers. I move beyond their statements, or even their conscious understanding, to fill out the perspective from which they view the novels, positing certain emotions, attitudes, and understandings not explicitly stated but a necessary part of a comprehensive explanation. I notice first of all a note of incomprehension on the part of these women reviewers who are clearly on the outside of the women's liberation movement. The reviewers, firmly located in traditional or middle-class social and family life, simply do not understand what the early feminists who made such radical criticisms were talking about. Traditional women felt they already had equality and opportunities for the growth and fulfillment of the self. They saw those who mounted a radical critique of social and family life as narcissistic and called their view of the world solipsistic. The complainees had only themselves to blame. Why didn't they accept the perfectly reasonable and valid social structures that existed? If one cannot have everything, that too is reasonable in an imperfect world.

Although one might expect that age might be a factor in ability to sympathize with the feminist movement, an examination of the ages of the reviewers (see notes) reveals that ages vary widely. The position from which they read the novel is, however, characterized by an acceptance of a traditional view of women's nature and role in society. The women have no sympathy with the feminist protagonist, who demands sexual freedom, talks freely about intimate physical matters—sexual feelings, menstruation—and is very vocal in her complaints about individual males and about the male-centered institutions of society. They are made uncomfortable by bold discussion of women's bodies. They are made uncomfortable by bold women brazenly defying the centuries-old canons governing ladies' behavior. The new protagonists, instead of being modest, supportive, and gentle, call attention to themselves in every way, engage in sexually "promiscuous" behavior (or at least fantasize about it), and make demands on individual men and on society that they seem to think should be acceded to. Thus one reviewer, Millicent Dillon, expresses a note of horror, but also incomprehension, at women who think they "can have everything" (220). Another reviewer, Jane Larkin Crain, expresses the idea that women have only themselves to blame for their troubles. The implication is that they should have been satisfied to live within the constraints imposed on them by society. The reviewers' defense of psychiatrists—harshly satirized by Jong as well as other feminist novelists of the early seventies—signals a lack of sympathy with the feminists' rejection of Freudian psychology, with its norms for female sexual response. The conservative female reviewers are what the feminists call male-identified, and their adoption of male cultural attitudes is reflected in an attitude of contempt for the traditional female activities and concerns dealt with in the novels. They share the longstanding view that such activities as housework are not valuable. Such an attitude is revealed in condescending references to the concerns of ladies' magazines being transferred to the novel (Crain 58). These women have an investment in keeping society the way it is. Understandably, they see no reason to change a world in which they are comfortable, understand their roles, and, in fact, occupy positions of privilege.

Jane Larkin Crain,[12] writing in *Commentary*, a journal noted for its conservative viewpoint, is emphatic about her opinion of "feminist novels": "Taken one by one, no feminist novel really rewards critical scrutiny" (59). She is consequently fascinated but also dismayed by the fact that "these novels have not only sold extremely well but have been widely, respectfully, and even enthusiastically reviewed" (59). She finds Jong's novel (along with several other novels by women discussed in the same review) "too steeped in ideology to pay the elementary respect to human complexity that good fiction demands" (59). Crain sees and deplores an attack in the novel on marriage as an institution. She is annoyed by an absorption in the woman's point of view and asserts that Jong "falsifies reality irrevocably" (61) by depicting women as victims of forces they cannot control. The central characters are one-dimensional, and the author has no capacity for irony. Crain insists that it strains credibility to suppose that an intelligent woman such as the protagonist of this novel would put up with so much abuse. Why would such a person endure "grotesque domestic unpleasantness" and then, searching for help "pay good money to a buffoonish quack disguised as a psychiatrist?" And furthermore, she doubts whether "if this were what psychiatrists did there would be any still practicing today" (61).

With heroines who suffer "for no apparent reason" (61), the reviewer concludes that ''there is something repugnant in all this celebration of cowards, cripples, and losers. It is an offense to the memory of Natasha Rovtov, of Jane Eyre and Emma Woodhouse, of Isabel Archer; it reeks of the hatred of women'' (62). Crain, like some other women reviewers, is adamant in her contention that Jong falsifies reality. She explicitly rejects ''the world [the feminist novelists'] bitter fantasies have created'' (62). Her evaluation of the novel is presumably related to her conviction that a woman can find fulfillment in society as it is presently constituted. This reviewer clearly supports the status quo: society's gender roles, the institution of marriage, and other institutionalized practices, such as psychiatry. Her criticisms—misrepresentation of reality, one-dimensionality of character, and lack of irony—are voiced by other reviewers in this group, as we shall see.

A review by Patricia S. Coyne expressing views similar to those outlined above appeared in the *National Review*. This journal, along with the *American Spectator*, is probably the most ultraconservative dealt with here. Coyne identifies the book as a document of the ''Woman's Lib'' movement, suggesting that the novel is leading the pack in the race for the ''woman's novel of the year'' award because ''the author sees in life precisely what the women's movement has told her to see'' (604). She remarks glibly that the women's movement has said all it has to say, ''but popular fiction tends to suffer from cultural lag'' (604). The protagonist's story might have been good ''if only the author had been able to see it in relation to the rest of the human condition'' (604). But Coyne suggests that this author, with the characteristic lack of ironic vision of the feminist ideologue, cannot manage this. For Coyne, the book has no shape—the author ''spills it all out,'' and the novel does not ''dramatize any real development'' (604).

A similar critique is made by Ellen Hope Meyer,[13] writing in the *Nation*. It says something about the complexity of factors involved in literary evaluation that the opinion expressed about a controversial book by a woman in the conservative press should match so closely the views expressed in the *Nation*, which is thought of as the most progressive of liberal journals, comparable to the *New Statesman* in Great Britain. Clearly the bastions of male liberalism were not showing support for feminism in 1973.

Meyer laments the increase of ''missionary autobiographies masquerading as novels'' (55). For Meyer, Jong's novel belongs to a ''Dear

Diary'' genre in which a solipsistic world is created. The novelist cannot connect the self-indulgent subjectivity of the heroine with the real world, and thus the novel can do nothing to advance the cause of women: "The cause of women's liberation has given rise, thus far, to a good deal of *dear diary.* . . . The genre's narrow focus makes liberation unattainable. It expresses the author's indisposition to get out of the prison of herself'' (56). In the novel Jong gives us that "old chestnut, growing up Jewish in America,'' but it's "a good read, falling somewhere between educated jet-set 'in' talk and well-written true confessions'' (56). She cannot, she admits, see coherence in the novel. The book "becomes a reformist tract on the one hand and on the other a highly personal account of one women's reactions, digestion and tastes. There is no artistic distance between the author and her subject, and hence no objectivity'' (56).

Writing in the same journal one year later, Millicent Dillon[14] presents a similar message. In a review called "Literature and the New Bawd,'' Dillon laments the passing of the old bawd who was lewd, mercenary, and vulgar, but unpretentious. Dillon announces the creation of a new bawd by Jong and others, equally lewd, but also claiming to be "superior in intellect, sensitivity, and perception'' and "in search of the ultimate truth, within herself'' (219). Dillon finds impossible this fusion of "vulgarity'' and "self-conscious art'' (220). Artistic failure stems from self-absorption, which permits the novelist "no window on the world'' (220). For Dillon, we are living in an age of decline: "But now we live in a world that distrusts distinctions, such as purity as against baseness, innocence as against evil. No clear lines can be drawn in words or actions. And there is nothing to be attacked that cannot be overcome. So even vulgarity becomes debased and ultimately useless, only more pap for the leveled multitude we are all supposed to be'' (221). The feminist agenda is seen as liberation from society's constraints, with an emphasis on sexual liberation. For this reviewer, feminists' goals can be achieved only at a cost—"if there are barriers being broken, we have also lost a sense of community'' (220).

In connecting feminism with loss of community and breakdown of society's forms, Dillon sounds very much like the cultural conservatives, male and female. But since this reviewer (who is also a fiction writer) writes for other publications whose editorial policies identify them with the left, e.g., the *Threepenny Review*, we infer that she shares their general ideological stance. We know, however, that the critique of contemporary society mounted from the left can sometimes sound very much like that mounted from the right.[15] Relevant also is the point Barbara Herrnstein Smith makes about the conservative nature of the professional humanist,[16] who, as the guardian and transmitter of cultural values, can quite naturally adopt the views expressed here about the necessity of cultural continuity while at the same time supporting political causes endorsed by the journals they write for. Although both Dillon and Meyer appear to have associations with the left, their reviews make clear that they are not sympathetic to women's liberation as represented for them by a number of women novelists of the time. Meyer criticizes Sylvia Plath, Sandra Hochman, Anne Richardson Roiphe, and Alix Kates Shulman while Dillon mentions Hochman and Lois Gould, along with Jong.

Patricia Meyer Spacks,[17] professor of English at Wellesley College at the time she reviewed *Fear of Flying*, is well known among academics. Spacks, whose books on women writers are included under the umbrella of feminist criticism, describes the genesis of her interest in ''reading as a woman.'' In 1969–1970, while she was engaged in writing a book on Pope, a librarian at the Houghton Library asked her to look at a manuscript of Mrs. Piozzi's journal (''The Difference It Makes'' 22). From then on, she says, she began to read writers such as Jane Austen in a new way. Spacks, who finds a ''poverty of literary value'' (283) in novels by Jong and four other women, has, however, no empathy with the viewpoint expressed by the feminist heroines of the early seventies. She comments, ''Endless discontent and an accompanying sense of entitlement: that's what heroines are made of'' (284). She is troubled by Isadora's self-display, her unsupported claims of victimization, and her sensibility—''too crude to justify any profound concern with her plight'' (284). The effect of these novels on Spacks is to create ''old-fashioned longings: for art as criticism of life, for writing which offers more than self-indulgence or pretentiousness, for authors who suggest attitudes more meaningful than self-pity and self-display'' (285). Spacks finds the authors' purposes intrusive in all of the novels she reviews—''people *reading* novels have not always had to be so sharply aware that women's lib . . . [is] selling this season'' (291). Clearly Spacks sees the novel as an example of declining literary quality, a decline that seems to be related to a lack of moral seriousness in modern society. According to her account of *Fear of Flying*, the novel does not take shape for Spacks as a work of art. She finds it "irritating" and incoherent, pointing out that the heroine claims to be victimized but is, in fact, manipulative. Her summary of events in the novel follows a this-happened-and-then-that-happened pattern, ending with the statement, "She goes back [to her husband]—after a brief and unconvincing bout of psychic anguish—and . . . takes a bath" (285). Spacks sees no relation to reality in Jong's depiction of her heroine's plight. Born in 1929, Spacks is a woman who has made it in a male-dominated establishment and who has a view of literature firmly rooted in high culture.

The reviewers discussed above, all of whom are women, do not share the ideology of Jong's novel and thus find it ideological. They consequently find that the world of the novel bears no relation to reality and that the heroine's reflection on her situation is self-indulgent (and vulgar). These reviewers connect the novel with characteristics of modern life they deplore and which they label self-indulgence and solipsism. In their view, individual responsibility and loyalty to a tradition have given way to the pursuit of sensations and the acceptance, even celebration, of fragmentation. The feminist movement, in their view, emanates from these tendencies and strengthens them at the same time. Women as exemplified in these "feminist heroines" blame society instead of themselves for their unfulfilled lives. As a description of modern life, Jong's writing "falsifies reality irrevocably" (Crain 61) and at the same time somehow tends to weaken society. These reviewers make it clear that they believe Jong and others are hurting rather than helping the cause of women, feeling that the traditional forms of society (with which they are evidently personally content) are preferable to what is suggested by Jong's vision. Criticism of society's institutions, celebration of female appetite, and sexually explicit descriptions are not welcome. Thus we see as one cluster of ideas women's liberation, ideological writing, narcissism, lack of truth to reality, vulgarity, and bad writing. The novels are seen as incoherent and falling woefully short of artistic success.

Male reviewers are also troubled by the brave new world the feminists are advocating. Especially evident in the reviews is the unease men feel with feminist challenges to existing norms of sexual behavior. Men, who, according to Ehrenreich et al., had been in control of the sexual act and of definitions of male and female sexuality, might well feel challenged or threatened by women who talked openly about their sexual needs and desires, advocated experimentation with sexual techniques, and, in the case of Jong, wrote novels in which male impotence played an important role. The reviews by male reviewers discussed below illustrate the reception of work by a woman writer who describes a woman who experiences herself as sexual, rather than depicting a woman's sexuality "from the standpoint of the outsider who experiences the sexed woman as an object of desire" (Hite 121). Molly Hite has noted that "such works are transgressive inasmuch as they are aggressive, asserting female desire in a culture where female sexuality is viewed as . . . inextricably conjoined with passivity" (121–122).

In many instances, as in the case of Alfred Kazin,[18] personal, social, and cultural threats go hand in hand. In Kazin's article, "vulgar" is a key word. Kazin is appalled by a woman who would deal as openly with sex as Jong does. Such behavior is socially vulgar, and a book about such behavior is vulgar in a literary sense. The high ground of literature, Kazin seems to assert, should be occupied by those with the proper aesthetic values and manners.

Kazin's article appeared in 1975 and is not, strictly speaking, a review. Its purpose, though, is evaluation, so I have discussed it here instead of in Chapter 3, where it could also serve as an example of one of the attacks that came after Jong became successful. Critic and scholar Alfred Kazin has also been identified with the left, but he here sounds the note of a cultural conservative. Indeed, his recent pronouncements on the contemporary scene have been characterized by mounting pessimism, and in the remarks on women writers in the article discussed below, appear indistinguishable from those of other cultural conservatives. In an article entitled "The Writer as Sexual Show-Off: Or, Making Press Agents Unnecessary," published in *New York* in 1975, Kazin describes Jong (along with Mailer and Vidal) as part of a trend of the self-debasement of the modern writer, whose integrity has been compromised or thrown overboard to facilitate self-promotion. Although Kazin suggests that Mailer, however shallow his work has become, began with promise as a writer and that Vidal is a "natural entertainer" (38)—they are "pros with a respect for the intricacies of narrative" (40)—he sees no redeeming qualities in Erica Jong. Jong is described as "as commonplace a mind as ever appeared on the best-seller lists, but a woman novelist who obviously speaks for all the oppressed women writers in this country." (39). He emphasizes Jong's vulgarity, made particularly unacceptable because of her literary pretentiousness, exemplified for him by her prolific quotation—"From now on, English majors will be able to give a high class flavor to sexual reminiscences" (40). Jong proves "Creativity is Easy" (40) while exploiting "a woman's parts, a woman's fantasies" (40). Kazin takes particular note of the fact that Jewish writers, and especially Jewish women writers, exhibit the characteristics he deplores. Kazin sees these novelists as expressing "disaffection of a strictly cultural-introverted kind" that is "ripe in this class—just now especially among women—and the sounds of incipient *personal* revolution are heard in the bedroom" (37). He refers elsewhere to "our disturbed, confused culture" (36) and suggests that Jong and others have no vision beyond cultural disruption (and have the bad taste to use sex for such a purpose). Describing Jong's form as "*True Stories* mixed with Masters and Johnson" (40), Kazin makes it clear that he finds no literary value in Jong's work.

Benjamin DeMott,[19] another noted academic, also sees the novel as a sign of the times in a review in the *Atlantic*. So troubled is DeMott by changes in the relationships between men and women looming on the horizon that for him a "chill . . . permeates" the novel, which he describes as a "diatribe against marriage" (125). For DeMott, who also identifies the novel with "The [women's liberation] Movement" (125), the relationships in the novel are a study in " 'managed' remoteness" (125), in spite of the abundance of sexual affairs (which he exaggerates as he recounts the plot). Personal creativity is all, he laments. DeMott sees the novel as a document in the women's movement and hardly as fiction at all, as we see by the nature of his comments and by the fact that he brackets the novel with nonfiction works dealing with the changing lifestyle of couples. DeMott reviews Jong's novel and several others along with a book on marriage by psychologist Carl R. Rogers and a nonfiction book on a "free" marriage.[20]

The response to Jong's work of the British reviewers provides further insight into the contingencies of value. Various aspects of British-American relations come into play: the attitude of an old world power to a new one, the competition for cultural prestige, and the disgust of those who represent a national tradition founded on a class-based elite culture for a society dominated by popular culture and commercialism. Certainly the British have taken up Jong as an embodiment of something hated and possibly feared. She is seen as embodying all the negative values associated with America—vulgarity, breakdown of traditional values, commercialization of literature, and feminist disruption.

Three male reviewers writing in British journals respond to Jong's novel with disgust and dismay. For them, as for Kazin, the novel is vulgar and exhibitionistic. In a review entitled "Altitude Sickness," the anonymous reviewer for the *Times Literary Supplement* identifies the novel's central concern as "sexual promiscuity" and pronounces the novel "difficult to review in a gentlemanly manner" (813). He can respond to the novel only in terms of its depiction of a woman's sexual exploits. His reading of the novel is colored by the fact that he disapproves of the protagonist and the author as women. This reviewer finds himself so at odds with the novel that he generalizes "almost everyone and everything Miss Wing describes with enthusiasm is disagreeable, and whatever she sneers at is generally rather pleasant" (813). Thus he demurs from the narrator's "[attempt] to mock the American servicemen's wives in Heidelberg—'25-year-old freckle-faced matrons from Kansas wandering about in housecoats and hair rollers, always awaiting that Cinderella evening for which it will be worthwhile to comb out their curls.' " He comments, "This description presents a more pleasing picture than the narrator seems to realize" (813). The reviewer prefers such descriptions to the other descriptions he finds more prevalent, of "[the narrator's] own private parts . . . or the unsuccessful physical performances of her lovers, described with a depressing cheeriness" (813). This reference to the subject of male impotence deserves further comment. Surely it is Jong's willingness to bring into the open aspects of male sexual performance that had previously been discretely ignored by women (and men) novelists that particularly angers some male reviewers. This reviewer is quite candid about his inability to see the novel as a coherent artistic entity: the narrator tries to be appealing, but "it is not clear whether her creator is fully aware of the poor girl's failure" (813). The overwhelming impression is one of bewilderment and shock at what has appeared on the literary scene.

Two other reviewers are so irritated that they have evidently given up all attempts to review the book in a gentlemanly manner. In a review entitled "Hapless Organ," Paul Theroux,[21] an American writer living in Britain, appears to identify with British values. Timothy J. Evans describes Theroux as concerned with the "chaos of society" and charac-

terizes him as "increasingly bitter," saying that Theroux "lists his politics as socialist [but he] could be a Tory, viewing society as decayed
and all changes as encouragements to that decay" (483). Theroux succeeded in seriously annoying Jong, who has referred to his review many
times and nominated it as her least-favorite review in *Esquire*'s "Revenge Symposium." Theroux writes in the *New Statesman*, "Erica
Jong's witless heroine looms like a mammoth pudenda, as roomy as
the Carlsbad caverns, luring amorous spelunkers to confusion in her
plunging grottoes" (554). To Theroux, Jong is a vulgar sexual exhibi-
tionist. He is also put off by the fact that

> Isadora is also a feminist, interlarding her memories with grim
> quotations from Sylvia Plath and Anne Sexton, and tendentious
> ones from Freud and Rudolf Hess. She said she "wanted to write
> *War and Peace* or nothing," and having chosen the latter, seems to
> have settled for the ambition of being gamahuched from here to
> eternity. (554)

His final judgment is outspoken: "This crappy novel, misusing vulgarity to the point where it becomes purely foolish, picturing woman as a
hapless organ animated by the simplest ridicule, and devaluing imagination in every line . . . represents everything that is to be loathed in
American fiction today. It does not have the excuse of humour, nor is
its pretense to topicality anything but tedious" (554). There is no way
the work can come into focus for Theroux as a novel.

Theroux's language of denunciation is closely matched by another
review written by Martin Amis,[22] novelist son of the novelist Kingsley
Amis. Amis's status as a spokesperson for the reviewing establishment
in Great Britain is signaled by the fact that he has twice been the recipi-
ent of British Press Awards, an indication that the contingencies that
govern his preferences are also operative for many others in places of
influence. Richard Poirier describes him as a "sort of neoclassicist
manque, distressed by a force of monstrosity, appetite, and vulgarity
which he calls America" and identifies him as a "voice of contemporary cultural conservatism" (785). Like others, Amis, writing in the *Observer*, seems to be responding to the fact that the book describes in
graphic detail the sexual exploits of a woman. He also makes explicit
connections between the protagonist of the novel and the author. "One

or the other of them," he writes, undertakes an odyssey around Europe with her lover, finally returning to her husband "with all fellatio, illicit sex, introspection, retrospection, Laingian duologues [*sic*], beefs about women's lib, creative commitment, dieting, orgasms, periods, etc., spent" (37). He then says that he neither knows nor cares whether all this "actually happened to Miss Jong." For him any merit the book has is in "telling moments" or vignettes that reveal the bleakness of modern life, particularly in America ("witness its American success"), giving the novel a "fleeting documentary interest" (37).

Amis's response appears to be mediated by the fact that he imagines the author might have done the things she writes about. He clearly disapproves. Further insight into Amis's response is suggested in a review of one of his books in *TLS* by Adam Mars-Jones, who comments that Amis may consider the "breakdown of sex roles a consequence of a deeper breakdown . . . but he can still seem to use sexual irregularity as a scapegoat, in a way that is highly conventional despite his career of iconoclasm" (457).

All these reviewers react to a greater or lesser degree to what they call the vulgarity of the novel. Some, especially the British reviewers, can hardly respond to anything else. Theroux depicts Jong as a Lamia-like sexual temptress, a threat to men in her destructiveness. Martin Amis, the chronicler of a cultural breakdown that he deplores, focuses mainly on Isadora's (or Erica's) sexual exploits. Clearly he has a negative response to a woman's doing such things, or perhaps just to a female subject telling about them in an assertive and unapologetic way. Kazin's attitude appears to exemplify in part the dismay of the Jewish patriarch at the self-assertion and iconoclasm of the "nice Jewish girl," as he ironically describes Jong in his remarks on the novel. In general, in this set of reviews the reviewers seem more intent on reviewing Jong than on reviewing her book.

These reviews project a deep uneasiness with changes that have characterized modern life, and in their indictment of modern culture they associate feminists with what they view as degenerative changes. For a number of the reviewers aggressive female sexuality and aggressive female authors are associated with a modernity that deconstructs fundamental verities: the "natural" roles of men and women and even the "natural" institutions of a mythic past. In *Nostalgia and Sexual Difference*, Janice Doane and Devon Hodges identify a "nostalgia" for a lost culture in which "men were men, women were women, and reality was real" (3) that preoccupied some fiction writers and social and cultural critics beginning in the early 1970s. (Their analysis is in fact a fleshed-out version of Adam Mars-Jones's comments on Martin Amis, cited above.) The work of Doane and Hodges suggests that Jong's reviewers were part of a much larger group, all of whom present a "sexualized" critique of culture. According to Devon and Hodges, Christopher Lasch, John Irving, Thomas Berger, and others attribute vast negative cultural changes to the influence of feminists. These purveyors of "nostalgia" mount a critique that aligns the female with narcissism, moral decline, and the disintegration of the self.[23]

It is an illustration of the gendered nature of responses to sexually explicit writing that such writing on the part of a woman can arouse great ire while it is acceptable and even welcome from a male writer, as we see, for example, in this review by Gore Vidal of a volume of Henry Miller and Lawrence Durrell's letters. Vidal writes that the book's dust jacket shows the three protagonists sprawled in the sea—Durrell, Miller, and Miller's "numinous cock." Vidal continues

Needless to say, it is the third that not only rivets attention but commands nostalgia and, well, let us be honest, pity and awe. Like so many celebrities caught off guard, the protagonist of a million words looks slightly exhausted and rather smaller than one recalls it from Literature; and yet even in its fragile state one senses that humming hydraulic energy which made it the stuff of legend in the first place. (979)

It is impossible to imagine a female writer described in this way. Indeed, the reviewers quoted above have used Jong's sexual content against her, whereas men can write about male sexuality or explicitly about their own sexuality without jeopardizing their standing as serious writers.

Male critics have something of a double standard in their views of the appropriateness of literary treatment of female versus male bodies. The intimate details of female bodily processes, so shameful that they were socially unmentionable for centuries, cause male reviewers annoyance that is most accurately described as misogyny. Jong's mention of the unmentionable is an important factor in the assessment of her literary reputation, as we see in the mocking allusions to periods, orgasms, and "parts." To provide a further gloss on this topic, let me quote British cultural critic and philosopher Roger Scruton, who was very explicit about his distaste for what he called "the gynecological novel" in a 1982 *TLS* review of several novels by women. Scruton expresses the view that the emergence of the gynecological novel should come as no surprise:

> For some time now feminists have been claiming that women should cease to be ashamed of their natural condition, and that they should integrate their urino-genital tracts into the totality of their experience and so resume "control" over bodies which have for too long been obedient to the whims and fantasies of men. The result leads one to think that it was not only shame that led the female novelists of the golden age to pass over these matters. The issue is ideological, and it is probably necessary for a reviewer to protest that he is not against menstruation, that some of his best friends even menstruate, before suggesting that it requires more than ordinary literary skill, whether lyrical or dramatic, to evoke an interest in its description. The poetry of Bloom's defecation is one of the great achievements of English literature; the aspiring feminist writer should study it, and take care. To incorporate such details into a narrative without detracting from the gentle irony and touching emotion which pervade it, Joyce had to remake the entire structure, form and purpose of the novel. (807)

Scruton evidently finds the women's treatment of the female body too crude, but his review as whole suggests—as do the reviews of Jong's novel cited here—that any treatment of the female body is unwelcome.

To compound her offenses, Jong stresses the literary nature of her work by numerous literary allusions and quotations. A number of reviewers are incensed by Jong's prolific literary quotation, in epigraphs and in allusions scattered throughout the novel. Perhaps these reviewers, like Kazin and Theroux, are annoyed at the co-optation of the literary heritage by one not qualified to be among its inheritors. One might think that, all other things being equal, quotations from one's favorite authors would add value to a literary work. In his discussion of the social construction of taste, *Distinction: A Social Critique of the Judge-*

ment of Taste, Pierre Bourdieu refers to those "intertwined references" that "cultivated pleasure feeds on" (499). He argues that cultural allusions "reinforce and legitimate each other, producing, inseparably, belief in the value of a work of art" (499). But apparently a work has to be granted the status of art before such an effect is achieved. Those who view the novel favorably either do not comment on the quotations or else regard them favorably.

Thus there are a number of factors that figure in the devaluing of Jong's novels. Jong does not appeal to the taste of many readers, especially British readers, who prefer a more restrained and genteel mode. For them, Jong's novel lacks restraint and her central character is too self-dramatizing and self-revealing. We may note here Pierre Bourdieu's discussion of the link between taste and class identity. Standards of taste, learned in formal and informal educational settings, are experienced as natural preferences and are the basis for one's "distinction," to use Bourdieu's term. Bourdieu explains that the seeking and proclaiming of one's elite status through the display of one's taste is most often exhibited first in disgust and revulsion at the tastes of others. Book reviewers, whose tastes are institutionalized in the literary establishment, jealously guard their positions as brokers of literary value. Some reviewers are particularly incensed at the possibility that Jong's work could be considered a part of legitimate culture. (This subject is discussed more fully in the next chapter in connection with the very negative reception of Jong's second novel.)

Reviewers who experience the novel as valuable speak to the same issues as those who dislike it but react very differently to what they perceive. The most influential favorable review was written by novelist John Updike[24] for the *New Yorker*. Updike said, in a comment subsequently taken up by many others, that *Fear of Flying* "feels like a winner. It has class and sass, brightness and bite" (149). Updike's review does strike the reader as generous in the sense of goodwill it exudes. The few critical comments it contains are muted. It ends with a blessing for Jong, who is seen as a reincarnation of the Wife of Bath: "Fearless and fresh, tender and exact, Mrs. Jong has arrived non-stop at the point of being a literary personality; may she now travel on toward Canterbury" (151). Updike responds positively to the "cheerful, sexual frankness," which "brings a new flavor to female prose" (149). In fact,

Jong "sprinkles on four-letter words as if women had invented them" (149). While identifying a feminist note in the novel, Updike sees the work as an imaginative triumph: "Containing all the cracked eggs of the feminist litany, her souffle rises with a poet's afflatus" (149). His high praise is signaled by the fact that he compares the book to *Portnoy's Complaint* and *The Catcher in the Rye*, asserting that it has a slight edge on both of those modern classics in that it "remains alert to the world."

Updike is clearly not offended by the sexual content of the novel, and in fact one could identify a similarity in the fictions of Jong and Updike in that each seeks to define the identity and creativity of human beings in terms of their sexuality. That Updike perceives the book as comedy is also an important factor in his evaluation, and again one thinks of Updike's own comic imagination. Valorization of the comic mode is a factor in several positive reviews, in this novel as well as in other Jong novels. Updike identifies the novel as being about "the family slapstick of growing up" (149). Updike's plot summary reads like comedy, in which, he makes clear, "a pattern and a person emerge" (149). For Updike, "the smaller discomforts of femininity are vividly, comically detailed" (149). Here, of course, he stands in contrast to other reviewers who are offended by the novel's candid treatment of menstruation and other intimate details. Also in contrast to reviewers who complain about a lack of contact with reality, Updike remarks that the upper-middle-class milieu of the heroine insulates her from some of life's horrors. He suggests a reading that views the heroine as "a spoiled young woman who after some adventures firmly resolves to keep on spoiling herself" and pronounces her "for all her terrors . . . the heroine of a comedy" (150). Updike also has praise for Jong's style: "The prose flies. Throughout, the poet's verbal keenness rarely snags the flow of breathy vernacular." (150).

To fully understand his attraction to the novel, however, we must look to Updike's explicitness about his enjoyment of the book as a male. His review suggests that the novel is a delicious bonbon for the male reader and reviewer. Updike's response is an interesting one, because many critics feel that his attitude toward women is ambivalent at best. John Leonard has remarked that "Updike thinks he loves women, but they emerge from the condescension of his novels . . . as merely cute, like poodles" ("Bad-Boy Books" 124). Even his attempts to give a sympathetic portrait of a liberated woman is a failure, Leonard suggests, in comments on the novel *S*.[25] Alfred Kazin characterizes Updike's enjoyment of *Fear* as a kind of sublimated sexual pleasure: "It was not clear from Updike's excitement whether he was reviewing Jong or tasting her" (39). Updike did mention the photograph of the author on the novel's book jacket: "On the back jacket flap, Mrs. Jong, with perfect teeth and cascading blond hair, is magnificently laughing, in contrast to the sombre portrait that adorns her two collections of poetry" (150).

We note also that Updike evidently welcomes the fact that Isadora has an abundance of kind words for the male body. For Updike the novel suggests the possibility of greater understanding between the sexes rather than greater polarization: "while not exactly a flag of truce in the war between the sexes, [the novel] does hold out some hope of renewed negotiations" (149). Updike's response is a complicated one, but unusual in that he apparently does think "sexual woman" and "good writer" at the same time.

In the *New York Times* in 1974 Henry Miller[26] made a response similar to Updike's in an article about Jong that appeared side by side with an article by Jong about him. In the introduction to the fifteenth-anniversary edition of *Fear of Flying*, Jong attributes the increased visibility of the novel to Miller's endorsement along with the Updike review. Miller extends to Jong "a warm, heartfelt tribute to a woman writer, the like of which I have never known" (27). Finding Jong "more forthright, more daring than most male authors," Miller comments, "That's what I like about her. In short, she is a treat for sore eyes" (27). Miller is pleased by Isadora's frank sexuality: "We don't hear enough from women on this subject." He finds the novel "full of meaning and . . . a paean to life" (27). Miller says he shares in Isadora's exuberant self-discovery at the end of the novel and concludes, "I feel like predicting that this book will make literary history, that because of it women are going to find their own voice and give us great sagas of sex, life, joy, and adventure" (27). Miller and Updike seem to see Jong as joining in the same enterprise they are engaged in.

Benjamin Stein,[27] a writer and reviewer who has also served as a speech writer for Presidents Nixon and Ford, reviews the novel in the *Wall Street Journal*. He first finds the novel irritating and confusing (because it's about a confused woman, he explains), but he ultimately finds it interesting and even arresting. In the final chapters of the work a pattern emerges for him that he finds meaningful and significant: Isadora looks at herself through her own eyes and starts to generate her own ideas about who she is and where she ought to be going. Thus ''the book transcends being a woman's book and becomes a latter-day 'Ulysses,' with a female Bloom stumbling and groping, but surviving a hopeful symbol for confused people of either sex'' (20). This ''extra dimension'' of self-awareness and accountability on the part of the heroine separates Isadora's memoirs from ''the league of books by women'' who believe that they are victims of a conspiratorial male society. With such persons Stein has no sympathy. With a ''female Bloom,'' however, he can sympathize, and the creator of a ''female Bloom'' he can praise as a novelist.

Four reviews by women who implicitly identify themselves as feminists present distinct contrasts with many of the reviews discussed earlier. These reviews all center on Isadora's vocational aspirations (as a poet), largely ignored in the other reviews. The most admiring of them also find meaningful and important Jong's depiction of a woman's inner life and respond positively to the energy and self-assertion of the heroine. The evaluations made by these reviewers provide a striking contrast with those of the conservative women reviewers discussed earlier in this chapter. While solipsism was a key word for the negative reviewers, the feminists see Isadora as above all in the world they themselves know. They read the ''zipless fuck'' as a fantasy and see the book as about the disappointments of reality as compared to fantasy. Their estimate of the novel's literary quality is also 180 degrees away from the other estimates. They praise the novel for character creation and narrative devices and also see the novel as comic, commenting on Jong's gifts as a ironist and parodist. It is these readers who appropriated Jong's novel most fully and passionately.

To understand the responses of the feminist reviewers, we must consider the novel in the context of the feminist movement of the early seventies. The ideas of those who began to do feminist analysis in the late sixties soon spread to the larger society. Victoria Geng describes the involvement of many women in the movement:

Buoyed by the optimism and energy generated in the Sixties, radical feminism carried along many of us—for we had begun to think

of feminists as "us"—who never joined either a radical organization or NOW. Radical feminism—and this still surprises people
who misunderstand "radical"—did not ask us to start by getting
out on the barricades. It asked us to think, to talk to other women,
and to tell the truth, even if we weren't prepared to act on it. (52)

Consciousness raising (CR) groups invited women to rethink their relation to the men in their lives and to social structures. The female tendency to self-blame was directly addressed in CR, where women were
encouraged to think that what they formerly considered personal problems were, in fact, social problems (Echols 83, 87). Although there was
a difference of opinion among feminists about sex, with some suggesting that sex was something women needed to be liberated from, the
majority sought new sexual freedoms. Women were no longer allowing
themselves to be positioned by a dominant discourse but were positioning themselves in active roles. In 1975 Jong commented on the reasons
her novel struck a responsive chord: "Women are confronting their
own sexuality, dealing with things inside themselves they've been
afraid of dealing with before: their own aggression, their negative feelings toward families, possibly toward their men" (interview, *Playboy*
78).

Rita Felski has discussed the role of literature, both confessional autobiographical writings and realistic novels, in forming the political
consciousness of women.[28] Feminist confession reveals that most problems are not personal but communal and at the same time provides the
"cathartic release which accompanies speaking about that which has
been kept hidden and silent" (116). The novel spread feminist ideas to
people who might not have been part of an organized women's movement and enabled them to participate in the self-discovery imaginative
literature made possible. The realistic novel was an important means
of self-exploration and social criticism. Felski emphasizes the usefulness for feminist consciousness raising of the realistic novel, which
"[encouraged] a functional and content-based reading" (79). One is
struck by the degree of identification and the strong expression of social relevance on the part of the feminist reviewers of Jong's novel.[29]

Jong's novel offered women permission to indulge in or acknowledge
sexual fantasies. That there had been a denial of women's fantasizing is
indicated by the fact that many responded to Jong's novel with the

comment, "Women don't think like that." To many of Jong's female readers, however, the theme of sexual fantasy was an important part of the novel and told them that they were no different from other women. The phrase "zipless fuck," which names the central fantasy in the novel, has become notorious. It first named what was new about the novel's message and subsequently was taken up by those who used it as a pejorative. Naughty, original, and succinct, the phrase has become, much to Jong's dismay, a kind of shorthand for the novel and for its author.

Let us turn now to the feminist reviewers. Molly Haskell's[30] credentials as a feminist are established by her book *From Reverence to Rape: The Treatment of Women in the Movies*, in which she writes: "The big lie perpetrated on Western society is the idea of women's inferiority, a lie so deeply ingrained in our social behavior that merely to recognize it is to risk unraveling the entire fabric of civilization" (1). Reviewing *Fear* in the *Village Voice Literary Supplement*, Haskell identifies the protagonist as a woman poet and states her admiration for this energetic and assertive woman: "Erica/Isadora, siren-wit-poet, comes on strong, shrinking the shrinks with their own jargon, dominating her mise-en-scène as authoritatively as Mae West ever tyrannized a tacky saloon" (27). Haskell's plot summary suggests immediately that she has constructed a coherent account of what she sees as events of significance: "The journey begins in the air of uncertainty—with the heroine's fear of flying a metaphor for woman's alternate longing for and fear of independence—and ends in the muddy bath water of self-acceptance, in the bath of her husband's London hotel room" (27). Haskell identifies with the heroine, saying that Isadora is "caught, like most of us, between the need for a mate and the need to be free," and then "turns to women's fantasies in her quest for the free and anonymous 'zipless fuck'" (27). Thus Isadora's fantasies are seen as a response to women's peculiar situation in society and not as vulgar sexual showing off. Her problems are real to the reviewer and "intersect with that common fund of experience that we think of as distinctly and generically women's" (27). But Isadora is not a victim: "somehow the very hand that writes, having writ so boldly, erases the image of victim" (27).

This reviewer, who describes the novel as a type of *Bildungsroman*, finds successful all the aesthetic and formal elements. She sees it as characteristic of the modern confessional novel that there's not much room for anyone else besides the protagonist. Hence the heroine's pre-occupation with herself is not seen as an inability to relate to reality. Haskell is not offended by the language or the sexual content but welcomes a woman's ironic use of these devices: "Here she comes . . . her cunt up front (in a comic reversal of those pornographic cartoons in which erect phalluses lead the way)." Jong has scored an artistic triumph, according to Haskell, in her story of a woman writer; "The writer and the woman work different sides of the street: they are a comedy team, the straightman getting into scrapes to give the writer (the ironist) material" (27).

Rosie Parker,[31] writing in the British feminist magazine *Spare Rib*, also sees Isadora's sexual fantasies as related to the actualities of married life. The fantasies arise from "the baggage of guilt, insecurity and romanticism planted on a girl growing up in the fifties and sixties" (42). Parker further notes that the book is about the unromantic nature of realized fantasies. The reviewer admires the wit and energy of the narrator and identifies the tone as "superficially naive" and hence as an artistic device on the part of the novelist, using as illustration quotations that are cited by some negative reviewers as evidence of Jong's shallowness and lack of talent. While some reviewers mentioned earlier express admiration for Jong's descriptions of European life, for Parker such descriptions "seem trivial in comparison to Isadora's inner experience" (42), particularly as she recounts her search for a female artist role model. Parker also responds to the book as comedy, admiring Jong's sense of the ridiculous as Isadora mocks herself even while suffering, and all in all, finds it "an impossible book not to like" (42).

Another reviewer who expresses an experiential relation to the content of the novel and explicitly identifies herself as a feminist also has high praise for the novel. Ghislaine Boulenger,[32] writing in the *Washington Post*, accepts Jong's portrayals of her encounters with the psychiatric profession as emblematic of her sufferings at the hands of a male system and remarks that Isadora "certainly has reason to be a feminist; so do we all" (D13). Like other feminist reviewers (and unlike those who have ideological conflict with the novel) she finds in Isadora's inner life a convincing depiction of female confusion in a transitional age; she is sympathetic to Isadora's fear of freedom (or flying) and applauds her insight that she must create meaning in her own life rather than depend on a man to do it for her. The reviewer does have one serious reservation about the novel—its class bias and intellectual elitism. The reviewer believes that Jong has inadequate sympathy for those who choose to be secretaries or "safe little wives" (D13).

A feminist with more serious reservations about the novel is Elaine Reuben,[33] who describes the novel in a review in the *New Republic* as a "painfully witty portrait of the author as a nice Jewish girl" (27). Reuben doesn't find Isadora's problems as a woman very convincing and praises only the portrayal of Isadora the artist: "Her accomplishments are real and the flashbacks in *Fear of Flying* which deal with her work, rather than her men, are the most satisfying in the novel" (27). Reuben then states a criticism that is repeated by some feminist reviewers of subsequent Jong novels: except for several brief comments, Jong does not hint at "the possibility that 'liberation' might have more to do with women caring about each other, in their lives and in their work, than with their caring, or not caring, about men" (27). Reuben's review, placed side by the side with the feminist reviews immediately above, reveals the tensions within feminism, tensions also seen in the reviewing of Jong's subsequent novels.

Those who praise the novel see more artistic complexity. They often see irony, comedy, wit, and a difference between the narrator and author. Especially in the reviews I characterize as feminist, the reviewers see what is often called criticism of life. For them, the novel concerns not narcissism and solipsism but a relation between reality and fantasy, not wallowing in self-pity but the achievement of mastery and control. To a large extent those who praise the novel value the same literary qualities (those in vogue in our day) as those who damn it—complexity of character and idea, irony, wit, coherent design, and skillful use of language. But the former find those qualities in the novel whereas the latter do not. The connection the favorable reviews make between what they see in the novel and the traditions of English and American literature are especially significant. Descriptions of the novel as a *Bildungsroman*, or location of the novel in the tradition exemplified by works considered classics, such as *Huck Finn* and *Ulysses*, if mentioned by the right people, mark the novel as a candidate for precanonical status.

Those readers who can connect the characters, situations, and events with their own experience of life and who recognize in the novel congenial ideas or ideological perspectives find the novel fills a need or serves a purpose for them, and thus they value it. It seems the novel also fills a need for the hostile reviewer. For some Erica Jong becomes the author they love to hate. An author who can be seen to embody "everything that is to be loathed in American fiction today" (Theroux 554) and perhaps much that is to be loathed in American society has a species of negative value.

Thus Jong seems to be a useful example for study of the constitution of literary value. As we unpack the contingent judgments of each reviewer, we find that he or she has much in common with others. The proverbial *De gustibus non disputandum est* does not apply. The results of this study illustrate or support Barbara Herrnstein Smith's belief that an investigation of the dynamics involved in evaluative judgments "would, I believe, reveal that the variables in question are limited and regular—that is, that they occur within ranges and that they exhibit patterns and principles—and that in *that* sense, but only in that sense, we may speak of 'constancies' of literary value" (11–12).

Jong's work was regarded as unquestionably literary in the early years after the publication of *Fear of Flying*. She was invited to appear at the Modern Language Association convention in 1974; she was invited to the Smithsonian to participate in a "distinguished women of letters" series (Jong later rejected the invitation, as I describe in the next chapter); she was invited to the nation's most prestigious colleges to read her work. The novel gained recognition as a literary success, and its author was regarded as a woman of letters, befitting a writer who made her first success as a poet and who had received support from the National Endowment for the Arts to write *Fear of Flying*.

As we look more closely at the dynamics of visibility, we may note some interesting facts about the construction of the novel's early reputation and specifically about the role of gender in the novel's early history. Jong's novel was first lifted from literary obscurity by notice from two males, Updike and Miller. The novel was given its first, and essential, boost by males, who, incidentally, validate the book by comparing it with other books written by men. Because of their stature in the literary establishment, Updike and Miller may well have done Jong the essential service of making it possible for *Fear of Flying* to be regarded as literature, and indeed as literature of a high order. The endorsement of these two men is mentioned over and over again in reviews and articles and by interviewers in published interviews with Jong. In almost every article about Jong, one reads that Updike has praised Jong and that Miller has claimed Jong as an heir. Updike's influence becomes clear when his terms of praise are taken up by subsequent commentators. Like DeMott in his review of *Any Woman's Blues* (Chapter 5), they often attribute "sass" and "bite" to the novel even when they do not mention Updike. The Chaucerian analogy employed by Updike and his comparison of Jong to the Wife of Bath (suggested by Jong herself in the novel) have also been repeated. The comparison is of course important because it removes Jong's novel from the realm of pornography and positions it in the realm of literature. Updike also contributed to the respectability of the novel by implicitly categorizing it as a *Bildungsroman*, thus positioning it in a way that would allow it to be picked up by academic commentators.

But it is doubtful whether Updike's or Miller's endorsement would have made the novel a success if it had not already experienced tremendous popularity. The nature of the celebrity of the novel made it more than simply a best-seller. It was taken seriously by male as well as female readers—in the *Playboy* interview Jong reports that fan letters were equally divided between men and women (76)—and it was talked about as something new and remarkable. These factors gave the novel its visibility, and the praise by Miller and Updike gave permission to call it good "literature." Soon the general impression was that the reviews of the novel had been good, or more than good, overall. *Playboy* reported in 1975 that the novel "was greeted by a chorus of rave reviews (and a gaggle of horrified ones. . .)" (61). The success of the novel gave a boost to recognition and sales of Jong's poetry. (Two books of poetry came out in 1975, and one of them, *Loveroot*, was chosen as an alternate selection by the Book-of-the-Month Club.)

Although the novel has surely been read widely and greatly enjoyed by both male and female readers, women seem to have been among its most passionate readers. Evidence found in the reviews and in anecdotal evidence (some of it supplied by Jong in the introduction to the fifteenth-anniversary edition of *Fear*) points to the importance of the novel to its women readers. In my discussions with Jong's readers I still find many female partisans of the novel, such as a woman professor who told me she had observed a moment of silence in her classroom on the fifteenth anniversary of the novel's publication. Jong's standing with feminists in the first years after the publication of the novel is indicated by the fact that she was interviewed in 1974 for the *Columbia Forum* by professor and feminist-critic Elaine Showalter (along with Carol Smith, then head of the English Department at Rutgers' Douglass College) and asked such questions as "How do you see the future of feminist writing?" (17).

However, all this happened in 1973–1975. What has happened since then illustrates the mutability of literary value. Feminist criticism has moved on since 1975. Jong's first novel still has its loyal admirers, many of whom honor it for what it meant to them in 1973 and others for its present value. But Jong's work is now largely ignored by the feminist establishment. The institutional authority that feminists have gained is advancing the fortunes of other women writers but not Jong's. Jong's novel had some male admirers in high places, who welcomed the woman writer to the domain of sexual fiction, but we have not heard from these men lately. Updike has never made any subsequent endorsement of Jong though he included his review of *Fear* in *Picked-Up Pieces*. Miller, elderly at the time he was associated with Jong, has since died. Since reputations are always mediated by institutions, a crucial matter for the future of Jong's novel will be the extent to which it is championed by the literary and academic establishments. The following chapters, tracing Jong's reputation history to the present, will tell this story.

3 / How to Save Your Own Life: Mass Culture, Gender, and Cultural Authority

In its reassessment of cultural production and use, postmodern theory calls into question the modernist opposition between high culture and low or mass culture. Postmodernist remapping of cultural terrain eliminates the old hierarchies and substitutes a notion of culture as decentered and fragmentary. Jim Collins says in *Uncommon Cultures: Popular Culture and Post-Modernism*: "Cultural production is no longer a carefully coordinated 'system' but provides a range of simultaneous options that have destabilized traditional distinctions between High Art and mere 'mass culture' " (2). Collins notes that few models have been developed to describe the new understanding of culture. I contend that any new models will have to include attention to gender, since the place accorded women writers in the postmodern world bears some remarkable similarities to the former world.

In my study of the reception of Jong's work, I have found that binary oppositions of "high" and "low" have a sturdy resilience that has affected the reception of Jong's work. Her example suggests that popular works by women may be denigrated as mass culture by the literary establishment. As Pierre Bourdieu says, the status of a cultural object is conferred by the form of consumption (327), and Jong's critics set out to control how her work was consumed. The reception of Jong's work has been adversely affected by the association of low culture with women. Attacked, even vilified, by the literary press for her sexual fiction, Jong has found little favor with the cultural elite. Her reception as a fiction writer and a poet offers insight into problems of reading mass culture within the institution of professional literary studies and reveals the element of misogyny shared by the cultural elite and popular journalism. Although offering a striking example that may serve as a basis for redefining the notion of literary value, Jong's reception also reveals that the establishment continues to have difficulty according "literary" status to popular works by women.

Attacks on Jong over ostensibly aesthetic matters were, I argue, really conflicts over cultural authority. Fears that their authority was threatened by a wave of female, possibly feminist, authors and readers sent reviewers into a tailspin, and these fears were displaced onto "aesthetics." The example of Jong's reception reveals not just how deeply embedded literary reception and evaluation are in social processes but how deeply implicated are matters of gender in any discussion of literary value. As Janice Radway points out, the dominant discourse of the cultural establishment "[predicates] the individuated male subject as the fundamental cultural norm" ("Male-Order Culture" 515).[1] And the naturalization of the male subject as norm is tied to a cluster of assumptions about popular culture, including assumptions about male and female forms of consumption, with female readers seen as capable only of uncritical ingestion while male readers are associated with the respected activities of discrimination and critical use. These points are abundantly illustrated in the reception of Jong's second novel.

Let us turn now to the case at hand, the reception of *How to Save Your Own Life,* and place it in the context of the media attention Jong received after *Fear of Flying* became well known.

When *Fear of Flying* hit number one on the best-seller lists, about January of 1975, Erica Jong became a celebrity. In a matter of months she was transformed from an unknown, whose first publicity visit to Chicago in the winter of 1973–1974 was "the non-event of the season" (Colander E10), to a media star. Her name, her activities, her opinions on any subject were hot copy for newspapers and glossy magazines. She was suddenly inundated with requests for magazine articles, and the TV networks, which had, without explanation, refused even to carry ads for *Fear of Flying,* were eager to have Jong appear on talk shows (telephone interview, April 13, 1991). In a 1975 article on the new feminist novels, *Newsweek* called Jong "the most visible star in the new galaxy" (Peer 70). The story was accompanied by a sidebar captioned "Lusty Lady with Talent Too" and a photograph of Jong standing over her kitchen sink wiping her hands on a dishtowel. The first of the many interviews began to appear in popular publications such as the *Chicago Tribune,* the *Los Angeles Times, Playboy,* and *Mademoiselle.*

The introduction to the *Playboy* interview recounts some of the many current published reports about Jong: "She was in a deep depression; she was bubbling with happiness. Her marriage was on the rocks; it was stronger than ever. She was writing; she wasn't" (61). In a *Los Angeles Times* story she comments on her celebrity: "This morning I had a call from an editor at *Vogue*. 'We want 300 words from you on "Optimism about Marriage,"' he said, and we need it by the day after tomorrow.' . . . Last night *Ingenue* called to say they were doing a list of writers' favorite books" (Wilson 10). Jong is quoted as saying: "At a certain point, when your name is 'hot,' you become a commodity and people will publish anything by you—laundry lists, anything. You have to say no—otherwise they'll eat you up, and your by-line's going to be worth nothing" (10). Jong became an "instant sexpert," in the phrase of Pat Colander of the *Chicago Tribune*, who also labeled Jong "newly appointed guru of interpersonal relations" (E10). Among the articles Jong wrote in 1975 are "Daughters" in the *Ladies' Home Journal*, "Marriage: Rational and Irrational" in *Vogue*, and "Notes on Five Men" (an appreciation from Jong as the fan of five leading men of the cinema) in *Esquire*. In 1977, when excerpts from the second novel, *How to Save Your Own Life*, began to appear in *Vogue* and *Mademoiselle*, she wrote "Writer Who 'Flew' to Sexy Fame Talks about Being a Woman," also for *Vogue*.

The many articles about Jong that appeared around 1975 suggest the star quality Jong had at that time. In one article about unmarried celebrity couples, entitled "The Pleasures and Problems of Living Together," Jong and her lover (later her third husband) Jonathan Fast are pictured and interviewed along with three couples from the entertainment world (Selden). Another story brings Jong and Liv Ullmann together for "An Intimate Conversation" ("Two Women"). Jong had spent time in California working on a film script for a film of *Fear of Flying*, but in 1975 Jong sued Columbia and Julia Phillips, stating that Phillips was not qualified to direct the film. Jong lost the lawsuit, but the film has never been made.[2]

Jong remembers making numerous television appearances[3] including, among the earliest, interviews with Barbara Walters, Tom Snyder, and an appearance on *Sixty Minutes* with Henry Miller (August 17, 1975). *Sixty Minutes* host Mike Wallace introduced the segment with a brief history of Miller's battle with the censors and with poverty and then commented on Jong's success:

Well, now, 40 years later, came a book called *Fear of Flying* written by a young woman named Erica Jong. Her obscenities, her explicitness—in some ways more graphic than Henry Miller's. But Ms. Jong is feted, celebrated, and her bank account swelled, by the reception that she and her literary endeavor have received from the critics and at the bookstore. (19)

In the conversation that followed, Miller credited Jong with liberating women writers in the same way he liberated men writers to write freely about sex and the body. Miller and Jong ended up agreeing that they are romantics at heart and that sexual fantasies, when realized, are disappointing and a poor substitute for love.

Jong also made many personal appearances at this time. One scheduled appearance at the Smithsonian caused quite a flap. Jong was to appear as the last guest in a series of "distinguished women of letters" that had featured appearances by Lillian Hellman, Anaïs Nin, and Nikki Giovanni. Giovanni had embarrassed officials by making a remark questioning Gerald Ford's ability to be president at that time in history, so, trying to avoid further embarrassment, staff members warned Jong not to talk about politics or sex (Shales, "Propriety vs. Censorship" B1). Jong then declined to appear on the grounds of censorship. Jong had been welcomed at many college campuses, including the University of Chicago, Vassar College, and Marymount College, named in a *Washington Post* news story (Shales, "Smithsonian" B1) as places where she had made the same presentation she was to have made at the Smithsonian. (The Smithsonian subsequently instituted a policy not to schedule talks by contemporary writers.)

For a time in 1974–1975 Jong would have been justified in feeling that she could have it all: fame, wealth, and literary reputation in the bargain. Not only was her novel selling like the proverbial hotcakes, not only was she in demand by the print and electronic media (who seemed to treat anything she said like pure gold), she was also receiving plaudits from those whose opinions counted in realm of legitimate culture: she was invited to read at prestigious colleges; she was invited to appear at the Modern Language Association Convention (in 1974) and at the American Bookseller's Association convention, and her remarks to the booksellers were reprinted in the scholarly journal *Twentieth Century Literature*; her poetry was selling astonishingly well for poetry, and her new poems *Loveroot* were chosen as an alternate book club selection (her novel had already been selected by three book clubs); her novel was being taught in literature courses at highly regarded universities such as Rice University and the University of Wisconsin (and also in sociology courses at other schools, such as UCLA); she was publicly praised by important writers such as Miller and Elizabeth Janeway (Peer). These heady days came to an end, however.[4] Not surprisingly for those who have studied the dynamics of fame and its seemingly inevitable transformation into notoriety, Erica Jong the fairy princess was soon transformed into Erica Jong the witch.

It would be impossible to overemphasize the role of the media in Jong's literary reputation. The media's focusing on Jong as a newsworthy commodity made her into a celebrity, and it is a law of media fame, in modern America, at least, that what goes up must come down, or, more accurately, what is raised up must be pulled down. Leo Braudy writes in his anatomy of fame, *The Frenzy of Renown: Fame and Its History*, that "modern fame is always compounded of the audience's aspirations and its despair, its need to admire and to find a scapegoat for that need" (9). In contemporary society, Braudy tells us, "much of our daily experience tells us that we should [be famous] if we possibly can, because it is the best, perhaps the only way *to be*" (6). The famous are the apotheosis of success in a competitive, achievement-oriented society. They are liberated from the anonymity that dogs the rest of us, the myth goes, and transported to "a quiet place where one is free to be what one really is, one's true, unchanging essence" (6). Especially in America, where everyone aspires to climb the ladder of success, the famous epitomize our aspirations and must also become scapegoats for our failures. Media interests in all this are clear. In an industry dominated by the need to entertain, every new day brings the necessity for a new story. When the story of Jong the princess got old, it was time for the story of Jong the witch.

Attacks on Jong began as early as 1974 in a *Newsweek* article of December 16 which begins, "Poor Erica Jong. The two telephones in her New York apartment peal like maddened metronomes. Her fan mail fills a cardboard box in the corner and overflows onto the chaos of her desk" (Francke 65). A *Time* article in February 1975 suggesting that Jong is persona non grata to feminists quotes Becky Gould of NOW who says that Jong confuses the liberated libido and the liberated self. Gould's most positive comment is that "it has to be some kind of breakthrough for a woman to cash in on this kind of tripe; men have been doing it for so long" ("The Loves of Isadora" 70). Most outspoken was Burt Prelutsky in his regular literary column in the *Los Angeles Times* on May 25, 1975, which he titled "Kicking Jong Around." Prelutsky, who says he tries to postpone reading a book until it is at least three years old, broke down and read Jong's novel before the scheduled time because of all the talk he heard about it. Prelutsky's purpose, it seems, is simply to indicate that Jong does not deserve the recognition she has gotten. He makes a point of refusing even to deal with what others named as a distinctive feature of the novel, that is, a new way of writing about female sexuality, and implies that the novel has no originality or distinction whatsoever. He denies that Jong's book is either dirty or antimale, implicitly questioning why it got attention on those grounds (and thus why it got any attention at all). He then charges that the book is badly written and old-fashioned in its approach to female options. Prelutsky ends with an insult to the author, based on a statement made (and quoted in the column) by the novel's protagonist-narrator. He makes the judgment that the novel is a "trashy and unworthy book, not because of a smattering of four-letter words, but because it measures untold millions of women against its author—and finds them, of all things, beneath her" (75). He bases his conclusion on a passage in *Fear of Flying*, in which the protagonist wonders if the husband she has left has found happiness with some "ordinary girl" and then has a fantasy of herself as a happy housewife. The passage is admired by some feminist reviewers and commentators for what they see as truth to female experience in the portrayal of conflicting desires to pursue self-development and to follow a marked-out feminine path of service and subordination.

A *Los Angeles Times Book World* review of the two books of Jong's poetry published in 1975 prefigures many of the reviews of Jong's second novel, published in 1977. The reviewer is Marjorie Perloff, at that time professor of English at the University of Maryland. She speaks for that segment of the academic world that was horrified that Jong could become "an integral part of the academic establishment" (2), as indicated by the fact that Jong's novel is required reading in many courses and that the address to the booksellers was reprinted in *Twentieth-Century Literature*. Perloff says she almost feels sorry for Jong, but her compassion is tempered by her knowledge of the many deserving writers whose work goes unpublished.

At the same time Jong had defenders, such as Robert Kirsch, *Los Angeles Times* book critic, who defended Jong in the column "The Book Report" in connection with the publication of the volume *Here Comes and Other Poems*, a reissue in 1975 of Jong's first two volumes of poetry along with several prose pieces and an interview. Kirsch expressed pleasure at the fact that Jong's celebrity would have the beneficial effect of making her "impressive poetry" accessible to many readers. He predicts that she will not be "a victim of success" but will "almost certainly transform it into the matter of art" (D5).

Jong reports that when she began to appear on television in 1975, many writers still refused to make television appearances, seeing them as a breach of writerly decorum. Jong says that she too had reservations about appearing on television because she shared the values current in the grad school and poetry circles she frequented at the time. But, feeling under attack by the print media, she decided to take advantage of the opportunity to defend herself on television, in spite of the fact that many literary people had cautioned her against it. Jong says she felt that

I could be a good advocate of my work on television because when people saw me on television, they saw that I was a perfectly reasonable person, articulate and with a sense of humor, and they had a better take on who I was than if they were just reading printed attacks. The printed attacks made me out to be some kind of Valkyrie/monster. I seemed strange in the reviews. People would meet me and say, "But you're so short," or "You're so nice." So I understood that the Erica Jong in the press was so far from who I was that I really had to go on television and be who I was since I could do it with ease and humor. (telephone interview, April 13, 1991)[5]

Jong has also said in a published interview that she welcomed the opportunity to go on television to make her books better known and improve sales and in that way obtain the security and freedom to do "my thing" (*Mademoiselle* 98). She has said that the greatest freedom of all would be to be able to sell millions and millions of books without having to be on talk shows (*Mademoiselle* 98), but it's possible that Jong enjoys spectacle. She has described herself as a "people person" and compares herself to Norman Mailer in this respect (telephone interview, April 13, 1991). She has given many interviews, made many publicity tours, and made charitable appearances for PEN and other groups. In one such appearance she rode an elephant, and in another she made her singing debut at the Algonquin Hotel.[6] Those who have seen her on television and in personal appearances describe her as glamorous, sometimes flamboyantly dressed, and sexually attractive. An academic friend of mine remembers being horrified when she saw Jong read a poem about the joys of fellatio on a late-night show in the seventies. In her appearances and print interviews Jong has spoken out on the subjects of female sexuality and society's puritanism. In her personal appearances she does not back down from what she has said in her books. Some who react negatively to Jong's books for all the reasons I have discussed are probably even more put off when they see Jong in person, since in many ways she personifies the qualities associated with her books.

The extremely negative response to Jong's second novel was the high point of the backlash caused by resentment of Jong's success, but those who turned on Jong were attacking more than just one woman. The virulence of the attacks can be accounted for in part by the fact that Jong was made to stand in for the great successes of feminism in the mid-seventies. In August 1975, Laurel Graeber wrote in *Mademoiselle* that the popularity of the women's movement was so great that to voice support for the movement was an act of gaucherie: "To say that I'm a feminist has become as bland as to say that I'm a person who likes jazz. 'Isn't everyone?' is the presumed reply" (42). A 1975 survey of college students published in the *New York Times* on January 11, 1976, revealed that college freshman were more likely to accept the goals of the women's movement than any of their predecessors ("Freshman Survey Finds New Trends" A45). The newspaper files in the years 1976–1978 reveal successes for women's studies, widespread interest in feminist causes by politicians (or at least the desire to appear interested), Equal Rights Amendment (ERA) endorsement by both the Democrats and Republicans at their national conventions, preparations for the international women's year in 1978, and names of prominent feminists popping up everywhere—activists Eleanor Smeal, Betty Friedan, and Gloria Steinem, politicians Bella Abzug, Barbara Jordan, Elizabeth Holtzman, and a number of women writers.

Success provoked a backlash. The moribundity or even the demise of the women's movement has been a media headline all through the years of its success, but the fact that by 1976 the ERA had been voted down in several states gave people a new opportunity to ask "What Has Gone Wrong with the Feminist Movement?" the title of a *Harper's Bazaar* article that deals, not with the failure, but the success of the movement. A number of well-known spokespersons including Jong, Betty Friedan, and Elizabeth Holtzman make the point that the problems of the movement have to do mainly with communication that must go through media channels.

When we consider how strongly Jong has been identified with feminism, it is not surprising that those who sought an outlet for their anger at feminism's success directed their attacks at Erica Jong. As we have seen, Jong's first novel was viewed as a document of the women's liberation movement by reviewers. But let us note also that almost every interviewer asks Jong to comment on the progress of the feminist movement and that over the years Jong has been invited to review books of feminist interest and to appear on television talk shows to comment on the movement. Jong has sometimes expressed impatience, especially in the early years, with this role as spokesperson for all women along with incredulousness and annoyance at being blamed for women's leaving their husbands.[7]

All through her career Jong has had to fight the tendency of the media to simplify and distort the messages they transmit. The media prefer ideas that are easily assimilated and do not challenge the status quo. Certainly the media have had a difficult time reporting on feminism. Though sometimes feminist ideas have been reported in a positive light, just as often caricature and stereotype have characterized media reporting of feminism. Given the tendencies of media to simplify, we can see the strong potential for distortion in their coverage of Jong. The most common approach was to depict feminism as a rebellion against men without exploring the complexity of issues in a sexist culture. Jong was also taken to represent women who saw feminism mainly as an ideology supporting greater economic opportunity for women. But the most common stereotype applied to Jong was that of "sexy broad." It was easy to overlook any possible complexity in Jong's sexual theme and revert to old stereotypes.

Jong's role as the celebrity of feminism and women's new sexual status along with the enormous success of her first book had a negative effect on the evaluation of her second novel. *How to Save Your Own Life* got overwhelmingly negative reviews, even though by the time of its publication, Jong's first novel had acquired a reputation as a success— not just popular success, but literary success as well. As the reviewers look back on *Fear of Flying*, which received more negative than positive reviews, they often speak well of it. Lance Morrow comments in *Time*: "*Fear of Flying* possessed a bawdy exuberance, John Updike even found it Chaucerian" (75). He also remarks at the end of his review that "actually, *Fear of Flying* was extravagantly overpraised" (75), a statement that could refer to Updike's review, but which could hardly refer to published reviews in general. In her review, Diane Johnson refers to Jong's "exuberant" (6) *Fear of Flying*. D. Keith Mano says (somewhat condescendingly, to be sure) he found *Fear* as "cute as baton twirlers: likeable, humorous, adroit" (498). John Leonard refers to the "energy and irreverence of *Fear of Flying*, the Huck Finnishness, the cheerful vulgarity, the eye for social detail" (40). After four years, these reviewers, none of whom like Jong's second novel, claim to have an affection for her first book. Leonard's comparison of *Fear* to *Huck Finn* is especially telling, since it is this kind of comparison that marks a new book as a candidate for precanonical status. Would these reviewers have made the same evaluations of *Fear* if they had reviewed it when it first appeared? One cannot imagine Jong getting a positive review in, for example, the *National Review*, Mano's publication. But *Fear of Flying* had become known as a cultural phenomenon, had won the respect of some important authorities, and a new consensus about the value of the book had emerged. It is also a handy rhetorical ploy to praise the first work at the expense of the second.

In the foregrounding of the issues of mass culture and cultural health, the response to Jong's second novel opens another chapter in the study of literary reception and reputation. As the female celebrity author of a sexually explicit best-selling novel dealing with a woman's search for identity, Jong became a symbol, for high culture reviewers, of a cultural decline. Those who thought of themselves as guardians of and spokespersons for legitimate culture responded negatively because, I believe, they felt threatened by a possible shift in cultural power denoted by Jong's appearance on the scene. They presented *How to Save Your Own Life* as a sell-out, a pandering to a mass audience, and an illustration of the poverty of the cultural values of a society that could choose to reward this particular novelist. Because of her best-selling first novel and the subsequent publicity, Jong became identified with popular culture or, to use a more pejorative term, "mass culture." Many reviewers of *How to Save Your Own Life* seem to be reviewing the author—who is cast as the person responsible for dragging down cultural standards—rather than the book. The reviews emphasize the autobiographical nature of the novel and then turn to the author, often commenting on her status as a public figure, the amount of money she makes, and her perceived role as a culture heroine, a role resented by these reviewers. The British press was particularly hostile, seeing Jong as representing all that is wrong with women, America, and the modern world. Some reviewers on both sides of the Atlantic attack the audience, deploring their taste and lamenting the moral qualities of the consumers of mass culture. Some reviewers review the cover of the novel and see in that artifact all that is wrong with Jong and the world that has made her what she is. In fact, as I discuss more fully in a later chapter, Jong's reputation has never recovered from the circumstances of her debut.

The reviewers of Jong's second novel saw themselves as an elite threatened by a "mass," which Jong came to represent for them. In *Distinction: A Social Critique of the Judgement of Taste*, Pierre Bourdieu describes the construction of the social world as based on distinctions. "Social identity lies in difference" (479), he reminds us. By their tastes, chosen by them and legitimated by the institutions they control, the socially dominant classes declare their superiority, and the tastes learned by them in their social circles or through formal education are accepted by them and by the socially dominated classes as evidence of their superiority. Thus, a fundamental opposition is that between the " 'elite' of the dominant and the 'mass' of the dominated," viewed by the elite as a "contingent, disorganized multiplicity, interchangeable and innumerable, existing only statistically" (468). The defensiveness of the elite can give rise to "apocalyptic denunciations, of all forms of 'leveling,' 'trivialization,' or 'massification,' " denunciations that "betray an obsessive fear of number, of undifferentiated hordes indifferent to all difference" (469). Bourdieu's rhetoric captures very well the horror of guardians of high culture at a threat to their status.

Book reviewers, who, characteristically, are a part of the high culture establishment, see themselves as beleaguered defenders of the citadel of culture. The masses, who are lionizing Erica Jong, making her rich, and propelling her into the spotlight, or at least making her an object for the television camera and the journalist's page, are threatening high culture. The result is a lack of deference to the high culture establishment, and thus to the reviewers themselves. The theory at work here is that there may not be enough cultural deference to go around, and attention paid to Erica Jong detracts from the fund of deference to what these reviewers see as high culture. According to Bourdieu's analysis, the system of classification of cultural objects, usually internalized, is enunciated explicitly when it ceases to function below the level of consciousness. At this point, "the guardians of the established order must enunciate, systematize and codify principles of production of that order, both real and represented, so as to defend them against heresy; in short, they must constitute the doxa as orthodoxy" (480).

Jim Collins describes a postmodern universe of discourses in competition for a position as a privileged mode of representation, with culture becoming a field of conflict on which various players compete to win popular consent for their authority.[8] The cultural categories "popular" and "legitimate" or "high" and "low" are themselves subjects of contention. The contents of these categories are transferable, as Pierre Bourdieu explains: "the same object which is today typically middle-brow—'average'—may yesterday have figured in the most 'refined' constellations of tastes and may be put back there at any moment by one of those taste-maker's coups which are capable of rehabilitating the most discredited object" (327). In Bourdieu's analysis, status is conferred by the form of consumption and does not relate to "inherent" properties of the object consumed. For the tastemaking intellectuals of postmodern culture, matters of self-interest are not irrelevant. The stakes in the contest could not be higher or the situation more fraught with tension and anxiety, because what is being contested is their authority to dictate cultural values.

In the reception of Jong's novels, we have an instance of the problematics of cultural categories. Assignment of works to these categories is very much a social dynamic which, in the case of Jong, has to do with the perceived threat she poses to the high culture establishment and draws on the residual notion of low culture as female.

The reviewers, who have a binary view of culture and would be horrified by Jim Collins's vision of a fragmented culture, express the age-old attitude of contempt for a popular audience. In *Bread and Circuses: Theories of Mass Culture as Social Decay*, Patrick Brantlinger comments on the longevity of disdain for a popular audience, tracing it back to Heraclitus for whom, simply, "there are many bad but few good" (quoted in Brantlinger 54). Illustrating the persistence of this idea, Brantlinger comments, "Heraclitus matches one of his modern emulators, Friedrich Nietzsche, in his insistence that most people are blind to or even actively hostile toward moral and cultural excellence" (53). What can be enjoyed by many is, by definition, vulgar.

In our time there is a consensus of opinion emanating from segments of the right and the left that the mass culture created by the new technologies has a debasing effect on cultural life. In *No Respect: Intellectuals and Popular Culture* Andrew Ross gives a history of intellectuals that links the authority of intellectuals from the end of World War II to the 1960s to a rejection of terms like "class" and "mass" as reminiscent of the Marxism of the thirties. In the hysterical climate of the Cold War, the populace was seen as defenseless against mass culture, which was seen as a road to totalitarianism. The debate about mass culture that took place at that time "was conducted in a discursive climate that linked social, cultural, and political difference to disease" (43). As relentless as an epidemic, mass culture could no more be resisted than "germs." The intellectuals who gained prominence after World War II occupied an authoritative position that "depended explicitly upon the containment of intellectual radicalism and cultural populism alike" (47). With the end of the mid-century consensus in the 1960s and the rise of new voices supporting the various popular challenges to the establishment, those who still identified with the old consensus felt themselves to be under siege. Women seeking a share of cultural authority were one threat.

Jong's second novel is constituted as low culture by virtue of her status as a celebrity and the popularity of her previous novel (exacerbated by the fact that the novel was written by a woman and was explicitly sexual). The aggressive tone in the attempts to categorize the novel as low culture—which came in response to the literary success of *Fear of Flying*—can be seen as a move toward "containment" of feminist authors. Journalistic attention to Jong, including television interviews and appearances on talk shows, are mentioned or alluded to by Jong's American reviewers, while British reviewers more often allude to her commercial success. As Jong's novel is mediated by the reviewers' responses to her public persona as created in newspaper and magazine articles and in interviews and talk show appearances, it does not come off well. Jong the personality looms large, and the reviewers often respond to the novel as autobiography. Although we still hear the charges made by reviewers of *Fear of Flying* that Jong's work is marred by ideological feminism and presents an affront to traditional values, reviewers of the second novel are preoccupied most of all by Jong's personal style, which they find offensive, and by her success, which they find undeserved. Most of the reviewers make the same evaluation of the novel that they make of Jong the personality—shallow and trivial.

Jong's novel is denounced as an artifact of mass culture, but the novel has to be "placed" as mass or popular culture in a complex process that includes but is not limited to reviewers. Jong's second novel was reviewed in five of the eight journals mentioned by Ohmann as influential in moving a work to the precanonical stage (while *Fear of Flying* was reviewed in six). We must assume that the novel was regarded as at least a candidate for high culture status by the editors and reviewers of these journals. When *Fear of Flying* first appeared, it was reviewed along with other new novels, many of which could not easily be categorized as pop culture, including books by Patrick White and David Storey. *How to Save Your Own Life* was reviewed along with books by Joan Didion and Ingmar Bergman.

Also important is the status of the reviewer selected to write the review. Ohmann comments on the different treatment given books clearly regarded as ephemeral and those regarded as belonging in another, more exclusive category. Asserting that the *New York Times Book Review* leads the process of making distinctions between "ephemera" and "literature," Ohmann comments on the

marked difference of impact between, say, Martin Levin's favorable but mildly condescending (and brief) review of *Love Story* and the kind of front-page review by an Alfred Kazin or an Irving Howe that asked readers to regard a new novel as literature, and that so often helped give the stamp of highbrow approval to books by Bellow, Malamud, Updike, Roth, Doctorow, and so forth. (204)

Although *Fear* did not get special respect from the *New York Times Book Review* when it first appeared (it was reviewed on page forty by a little-known reviewer), it did receive a highly positive review from John Updike in the *New Yorker*. This review, along with the Henry Miller article in the *New York Times*, no doubt played a role in making the novel a candidate for the honorific category, literature. We should also note here that starting with *Fear*, many reviewers of stature have reviewed Jong's work, including many of the reviewers of *How to Save Your Own Life*. In the case of Jong's second novel, we have the following, rather anomalous, situation. The novel was reviewed in a large number of prestigious journals, sometimes with the tribute of a page-one review, by important reviewers. The attention given to the novel is underlined by the fact that it is often reviewed by itself, not along with other novels in a single review. The reviews place the novel and its author firmly in the realm of pop culture and in that way protect legitimate culture from an invasion. The vast majority of reviews I found undertake this defensive function, and thus the evaluative communities appear almost to have collapsed into one. There are, however, several exceptions, which I discuss at the end of the chapter, and from them we can infer the existence of larger evaluative communities sharing similar viewpoints.

Let us note also the identification of mass culture with the feminine, which goes back at least to Nietzsche, who said of the theater: "In the theater one becomes people, herd, female, pharisee, voting cattle, patron, idiot—*Wagnerian*" (quoted in Huyssen 51). Andreas Huyssen writes of the late nineteenth century that "the fear of the masses in this age of declining liberalism is always also a fear of woman, a fear of nature out of control, a fear of the unconscious, of sexuality, of the loss of identity and stable ego boundaries in the mass" (52). According to Huyssen, mass culture is the other of modernism: the powerful masculine mystique of modernism "has to be somehow related to the persistent gendering of mass culture as feminine and inferior" (55). Thus, says Huyssen, the "postmodern crisis of high modernism and its clas-

sical accounts has to be seen as a crisis both of capitalist moderniza-
tion itself and of the deeply patriarchal structures that support it" (58).
Feminist incursions into legitimate cultural arenas and the revaluation
of popular discourses are postmodern phenomena. Although Huyssen
asserts that women have now secured a place within high culture and
that consequently the gendering of mass culture as feminine is outmoded, the story of Erica Jong's treatment by high culture critics suggests that the place women have gained is tenuous and that the misogyny that undergirded modernism is not solely a thing of the past. Jong's
example suggests that mass culture is still seen as "woman" and is
consequently devalued even in a climate that is supposedly receptive to
new ways of defining culture.

Indeed the criticisms leveled against Jong are reminiscent of criticisms made about the women who invented the novel form in the eighteenth century, and *pace* Huyssen's optimistic view of the progress
women have made, the treatment of women fiction writers appears to
be an illustration of that old adage: the more things change, the more
they stay the same. As Terry Lovell in *Consuming Fiction* and others
have explained, as a new form the novel lacked a respected tradition,
and with women represented in large numbers among both authors and
readers, the novel was regarded as lacking in literary seriousness. It was
thought that it took little skill to write novels, which were often seen
as mere transcriptions of female experience. Viewed as escapist in nature and catering to the lowest tastes, novels were seen as having a pernicious effect on female character, and it was thought that this shallow
and purely entertaining form would drive out "good" literature.

The high culture honorific "literature" is the gift of reviewers and
critics. A work is constituted as "literature" through the process
Ohmann describes, from the response of the first reviewers through the
acceptance of a work by academics. Ohmann suggests that books that
are not taken seriously by high culture reviewers quickly fall into obliv-
ion, and little attention from reviewers means no attention from academics. The important question is where a work will end up, in Pierre
Bourdieu's words, in relation to that "sacred frontier which makes legitimate culture a separate universe" (5). For reviewers of *How to Save
Your Own Life*, it seems that celebrity and best-sellerdom militate
against Jong's chances of crossing over that "sacred frontier."

. Some of the complexity of the process of placing Jong is seen in the fact that she is included on Ohmann's list of forty-eight novelists whose work, by his measures, has attained precanonical status, having passed successfully through all the stages of selection, including appearances in scholarly bibliographies. Ohmann points out that his list excludes the "overwhelming majority of writers who regularly produced large best-sellers" (207), such as Puzo, Wouk, and Susann. Presumably Jong's inclusion is based on *Fear* rather than her second novel, but the point remains the same: the category "high culture" is fluid. Let us note also that seven years after its publication, Anthony Burgess included *How to Save Your Own Life* in his *99 Novels: The Best in English since 1939, A Personal Choice*. Neither *Fear of Flying* nor *Fanny* (the two novels that have gained the most approval from persons associated with the cultural establishment) is included in his list, which came out in 1984. Burgess, a fan of Jong who contributed cover blurbs for several of her publications,[9] describes in his introduction what he calls the "art novel," mentioning such familiar criteria as complex and believable characters, formal qualities, and philosophical exploration. In his discussion of *How to Save Your Own Life*, Burgess makes clear why it is for him an art novel. He especially praises Jong's language and even approves of the happy ending: "There is nothing wrong with a happy ending" (114).

The instability of cultural categories is continually illustrated. Herbert Gans points out that it is not uncommon for works originally identified as popular culture to be taken up as high culture at some later point. I was reading Gans's book early in 1985, on the Saturday of the radio broadcast of the Metropolitan Opera's first production of *Porgy and Bess*, an event that might be designated as the crossing of the sacred frontier.[10] In another example, singer Joan Morris referred to the songs of Irving Berlin (who had no musical training and was in his own day the quintessential popular artist) as "art songs," one hundred years after the composer's birth.[11]

Jong has stated that she was surprised by the popularity of *Fear of Flying*, thinking it too literary to have broad popular appeal. She comments further in an interview with Wendy Martin:

Fear of Flying was thought to be a very uncommercial book when it was first published in hardcover. It was all I could do to get the publisher to do anything for it, to advertise it, to publicize it. They were very wrong. The paperback publisher believed that it could reach an enormous audience and promoted it as if were very commercial—as indeed it proved to be. But all of that is hindsight; nobody knew that at the time of initial publication. (26)

Even the standard criteria of simplicity versus complexity, so often used to separate the sheep of high culture from the goats of low culture, are apparently not easy to apply to Jong's novels. Interpreters of the various novels come down on different sides of this issue. Does *How to Save Your Own Life* have a complex protagonist, effective social satire, and a philosophical "residue" (17), to use Burgess's term, or does it present a flat character and a banal view of life? As their responses to the novel are mediated by their responses to Jong's personality, the majority of the reviewers come down on the side of simplicity and pop culture. In the case of Jong's second novel, it is particularly significant that a part of the perspective brought to bear on the work by the reviewers is their cognizance of their role as brokers of value.[12]

As reviewers of *How to Save Your Own Life* make the point that Jong's novel is popular culture, not to be confused with serious literature, an art-entertainment dichotomy is set up, with Jong's novel classed as entertainment. The categorization of the novel as pop culture is based on the assumption that cultural objects must be arranged hierarchically and that the work itself dictates the way it is to be read. In the hierarchical classification of literature adumbrated by the reviewers discussed below, "good" literature offers a serious analysis of life that asks people to contemplate its painful features and places emphasis on a moral scheme that stretches or challenges people's moral or intellectual perspectives. Lack of a mature moral perspective is always revealed through inartistic language—cliché, and flat, uninteresting verbal structures. The invocation of the dichotomy "good" literature and "contaminating" mass culture owes much to literary modernism, but the attitude of many of Jong's reviewers, who emphasize the usefulness of literature to improve human character and deepen one's understanding of human life, would be better described as "middlebrow" than "highbrow." No doubt some reviewers would think it ludicrous even to consider Jong in relation to the true highbrow or modernist avant-garde, or perhaps some see their role as assisting the general reader to find books that have pragmatic value as guides to behavior or interpreters of a complex reality.[13]

Jong's readers are presented as strictly lowbrow, capable of appropriating literature only through consumption or ingestion. Metaphors of consumption pop up in the reviews, with both Jong and her readers described as greedy and gluttonous. The model of reading the reviewers attribute to Jong's readers has been called physical or biological by Janice Radway in *Reading the Romance*. In this model the act of reading becomes a "confrontation between two distinct objects, the text and the reader" (7). Rather than making or creating meaning by actually engendering signification, readers encounter a text that is fixed and inert and are able only to "swallow it whole, to incorporate its ideological content in unaltered form" (7). Responding to a group of readers they regard as their cultural inferiors, the reviewers posit for that group a consumption-based way of reading and implicitly express horror that such a way of reading could be considered legitimate.

In *Distinction: A Social Critique of the Judgment of Taste*, Pierre Bourdieu describes the hierarchy of tastes and readers on which social distinctions are founded. Jong's readers are seen by the reviewers as the "impure" readers at the bottom of the social hierarchy—readers not capable of the "pure" gaze of those who have acquired a taste for legitimate culture through formal or informal education. The taste of the culturally elite is founded on a refusal of that which is "*common*, 'easy' and immediately accessible, starting with everything that reduces the aesthetic animal to pure and simple animality, to palpable pleasure or sensual desire" (32). The refusal of such shallow pleasures "easily decoded and culturally 'undemanding,' naturally leads to the refusal of what is facile in the ethical or aesthetic sense, of everything which offers pleasures that are too immediately accessible and so discredited as 'childish' or 'primitive' (as opposed to the deferred pleasures of legitimate art)" (486).

Jong's readers ought to have better taste, the reviewers imply, than to indulge in the simple and undemanding pleasures provided by a book that is facile or "easy" morally and aesthetically: a plot that is not an imaginative structure at all but simply a transcription of experience, a story that offers not only "as much sex as punctuation" (Mesic 1) but also the elementary satisfaction of a happy ending, or in the description of reviewer Diane Johnson, that "peculiarly American and purely literary substance Fulfillment" (6).

To understand the reception of *How to Save Your Own Life*, we must recognize that Jong's readers are as fully under attack as Jong herself. As the reviewers see it, Jong has produced a commercial product—choosing to write about sex because sexual content would boost sales—and pandered to an audience that prefers an easily understood narrative that flatters their shallow view of life and encourages them to indulge in fantasies of fulfillment rather than to contemplate painful realities. I suggest, however, that the reviewers' real source of the resentment may be Jong's *readers*, with Jong and her readers easily interchanged in the minds of the reviewers. Jong, one woman, stands for a large group of noisy, demanding women whose latest and most heinous action has been to effectively redefine the category literature. The form the defensive maneuver takes is to characterize those readers as the robots and videots of mass culture—readers who eagerly welcome a narrative that requires nothing but consumption and that reinforces their inferior moral qualities.

Jong's success epitomizes the success of the women's movement, which threatens traditional cultural forms, having given the silent, unrecognized, and unrepresented female majority a place in the cultural sun, altered the meaning of the female body, challenged masculine sexual norms, and transformed social institutions. These changes released a flood of misogyny, and it is clear in Jong's reviews that the target of the misogyny is not only Jong but her readers as well.

The resentment of Jong's reviewers, as seen in the reviews of Johnson, Mesic, and others, is particularly evident in their attitude to the money Jong made on her first novel. The attitude that Jong is not morally deserving of wealth, so vociferously expressed, smacks of misogyny also and allows the reader to see that resentment of Jong is not simply a disinterested desire to protect cultural health, as the reviewers claim, but an interested response, perhaps a "normal" human response, or at least a common one, to a competitor, a person who has had a great success in the field of endeavor the reviewers themselves are identified with.

In *How to Save Your Own Life*, Isadora Wing, now the author of a bestselling novel, goes to Hollywood to write the screenplay for a movie of the novel and to negotiate the movie rights with a producer, one of several Hollywood types who are the subjects of satiric portraits. In the meantime, she has found out that her husband had an affair with one of their friends. This knowledge is the *coup de grace* for her dying marriage. She shuttles back and forth between New York and Hollywood, seeking consolation and distraction—including a lesbian affair—from friends and lovers, and eventually meets, in Hollywood, a man younger than she, with whom she falls in love.

Among the reviews that deal most explicitly with the issue of the destructive effects of mass culture is the review of Penelope Mesic,[14] which appeared on page one of the *Chicago Tribune Book World*. Mesic admittedly judges the book by its front and back covers—"Let us for a moment do something forbidden. . . . Let's judge a book by its cover" (1). The flesh and the "money-making name Erica Jong" on the front cover along with Jong's picture on the back cover tell her everything there is to know about the novel: it's an autobiographical book about sex written to make money. In Mesic's view, Jong has written a "lazy" book, one easy to write and easy to read. Mesic characterizes the novel as an "only-the-names-have-been-changed brand of fiction," which betrays a "poor imagination and a lack of decent reticence about others' private lives" (1). In a comment that illustrates the note of personal attack often found in Jong's reviews (and most often in the reviews of this novel), Mesic goes on to say that "Jong is either too lazy or too self-centered to approximate the thoughts and attitudes of people unlike herself" (1). Mesic comments on Jong's ability to make money and acknowledges that she has a huge audience:

There is undeniably a huge audience for Jong, an audience desperate to be rid of their guilt, glad to be told that they need not submit to boredom. Her books are read because they fill a need, because they are simple to understand, because they have a vitality so many "serious" books about entropy and impotence and balding academics clearly lack. (1)

Thus, for Mesic, the self-indulgence of Jong's audience matches Jong's own. The novel elicits criticism on moral grounds, with a moral judgment being made of both Jong and her audience. The novel does not qualify as good literature because it shuns painful truths about human existence and instead offers only the dangerous incitement to self-indulgence. It is not surprising, since she sees the content of this novel as both trivial and pernicious, that Mesic also experiences it as lacking any aesthetic or stylistic distinction: the style is glib and superficial, and the language is marred by clichés.

. In a review in the *National Review* (referred to in Chapter I), D. Keith Mano[15] charges Jong with having "cheapened the art of fiction" (498). Because of her status, her publisher would have published anything she wrote. Implying that Jong's confessional writing requires no imagination, Mano says that her success in the kind of fiction that she produces has had the effect of "[invalidating] the novelist-imaginator" (498). The existence of Jong's "easy" works, or their popularity, will drag down high culture in some way, he suggests. But Mano's entry into the discussion of low culture and cultural health is a very interested one. Mano's experience of the novel is mediated by his feelings about feminism and in some complicated ways about his feelings about a woman like Erica Jong, as we have seen in the discussion of this same review in Chapter I.[16]

Mano notes that while in *How to Save Your Own Life* Jong continues the "expressly autobiographical" mode of *Fear of Flying*, she now takes herself too seriously as a "fem-lib emblem" (498). For reviewers of this novel, the issue of autobiography looms large. Mano believes that Jong's novel is not a work of the imagination at all, and much of his review has to do, not with the book, but with Jong the person. The prominence of the autobiographical issue no doubt had something to do with the fact that, because of all the publicity she had received, Jong and her life story were well known. Dislike of the person, or resentment at the deference she was receiving, became the basis of dislike for the book.

But we must give proper emphasis to the fact that the reviewers' ways of looking at the novel as something less than art encouraged a view of the novel as a mere transcription of life. Jong, a woman writer whose previous novel had been a huge best-seller, was charged with inability to create imaginary fiction. But such assertions are not an uncommon response to the work of women writers. Others have commented on the fact that reviewers are much more likely to make the comparison of the author's life to the content of the novel when the author is a woman. Mickey Pearlman reports the comments of poet and novelist Susan Fromberg Schaeffer in *Belles Lettres*:

> Reviewers in [Fromberg Schaeffer's] opinion, don't "feel as free to investigate the personal lives of men and drag them into the reviews" because they "will be taken out behind a building and kicked in the mouth." There is, she suggested, probably "an underlying assumption that if a woman is going to expose herself to the public, she deserves what she gets. Nobody inquires about the relation between a man's latest marriage or affair and what's going on in his book, but this is a regular, chronic, reflex action when you read the reviews of a women novelist." The underlying message is that no woman could be inventive enough to imagine anything that does not hinge heavily on the details on her own life. (9)

Woman writers have been at pains to make distinctions between their fictions and their autobiographies. Margaret Atwood has commented at length on reviewers' tendencies to assume that what she writes has happened to her. No doubt anticipating what might be the response to her latest novel, *Cat's Eye*, about a young girl growing up in Canada, she has followed the prudent path of refusing to discuss or reveal events in her own life that might have parallels in the novel.[17] When *Fear of Flying* first came out, Jong acknowledged in interviews that the novel contained autobiographical elements, but in subsequent interviews she has emphasized the artistic transformation of her material, and she has also written several articles specifically addressing the continuities and discontinuities between art and life. In her interviews she began to use the term *myth*, to refer to the overarching meaning and unifying theme, suggesting that emphasis should be placed on the larger imaginative structures of her work instead of on parallels between her life and that of her protagonist.[18]

In fact, contemporary American fiction is often confessional in nature, sometimes self-consciously so. Norman Mailer, Saul Bellow, and other male novelists have used autobiographical material without apology—and without being subjected to the criticism that has dogged female novelists. In the case of Henry Miller, an author was given credit for writing fiction when he was not. Miller observes in the *New York Times* article that critics often assume that he invented the Henry

Miller he wrote about though in fact he did not: "in the case of 'Tropic of Cancer' . . . critics and readers alike were inclined to think I had *invented* Henry Miller. To this day many people refer to it as a novel, despite the fact that I have said again and again that it is not" (27). In a recent interview, novelist William Maxwell is totally unapologetic about his use of autobiographical material, remarking that "for me, 'fiction' is not whether a thing, the thing I am writing about, actually happened, but rather in the form of the writing. . . . The important distinction is between reminiscence, which is a formless accumulation, and a story, which has a shape, a controlled effect, a satisfying conclusion—something that is or attempts to be a work of art and not merely an exercise in remembering" (46–47). Maxwell is almost audacious in his assertion that fiction and real life can be identical: He says he "came to feel that life is the most extraordinary storyteller of all, and the fewer changes the writer makes the better, provided that you get to the heart of the matter" (47).

Unlike these men, Erica Jong became the target of much criticism for her use of autobiographical material. Many reviewers suggest that they are able to read *How to Save Your Own Life* only as autobiography. The *New York Times* reviewer, Christopher Lehmann-Haupt,[19] certainly indicates that his view of the novel is affected by his knowledge of what he considers the real-life protagonist and some of the other characters. He views the autobiographical elements as a "powerful incentive" to read the book "as gossip rather than fiction," a temptation he could hardly resist, he says, given the presence of so many "characters with keys sticking out of their backs" (C25).

His evaluation is influenced by another factor also: he finds the slang terms used to describe lovemaking offensive. Such terms may be used in emotional states of anger, fear, and so on, but "not love." For Lehmann-Haupt a work that employs what he considers obscene terms cannot be art. Other reviewers share his view and often comment specifically on Jong's use of what are considered obscene terms for female genitalia. These words are unmentionable for many. The perspective from which Lehmann-Haupt views the novel does not allow him to see it as a work of art. He not only finds no "transcendent meaning" in it; he finds so little to interest him that his mind wanders. The best he can do as far as an interpretation of the novel is concerned is to suggest that it adds up to a superficial cliché: "If by some supreme effort of the will one had to interpret what all this means, one would say that it over-leaps the narrower issues of women's liberation and comes down with a splash on the side of life, freedom and other such vagaries of passion'' (C25).

Lance Morrow[20] makes similar criticisms of the novel's vulgarity in a review in *Time* entitled "Oral History": "Erica Jong writes not so much novels as almost breathlessly up-to-date confessional bulletins" (74). While Morrow accords *Fear of Flying* the honorific ''bawdy exu-berance,'' he cannot find a way of looking at the new novel that permits him to see it as anything but vulgar: "The woman is enough to make readers think that sex really *is* dirty" (75). Morrow's plot summary sug-gests that he sees in the story no coherence but only a random pattern of events. As for any theme or meaning in the novel, like Lehmann-Haupt he finds only tedious cliché: "In Jong's wall-poster philosophy, today is the first day of the rest of your life" (75).

Isa Kapp,[21] writing in the *Washington Post*, also finds that the several ''creators and creations are look-alikes,'' (H1) and indicts the author and her character for the sin of ''Gluttony—for food, fame, flattery, gratification'' (H4). With such instincts, it is only a short distance to ''cornering the market on concupiscence'' (H4). Kapp identifies sex as the source of the book's appeal, but she herself finds nothing attractive in the book's ''raw vocabulary,'' which ''merely buries both sense and sensibility'' (H4). Jong's readers don't get any kind words either. She quotes Isadora's remark that her heroine's feelings were shared by ''the nation,'' and comments that ''the nation, or at least the female half, had been endowed with freedoms even the women's liberation move-ment was afraid to ask for and did not know it wanted: to bathe in steamy fantasies of seduction by strangers, and to turn the tables on men and treat them as sex objects'' (H4). Kapp's response has some-thing in common with the women who were so shocked and bewil-dered by *Fear of Flying*.

Finally, we see the outrage of the high culture reviewer in Kapp's comments on Jong's literary quotations: ''The 'outrageous' element of Jong's book lies in its pretentiousness, its gratuitous use of quotations from Byron and Chaucer, allusions to Whitman and Flannery O'Con-nor—to an imagined reputation for literary achievement'' (H4).

Janet Maslin[22] in *Newsweek* finds that Isadora only ''purports to be a fictional character'' (82). In Maslin's view, ''Jong has always been her own best—and only—object of contemplation'' and has written a novel that is "little more than a series of meanspirited attacks on the author's own enemies'' (e.g., the Hollywood producer who bought the movie rights to her last novel) (82). Once again the theme of the outrage of the high culture reviewer is evident as Maslin refers to the "literary pretentiousness'' of Jong's comparison of herself to Colette, which Maslin finds "outlandish enough to be momentarily diverting'' (83). For Maslin the novel has no pleasing aesthetic qualities but is characterized by "self-indulgence, solipsism, crankiness, and spite'' (82).

Roberta Tovey remarks in the *New Republic* on the "self-indulgence of the outpourings'' (34) of the novel and emphatically states that she feels no sympathy with the heroine who has to contend with the problems of being famous. She "can't stand'' Isadora: "I'm bored with her suffering, her orgies, her 'cunt,' her incessant self-righteousness'' (35). Finding the entire novel "self-indulgent,'' the reviewer predicts that feminists will be either "outraged'' or "bored'' by the ending (a love scene in which Isadora expresses a feeling of great need for her lover), which "endorses the Power of the Male'' (35).

In contrast to the reviewers above, John Leonard[23] notes in the *New York Times Book Review* that although the novel is autobiographical, he doesn't see that as a problem:

> If Jong wants to write a book about now bad it feels to be an unhappily married celebrity, and to put everybody she knows into it, and to tell us how she cured herself of fragmentation by finding herself a lover who was also a friend, she's entitled. Fame and its discontents, a dying marriage and a healthy heterosexuality are not unworthy themes. And what writer hasn't in some way exploited parents, neighbors, lovers, friends? (2)

Leonard provides one of the clearest illustrations in these reviews of a response to the novel made in the shadow of a response to the public personality. However, Leonard, editor of the *New York Times Book Review* at the time he wrote the review, is also a published novelist and moves in the same circles as Jong. Therefore his review may also reflect more personal feelings. He says he is put off by the sense that he is being addressed by a "public personality, Isadora/Erica, lecturing the whole world" (40). Leonard speculates that the private person got lost on the lecture circuit between talk shows. Clearly he has seen these performances because he makes detailed references to talk shows "where she was forever reading aloud the poems she had written while working on *Fear of Flying*, and the letters she had received about *Fear of Flying*, and the poems she had written about the letters she had received and her feelings on finishing *Fear or Flying*" (2). Leonard has praise for *Fear of Flying*, but he sees only shallowness and cliché in Jong's second effort. He detects laziness in language and character creation, and he finds only a simplistic theme: "Love is everything it's cracked up to be" (2). He concludes that "it is as if . . . Erica Jong had interviewed herself, when she should have been, sentence by sentence, writing a book" (2). The interviews ringing in his ears, he hears them again as he reads the novel.

The review of novelist Diane Johnson[24] in the *New York Review of Books* is an interesting example of a response by one novelist, who has herself enjoyed considerable critical success, to another novelist who has received a great deal of public attention and has a wide audience. Johnson has stated elsewhere that she is no admirer of Jong, commenting in an interview in the Janet Todd volume that she "hasn't really taken Jong seriously" (130). That Johnson has Jong's monetary and media success on her mind is evident in her reference to "huge advances, 8 x 10 glossies despatched in kits to potential reviewers and interviewers, along with questions to ask Jong if—as seems likely—she comes by; excerpts appearing in *Vogue* and the rest."

In her review, Johnson predicts that readers will feel pity for Jong, though pity mitigated by the knowledge that she is getting rich. Jong "has trusted people too far" (6) and exposed herself too openly. Johnson sees no aesthetic qualities in the novel, unable to take it seriously as a didactic work, despite its title, and finding in it neither art nor entertainment. For Johnson the novel resembles "the ramblings of a deserted [wife] who has taken to the tape recorder and submitted the unedited manuscript" (6). She is finally unable to find a point in the novel—Jong's prescription for saving one's life is unclear. It is clear only that the subject of the book is "Fulfillment." Johnson mocks its easy achievement in the novel.[25]

The British reviews read like a series of exercises in novel ways to disparage Erica Jong. In her previous work, Jong was seen to represent

America. Now that she has achieved resounding success, she is an even more eligible illustration of the ills of commercialized literature, American style.

Attitudes to America have played an important role in both legitimate and oppositional culture in Great Britain. To the British cultural establishment, America is viewed with loathing as the epitome and the source of pop culture as a worldwide growth industry. America is also a reminder of the eclipse of British power and Britain's inability, after the decline of empire, to influence foreign taste. To compound matters further, a positive attitude toward America has sometimes been adopted as an oppositional strategy by those antagonistic to the British establishment. It is quite clear, for example, that such is the case in the admiration expressed by Anthony Burgess for things American, including Erica Jong. (See Chapter 4 for further discussion of Burgess's views.) In *No Respect: Intellectuals and Popular Culture*, Andrew Ross mentions British working-class kids' romance with America and quotes from the memoir of Ray Gosling, who wrote, "'There was a tremendous romance about America. America was the place we all wanted to be. America was closer than London'' (148).[26] When we contemplate the clustering of attitudes and values around the sign America, both in relation to legitimate culture and to oppositional culture in Britain, we can understand the complexity of responses to popular American works of literature on the part of representatives of legitimate British culture. The skeptical or negative attitude toward things American is indicated in the title of a feature story on Jong published in the *Sunday Times* in 1975: "Can a Million Americans Be Wrong?" (Brown).

The British reviewers dwell on a lack of literary quality, sometimes dramatizing Jong's inadequacies by comparing her to other writers who are generally recognized as only marginally literary. In a review in the *New Statesman*, a liberal journal whose reviews of Jong have always been very negative, Jeremy Treglown[27] exploits an opportunity created for him when Spiro Agnew's novel, *The Canfield Decision*, was released at the same time as Jong's novel. Reviewing the two novels together, he suggests that the two authors ought to team up. Jong would have more to gain from such a collaboration than Agnew, he says. Although she could teach him about sex, he outdoes her in narrative strategy and organization—"though it has to be admitted that a novel by both of them would be only marginally less unreadable than one by either'' (612). Jong's storyline is "bumpy," and there is monotony in the events depicted. The reviewer concedes only that Jong "is good at one-liners" (613). Although most of Treglown's review addresses "literary" matters, such as storyline, organization, narrative strategy, it is what the book is about that bothers him most. Jong's book is a woman's autobiographical narrative about sex and thus basically trivial. Given Jong's reputation as a writer of the sexual novel, no one "expected [her] to open out *Middlemarch*-like moral vistas" (613). Her novel has no more claim to literary recognition than Agnew's.

Peter Keating,[28] writing in *TLS*, places Jong in the tradition of the popular romance. "Romance is back!" Keating writes: "Within the world of this novel, and the literary tradition to which it belongs, sexual love is the only thing, ultimately, that matters. It is this that women desire above all else: it is this that gives meaning and justification to their lives" (545). Keating makes an extended comparison between Jong and romance novelist E. M. Hull. In Hull's novel (not named in the review), Sheik Ahmed Ben Hassan rapes Diana, a young English lady. Keating comments, "The real differences between the Diana who learns to like being raped and the Isadora who begs and pleads to be fucked are not great" (545). It is clear that what is noteworthy about the book for Keating is its sexual explicitness and the creation of a heroine in active pursuit of sexual adventure. Carrying the parallel between Jong and the romance writer throughout his review, Keating emphatically places Jong in the category of pulp fiction and thus trivializes her achievement. Like the writers of romance fiction, Jong has a message—be joyful and seek for true love. Again like romance writers, Jong's readers are personally drawn to her and seek her advice in letters. Keating comments that we cannot imagine readers of Henry James, Harold Pinter, or Joseph Conrad writing them for advice. Jong is no more serious a writer than E. M. Hull.

Peter Ackroyd,[29] who reviewed the novel for the conservative weekly *Spectator*, also sees Jong as exemplifying the ills of commercial success and indeed the deplorable state of contemporary culture. Ackroyd's own viewpoint is clearly expressed in the introduction to his book *Notes for a New Culture: An Essay on Modernism*, in which he explains that his work is "not a scholarly work" but a "polemic and an extended essay directed against our declining national culture" (9). Among these reviewers Ackroyd most clearly represents what

Brantlinger calls the apocalyptic mode characteristic of much of modern culture, in which "doomsaying" is the "chief mode" (37). He characterizes Jong as guilty of "pervasive self-adulation" and accuses her of pandering to the low tastes of a mass audience, doing a calculated repetition of *Fear of Flying* (which Ackroyd didn't like either) to reap the same rewards: "So what new monster was slouching toward Madison Avenue to be born? Now we know. It is called *How to Save Your Own Life*, and it continues the story of Isadora Wing, who is now rich and terribly famous" (24). Her book, based on her life, is about sex and hence marketable. Ackroyd, like Keating, is bothered by the version of female sexuality present in the novel. In one comment he writes, "the Female Orgasm manages to stagger on, from one American situation to the next" (24).

A self-obsessed writer with commercial motives cannot produce art, and Jong's greatest sin is against Art. Jong is incapable of making the transition from art life:

> And in this case, with a heroine who talks and acts like a Barbiedoll, all human life turns into a wooden and hollow effigy of itself. . . . But bad writing is even more insidious. The first and last rule of writing is that its reader becomes, if only for a moment, what he beholds—and in this case all of us are turned into horrified stone replicas of human beings, as if we had looked back too soon in order to get a glimpse of reality slowly disappearing. (24)

What the novel means the reviewer does not know except that "the novel is finished when Erica Jong's diary is exhausted" (24). Since the substance of the novel is inauthentic, the prose becomes so too. The style is cheap journalism and the language is tired. Ackroyd's own personal stake in all this is clear as he quotes a remark that "someone says to [Jong] somewhere, 'You're going to be the most famous woman writer of your generation!'" and adds, "What can a poor reviewer say, in the face of all this respectful attention and commercial success?" (24). In this final comment he laments the lack of influence of the reviewer who values quality but whose influence is diminished by the mechanisms of the marketplace and low public taste.

Lorna Sage,[30] writing in the *Observer*, also responds to the novel as a harmful artifact of mass culture. In a review entitled "Gobbling It All

Up," she comments on Jong's huge sales and attributes them to the novel's usefulness as an "elementary female ego-building exercise, a fantasy cure for the hereditary caste of under-achievers" (24). Jong is praised for her "canny, exuberant Shamela Andrews manner" (24), but Sage nevertheless finds the novel depressing. It is "too bland" to make a good fantasy.

For two male British reviewers, Jong is still framed explicitly by her feminist views. Their reviews echo some of the comments on *Fear of Flying* in 1973. The reviewer for the *Evening Standard* is Auberon Waugh,[31] son of the novelist Evelyn Waugh. Also a columnist for the conservative *Spectator*, he clearly represents traditional values in British society. His establishment connections are indicated by his attendance at Oxford and by his service in the Royal Horse Guards, a credential that confers prestige in Great Britain and is listed in all biographical entries about him. In his collected essays, *In the Lion's Den*, he shows little sympathy for the goals of the women's movement, commenting that he finds "profoundly disturbing" the "shift in the relationships between men and woman in our society" (137). For Waugh, Jong is a run-of-the-mill female/feminist confessional writer, set apart only by a sense of humor that "distinguishes [her] from a hundred other dirty-minded housewives" and "lifts the book (a little—not too far) above the common run, and relieves all the pretension, the bogusness, the aggressive hysteria and grinding selfishness which I am sorry have become inextricable from the literary section of the Women's Liberation Movement" (20).

Waugh concedes that the book may have some usefulness as a sex manual to "instruct men in the workings of the female sexual mechanism" (20). However, a sense of humor and some information do not constitute literary quality, in Waugh's opinion. In literary terms, "this book is an unqualified disaster" (20)—it generates no suspense and provokes no emotional sympathy. Waugh expresses the hope that "perhaps one day women writers will realize that the tired literary mannerism of telling stories backward works only in very special circumstances" (20). Finally, he quotes Jong's statement that "when men writers confess it's considered literature—when women writers confess it is considered garbage" (20) and concludes by saying that Jong has done nothing to remedy this state of affairs. Though Waugh writes of many literary matters in his review, it is clear he is simply not interested in a confessional novel by a woman writer.

Playwright Ronald Harwood,[32] writing in the London *Sunday Times*, concedes that Jong is a "story teller of considerable skill" but believes that her work falls short of success because she has "chosen not just to tell a story but to write a sort of manifesto for her sex, and the morality of her pleading seems to me, in every particular, suspect" (41). Harwood has found out Jong's secret, namely that she (or Isadora—he conflates the two) hates women, as revealed by her treatment of the lesbian episode in the novel and in her choice of a male lover, whom he characterizes as a *nebbish*, "less talented than she, less ambitious, less demanding, and yes, less manly" (41). He asserts that Isadora—"a 32-year-old-Jewish adolescent"—is living a lie: "She is a *poseuse*, spouting a doctrine of freedom for her sex while concealing a dreadful secret: she hates women. Isadora White Wing wants to be a man" (41). A comment at the end of Harwood's review anticipates criticism that might be made of his review on the grounds of male chauvinism. He allows that such objections may be made and then continues:

> But I am reminded that when I was at school and a master punished me or one of the other Jewish boys for impudence or deceit, we at once accused him of anti-Semitism. The last thing we wanted was to admit we were impudent or deceitful. The same is true of Jong's heroine. She conceals her double-standards behind hostility and her cause, accusing others where she herself is culpable. It is not so much a case of Women's Lib as Women's Glib. (41)

Harwood, like Waugh, is horrified by what the feminist movement has produced.

These reviews display a vigorous animosity toward Jong, related to her success and to the reviewers' identification of her with her audience, and a striking disgust at the taste of others, which Bourdieu describes as an intense, even visceral experience. The reviews have taken on an ad hominem (or ad feminam) character. Jong is criticized for being dirty-minded, self-centered, and greedy for food, money, and sex, and, in at least one review (as implied by Ackroyd), middle-aged. We may note here that the book review has been called one of the few socially acceptable forms of aggression.

Surely the book review editors, not just reviewers, have a share in the negative responses to Jong's novel. The editors are equally part of the cultural establishment and in fact occupy positions of greater power than most (not all) of the individual reviewers. I would by no means claim that editors determine the content of each review they assign by choosing the reviewer, but certainly this can happen. For example, Lorna Sage, whose reviews suggest that she dislikes Jong's work, has twice reviewed her novels for the same publication, the *Observer*, and made similar judgments. This fact illustrates that responsibility for the judgments expressed in the book review pages belongs to both the editor and the reviewer—the reviewer speaks for some powerful voices besides her own.

The reviewers who make these heartfelt denunciations are not just reacting to any work that has gained a large popular audience and has become the object of public discussion. They are reacting to a book by a woman, and moreover, a woman who, declaring not only her independence but explicitly her sexual independence, does so in a first-person narrative using sexually explicit language. The reviewing establishment, threatened by all the attention given to Erica Jong, reacts defensively. The heat of the denunciations of Jong suggests that the reviewers were indeed troubled about a possible shift in power and not simply reacting to the annoyance they suffered from one silly woman. If so, the stakes were indeed high in this conflict between the temple and the marketplace. Barbara Herrnstein Smith comments that a given

institutional-ideological opposition tends to be exacerbated historically whenever, and to the extent that, there is a sharp or acutely sharpening conflict between, on the one hand, the more or less conservative (normative, standardizing, controlling, classifying, supervising, maintaining, regulating) practices of the relevant community and, on the other hand, its destabilizing and transformative practices, mercantile or otherwise, including the more or less innovative, entrepreneurial and diversionary activities of those who stand to gain from a reclassification, circulation, and redistribution of commodities and cultural goods and, thereby, of social power—including the profit and power to be had just from *mediating* their circulation. (131)

In 1973, when *Fear of Flying* was published, Erica Jong was one of the first writers to emerge as a spokesperson for the women's movement, whether or not she sought such a role. The effect of Jong's books, far from causing torpor, moral laziness and intellectual passivity—the deleterious effects of low culture in the view of the high culture critics—was to energize her female readers. This effect is suggested both by the feminist reviews of *Fear of Flying* and by other evidence, including Jong's reports about her interactions with readers. In the fifteenth-anniversary edition of *Fear*, Jong comments indirectly on this phenomenon, describing how readers approached her at public appearances to ask for autographs of dog-eared and marked-up personal copies. Clearly the prospect of female or feminist writers gaining a large audience, and attention from some prestigious cultural authorities whose notice inflated their stock in the cultural marketplace, did not please numerous members of the cultural establishment, certainly not when the challenge came in the crude form of a woman talking bawdry.

It seems quite clear that Jong does not, or did not in 1977, qualify for membership in the club of high culture. The "club," made up of male and female reviewers, has vested interests to protect. Smith comments that "all normative theories of culture, including those mounted from or in the name of the political left, serve vested tastes and vested interests" (76). It follows for Smith that

> among the questions we are thereby (and otherwise) led to ask are whether nostalgic/apocalyptic accounts of popular and mass culture may not represent a reactionary response to the increasing contemporary destratification of cultural arenas and practices, and a misdiagnosis of the cognitive dislocation, dissonance, and nausea—literally, disgust—experienced as a result by high-culture cultural critics. (76)

Reviews that look at the novel from another perspective than that of the high culture reviewer deploring the influence of popular culture are rare but do exist. One such review is the work of Jean Radford,[33] writing in the British feminist magazine *Spare Rib*. Radford writes from a socialist-feminist perspective and also from a lesbian perspective. Socialist-feminist lesbians are not heard from very much in the book review pages and are hardly looked to as cultural authorities. Radford has serious criticisms of the novel, but they are totally different criticisms from the ones voiced by the high culture reviewers. She asserts that Jong's book "will make many women angry." She finds it "in some ways anti-feminist" while characterizing it as coming from "the fringes of the women's movement" (45). For her, the novel is a valuable document because it expresses "all the contradictions about sex and love which women have to live through" (45). However, for Radford the novel fails because the heroine "capitulates, without too much struggle, to an individual solution of phallocentric romantic love" (45). She criticizes Jong for "providing no serious alternatives for her heroine—the movement, women's groups, a sense of collective struggle are noticeable by their absence" (46). Noticeable by their absence to this reviewer, these alternatives were not missed by other reviewers. Radford also finds the lesbian segment of the novel "offensive and heterosexist" (45); Jong betrays unselfconscious hatred for the other woman's body and reveals her inadequate understanding of what lovemaking is to the lesbian. Still, for Radford the novel is useful, standing "as a testament to what women are up against personally and collectively, and how urgently we need to create different forms of love and validation; in short, alternate ways of saving our own lives" (46).

One interesting example of contingencies of value is the varied responses to the lesbian episode in the novel, ranging from Ronald Harwood's disgust to praise by others of Jong's exploitation of possibilities for humor in the lesbian love scene. Radford represents yet another perspective different from these two: the perspective that sees Jong's treatment of the lesbian relationship and scenes of lovemaking as inadequate because they demonstrate heterosexual failure to understand lesbianism.

Even of this negatively evaluated novel there are positive reviews to illustrate the contingent nature of literary judgments. However, both of the positive reviews I discuss below were written by persons less directly identified with the high culture reviewing establishment than most other reviewers, or with strong attractions to the novel that enable them to see it more positively. The first, by a woman librarian, appeared in the *Library Journal*. The reviewer, Marcia Fuchs,[34] praises the novel, responding positively to the exuberant self-fulfillment of the heroine. Isadora has "dropped her excess baggage of guilt and learned to live in and for the present moment" (218). The reviewer pronounces the novel a "joyous, exhilarating, miraculous novelistic flight, most breathlessly recommended" (218). This brief review is noteworthy for the complete empathy of the reviewer with the heroine.

One other review, written by Craig Fisher[35] for the *Los Angeles Times*, is noteworthy for its high praise of the novel. The reviewer, a journalist who worked for Earth News Radio at the time he wrote the review, is not at all preoccupied by the high culture critique of popular literature. He finds the novel a success as a whole and also praises many of the specific features condemned by other reviewers, thus offering an illustration of that law of book reviewing repeatedly illustrated in these pages: for every evaluation there is an equal and opposite evaluation by some other reviewer. Although Fisher finds it takes him a little time to "get in synch" with Isadora, he thinks the book takes off when Isadora hits the streets of Manhattan on visits to her friends, and confirms that "she has retained her wry humor, her snappy conversational asides and her brazen, clear-skinned candor" (1). Friendship is at the heart of this book for Fisher, who finds it "in many ways a paean to friendship" (13). This characterization provides a sharp contrast to some other reviewers who call the book nasty and vindictive, alluding not only to Jong's treatment of the husband but also her treatment of other figures. For Fisher Jong has a "gift for characterization," which she uses in the portrayal of her friends, "urban survivors, articulate and with odd edges, like people in life" (13). Fisher praises the portrait of Britt Goldstein, calling it the "meanest, funniest portrait of a New Hollywood 'producer' to have been created so far" (10).

Fisher finds in the novel criticism of life as opposed to the cliché and banality found by others. Fisher also likes the character Isadora. Far from seeing her as a foolish person, he values her for her "willingness to make a fool of herself" (13). In fact, Fisher finds the novel as successful as *Fear of Flying* and in the same way: "[Jong] cases this Coast as cannily as she cased the congress of analysts in the beginning of *Fear of Flying*" (13). Although Fisher stands almost alone among the reviewers in his praise of this novel for its artistic qualities, he describes it in terms of a successful realistic novel: Jong's work succeeds because it has wit, able character creation, and thematic depth.

Once again, it is clear that the relation to the content is crucial in forming the evaluation. Fisher, who lives in California, finds the novel interesting in part because he enjoys the recreation of the California scene. In a telephone interview he told me he did graduate work on film, follows the film industry, and had his own ideas about what Hollywood figures might be sources for some of Jong's characters. He also has a special fondness for comedy, enjoying new fiction that is "funny and smart" (telephone interview, May 19, 1991). Thus he is well situated to reap pleasure from a spoof of the Hollywood film scene.

The responses to Jong's second novel show that while an author's first novel may evoke varied and contradictory responses, a novel by a celebrity evokes an even more complicated response. By 1977 the figure of Erica Jong had become weighted down with a lot of baggage. The responses of the reviewers could not help but reflect this complication. Thus the reviewers respond not only to the issues raised in the novel, but to the novelist herself or, perhaps more pertinently, to the issues raised by her popularity and even to a social movement for which she had become a symbol.

In his book on the reputation of George Orwell, John Rodden raises the matter of the effect of a writer's public persona on literary reputation, noting that Orwell may have been more important as a man than as a writer. Rodden comments that "it is questionable, almost painfully so for some admirers, whether Orwell's literary achievement—except perhaps in essay form, where his compelling ethos so strongly appeals—can bear the weight of esteem and significance which successive generations have bestowed upon him" (x). Orwell may have been more important for how he lived than for what he wrote, and the admiration for the man may have prompted influential critics, who often took him for a moral guide and chose to see themselves in his image, to value the work as highly as they valued the man. Jong may be an example of the same phenomenon in reverse. Her high media profile may have done damage to her literary reputation. Through media exposure, she became an image to be shunned and a sign that few wished to appropriate.

Although Jong is not characterized as a feminist in these reviews as often as she is seen as a silly woman, the response to this novel appears nonetheless related to cultural perceptions of feminism. Jong may be seen as part of a long line of women writers (beginning with the "scribbling women" who so annoyed Hawthorne) who were popular, successful, and consequently resented. Jane Tompkins remarks that "the *popularity* of novels by women has been held against them almost as much as their preoccupation with 'trivial' feminine concerns'' (xiv). Jong, whose previous novel had received critical acclaim, had been touted as a feminist novel, and had sold millions to women readers,[36] appeared to be leading a movement that threatened the brokering function and thus the status of the high culture reviewers. We remember also that all this was happening in 1977 when the feminist movement was at its height. What made Jong's success so annoying—and very much influenced the evaluation of her second novel—was the fact that it evoked fears about a threat to the cultural authority of the reviewing establishment.

4 / Fanny: *The Anatomy of a Literary Success*

In 1980 Erica Jong abandoned the Isadora character and published *Fanny, Being the True History of the Adventures of Fanny Hackabout-Jones*, a novel set in the eighteenth century. Fanny, who tells her own story in this first person narrative, says she is the same character as John Cleland's Fanny and is going to tell her true story, not told by Cleland in *Fanny Hill*. An imitation of the eighteenth-century picaresque based on extensive research on eighteenth-century life, the novel is often referred to by its admirers as a novel of ideas for two reasons. First, it alludes to many eighteenth-century figures from literature and philosophy—Swift, Pope, Shaftesbury, Locke—and includes some of them as characters in the novel. Second, it espouses a feminist ideology and is indebted, in particular, to Margaret Murray's theories about witchcraft, which suggest that far from being a satanic cult, witches preserved ancient worship of a Mother Goddess.

In *Fanny* Jong tells the story of Fanny Hackabout-Jones, a beautiful young orphan who dresses in her foster-brother's clothing and rides off on her horse after being raped by her foster father, Lord Bellars, to whom she develops an erotic attraction when he reappears in the story. The consequence of the rape is a daughter for whom she writes the memoir that is the novel. She is initiated into a coven of witches, joins an outlaw band, works in a London brothel—where she meets Theophilus Cibber, Jonathan Swift, William Hogarth, and John Cleland—turns pirate to recapture her stolen child, and writes a best-seller. She falls in love with the outlaw Lancelot, converts him to heterosexuality, and returns to her Wiltshire birthplace where she finds that she has been bequeathed the estate by Lord Bellars, who is actually her biological father.

Though some reviewers have negative responses to the use of an eighteenth-century setting and regret the disappearance of Isadora, many
respond positively to the picaresque style narrative with a new heroine
(or hero, since Fanny is seen by many as having heroic qualities). For
many readers the introduction of a new heroine made possible a fresh
look at Jong and a revised evaluation of her work. In fact, only *Fear of
Flying* can be compared to *Fanny* in the response received, in the years
since its publication, from academics, writers, and literary intellectuals. *Fanny* differs from *Fear* only in that wide acceptance came
sooner—from a number of literary intellectuals among its first reviewers. Jong's literary allusiveness and the use of traditional literary forms
have caused *Fanny* to be favored, both by the academics among its first
reviewers and by those who write for literary journals. The interest on
the part of academics in *Fanny* and *Fear of Flying* is revealing because it
suggests one of the ways literary value is perceived and created. The interest of English professors in familiar literary forms and their ability to
apply methods of analysis ready to hand—and the ability to find mar-
kets for their work!—attracts them to these works, setting in motion a
dynamic that simultaneously discovers and creates value. Ohmann reminds us that a work gains the status of literature through the applica-
tion of conventional methods of literary analysis by academics.

The decision of Jong's publisher, New American Library, to promote
a trade-book edition of *Fanny* by sending Jong on a three-week tour of
college campuses testifies to the fact that the publisher was touting the
work as literary. The issuing of a trade paperback, more expensive than
a mass market paperback (which, in the case of *Fanny*, was postponed)
and aimed at a different audience, was a testing of the publisher's theory that Jong's novel could attract a so-called middle market audience
who would welcome an edition that set them apart from a wider popular audience and thereby defined them, and the novel, as a cut above
the mass ("NAL Aims").

Jong had long had ambitions to write a historical novel based on the
eighteenth century, a period she had studied in graduate school and
had always been particularly fond of. In an introduction to an excerpt of
the novel published in *Vogue*, Jong explains her attraction to eighteenth-century attitudes to sex—more open and direct before the Victo-
rian remaking of sexuality—and her wish to tell the story of the eighteenth-century woman, to recreate "the novel that slipped through the

cracks of history'' (280). In announcing a new moment in women's writing, Jong also dissociates her new novel from the confessional form that provoked so many attacks from reviewers of *How to Save Your Own Life*. She says: ''Having explored our right to anger and sexuality in literature, having asserted our right to tell the truth about our lives, we must now also assert our right to explore imaginary and invented worlds'' (280).

Responses to *Fanny* suggest that Jong's foray into costume drama was a very important factor in the favorable reception of the novel. Categories such as *Bildungsroman* and picaresque come immediately to the minds of reviewers. Both reviewers and later commentators comment on the wit of Jong's imitation of both Cleland's *Fanny* and Fielding's *Tom Jones*, noting the parallels between the seventeen-year-old Fanny, who flees home, taking the road for London in male disguise after she is raped by her foster father, and the young Tom Jones, who is kicked out of his foster father's home when he is wrongly accused of acts of ingratitude. Jong's story of the innocent country wench forced into prostitution also clearly recalls *Fanny Hill*.

Scholars have often singled out *Fanny* among Jong's novels for special attention. Ralph Gardner chooses to talk to Jong about *Fanny* for his collection, *Writers Talk to Ralph Gardner*, even though by the time of the interview, 1989, Jong had published two additional novels. Gardner mentions his enjoyment of Jong's recreation of the past, confessing having found himself ''deeply involved in this vanished world'' (192). In the bibliography of articles on Jong, a number of articles and parts of books deal with *Fanny*.[1] The transposing of one's setting to a distant time or place to make one's theme more acceptable is an ancient device and also as recent as Russian art under Communism. Jong's feminist theme was more acceptable when the heroine was dressed in eighteenth-century costume and spoke an eighteenth-century dialect.

But Jong was not only fortunate in her subject in *Fanny*. The timing of the publication of the novel in a moment of great cultural acceptance of feminism—perhaps the period of its highest public (not necessarily academic) influence—can only be called highly felicitous. An examination of events in 1979 and 1980 gives evidence of the growing cultural legitimization of feminism, seen in such things as the creation of presidential advisers on women's issues, formation of a National Advisory Committee for Women, and dedication of a National Women's Hall of

Fame (in Seneca Falls, N.Y.). Other evidence that feminism was gaining a cultural consensus was the growing number of women in politics— provoking complaints by female candidates of a double standard—and a substantial increase in the number of women working outside the home.[2] Women were featured subjects of regular newspaper columns with a feminist slant, such as those by Gail Sheehy in the *New York Times*, while special feminist publications were flourishing. One such publication, *New Directions for Women*, changed from quarterly to bi-monthly format in 1979.[3] Pollster Daniel Yankelovich found that in 1980 "the American public finally began to regard women for the first time as equals to men, entitled to the same jobs, pay and higher [*sic*] levels of responsibility" ("Poll Finds New View of Women" B12). A $500,000 gift by Norman Lear to the National Organization for Women Legal Defense and Education Fund was the largest corporate gift in the history of the women's movement and was used to create the Edith Bunker Memorial Fund for support of the Equal Rights Amendment and other women's rights causes. On a national level feminism became a business for the many advertisers who co-opted slogans from the women's movement, and in one local setting two enterprising women created "Supersister" trading cards for young girls (modeled on baseball cards) and got the project funded by the New York State Department of Education for introduction in Westchester County schools ("Trading Cards Introduced for the Young Girl").

While the late seventies and early eighties saw significant gains for feminism, these years were also marked by virulent attacks, such as that of R. Emmett Tyrrell, Jr., editor-in-chief of the *American Spectator*. Tyrrell wrote an article for the *New York Times* calling women's liberation the "most successful pestilence since Prohibition, a movement that was likewise under feminist stewardship" (A17). Such attacks were, however, evidence that feminism was gaining wide public acceptance.

In *No Respect: Intellectuals and Popular Culture*, Andrew Ross follows Gramsci in theorizing a concept of hegemony. According to this theory, a hegemonic moment occurs when a "historic bloc" succeeds in "containing and incorporating" the interests of various subordinate groups and "in articulating these interests along *with* its own" (55). In this way traditional intellectuals lend their support to the causes of other groups and help to secure popular support. In his discussion of

hegemony, R. Radhakrishnan remarks on the necessity for the dominant element to "sacrifice some of its specificity . . . in the name of a
wider and more inclusive commonality" (95). Radhakrishnan looks
forward to a "progressive *subalternization of the dominant discourses*"
(97) as elements formerly weaker or more oppressed are incorporated in
it.

The concept of hegemony is helpful in explaining the social acceptance of feminism and its endorsement by numerous intellectuals during the period in which *Fanny* appeared, and it can illuminate certain
facts in *Fanny*'s reception. *Fanny* was admired by influential intellectual male reviewers, such as Alan Friedman, Pat Rogers, and Anthony
Burgess, who articulate acceptance and support of feminism in their reviews. These men might be the analogue, in the cultural realm, to the
business community's Norman Lear, who supported NOW. As one further example of feminism's hegemony, let us note the growing acceptance of feminism in elite academic institutions as indicated by the institution of women's studies programs at Princeton and Yale in 1981.
(Women's studies programs had been introduced at less prestigious institutions before this date.) Nor is it insignificant that, in 1979, with
the introduction of the Susan B. Anthony dollar, a woman's head appeared on the coin of the realm.

Feminism's success was accompanied by an antifeminist backlash,
evidenced in part by difficulty in passing the ERA, with the deadline
approaching in 1982. (Issues surrounding the defeat of the ERA are discussed in Chapter 5.) The backlash was one cause of the soul-searching
feminists themselves were undertaking at the turn of the decade. A
new phase of feminism was explicitly announced by Betty Friedan's
The Second Stage, which appeared in 1981. Friedan declared that
women must move on from the first stage of the campaign for women's
opportunities for full participation in public life and turn to the family
as the new frontier of feminism and to women's need for a more fulfill-
ing personal life. Some feminists, such as Ellen Willis, loyal to the
older radical feminism, registered their disapproval, chiding Friedan for
the inadequacy of her history of feminism. Feminism, Willis insisted,
had always been concerned with "such issues as women's sexual freedom and satisfaction, equality and mutuality in personal relations
with men, and equal sharing of housework and child care" (494). The
threat to the movement, Willis claimed, came from pragmatists too

willing to make compromises to attain certain goals and from cultural feminists, more loyal to "female values"—strongly reminiscent of traditional criteria of femininity—than to feminism.

Cultural feminism was in the ascendancy, and emphasis on specifically female qualities and powers underlay the contemporary interest in women's culture, in uncovering an ancient matriarchal society, and in peace, ecology, and antipornography movements. Female bonding became an important subject of scholarly research and of imaginative literature. Jong's focus in *Fanny* on the mother-daughter relationship, her highlighting of Fanny's female virtues, especially her maternal qualities, and her invocation of witches as benign nature-worshipers was in line with the ascendant cultural feminism.[4] Reviewers do not often reveal a knowledge of the nuances of feminism, but it may well be that the dominant cultural feminism, with its view of female nature as nurturing and peace-loving, was less offensive to many than the earlier radical feminism, and that the centrality to the novel of the relationship between Fanny and her daughter facilitated acceptance, having the effect of muting the subject of sexual politics with which Jong had been (and still continues to be) associated.

Journalistic attention to Jong after *Fanny*'s release took a benign form. When *Fanny* was published, Jong was happily married and had become the mother of a child, born during the novel's composition. In a feature story in the *Washington Post* that appeared shortly after *Fanny*'s publication, Lynn Darling alludes to the new circumstances of Jong's private life: "She is married again and a mother now, no longer a wanderer in the dark libidinous woods" (D15). Darling remarks that Jong "doesn't even look the way she did" (D15), describing her as "solid and suburban, slow to laughter—the blithe spirit turned literary burgher" (D15). The story contains a reference to the positive reception given the novel, suggesting an interchangability between the public view of the book and the public view of the woman. A story in the *New York Times* "Style" section, by Judy Klemesrud, appearing about the same time, presents a similar image of Jong, identified in the headline as "That Suburban Matron, Erica Jong." Klemesrud describes a family lunch and remarks, "They looked and sounded like a typical upper-middle-class suburban family" (B6). Was Jong's image undergoing a (temporary) metamorphosis into a late-twentieth-century Mrs. Gaskell, a type of novelist-mother? Is a novel by a woman writer most acceptable when its release coincides with the birth of the woman's child? Klemesrud's article has two themes: Jong's family life and her interest, dating from her undergraduate days, in eighteenth-century literature. Jong says in the *Writer's Digest* interview with John L. Kern that she had immersed herself in the eighteenth-century idiom to the extent that she had to turn down magazine articles for years, unable to write in her normal style (24). This hiatus also gave the public a break from Jong and allowed her to emerge after *Fanny* as a more interesting figure.

The reviews of *Fanny* were more equally divided between positive and negative than the reviews of other novels, and the implicit and explicit endorsement of feminism appears in a range of publications. As in the response to Jong's other novels, judgments expressed tended to run to extremes. There were certainly those who felt strongly that modern civilization was marching toward perdition, with feminists leading the way, and they judged *Fanny* accordingly, but their voices were balanced by the novel's strong admirers. Thus reviews of the novel line up in two highly polarized groups. There are favorable reviews, including some by highly influential voices: novelist Anthony Burgess, eighteenth-century scholar Pat Rogers, academic critic and novelist Alan Friedman, and columnist and novelist Judith Martin. Highly negative reviews also include well-known reviewers: British critic and author Clive James, and playwright James Goldman. Some praise Jong's eighteenth-century imitation, complimenting both her scholarly accuracy and her success in creating an engaging fiction, while for others she is a "dumb blonde" (Gilder 36) whose eighteenth-century imitation is "bogus" or "phony" (Helgesen 81) and whose novel is a definite failure as an artistic effort.

The reviews of this novel are polarized according to certain issues that are seen as key matters (basically the same issues that were raised in response to *Fear of Flying*). These include the challenge to traditional values and the direction of modern civilization, the related issue of Jong's feminism, and often another issue—that same old issue that is a familiar refrain from the beginning of Jong's career—that is seen as related to the previous ones: Jong's sexual explicitness (or her salacious or pornographic effects, as some reviewers see it).

Those who see the novel as artistically successful find in the novel

those features that are valorized in twentieth-century fiction of the realistic school—architectonics and thematic coherence, lifelike and
multidimensional characters, and stylistic achievement. It is common
in the highly positive reviews for the reviewer to award Jong that laurel
so important in our time—praise for her language. Attention to language is appropriate for a novel that invents an eighteenth-century language for the twentieth-century, but the high praise accorded the novel's language also points to the higher aesthetic status accorded this
novel, for as anyone who reads literary criticism knows, a focus on language is a characteristic concern of essays dealing with authors who are
judged to be aesthetically superior.

A number of reviewers who focus on Jong's feminism call the novel
ideological or propagandistic. To these reviewers, Jong's feminism distorts or corrupts the novel form. These reviewers also criticize the eighteenth-century imitation, calling it heavy handed or untruthful. They
are particularly incensed at what they call the imposition of a twentieth-century consciousness on an eighteenth-century woman. They
sometimes also find the novel pornographic.

Some reviewers who express the views noted above are preoccupied in
particular with the liberties, as they see it, that Jong takes with history.
They take the position that it is possible to give one accurate or truthful
account of historical phenomena, or, in the words of Hayden White (who
doesn't himself see history this way), that history is ''a single definitive
account of what really happened'' (483).[5] Cultural conservatives, these reviewers sometimes explicitly identify themselves with a European elitist
view of tradition, as we see below in the review of Helgesen, who finds
America ''too eclectic, too diverse to imitate the cultural cohesiveness
that made European tradition great'' (81) and accuses both Jong and her
audience of ''profound historical ignorance'' (82).

Interestingly, a mirror image of the reviews described above occurs in
other reviews that identify the novel as a ''novel of ideas.'' Reviewers in
the latter group assert that the feminist elements in the novel work,
and finding the eighteenth-century imitation interesting and effective,
claim, as Pat Rogers does, that *Fanny* really does concern the eighteenth century or, accepting the idea that historical recreation is always a work of the imagination, are willing to entertain Jong's version
of the eighteenth century.

As we note the striking contrasts both in the overall evaluations of the novel and in evaluations of specific features, we may indeed raise questions about the constitution of literary value. What are we to make of the fact that the character of Fanny is praised as sympathetic and multifaceted by one group and criticized as narrow, tedious, and one-dimensional by another; that the novel is seen by some as pointless and interminable and by others as carefully constructed on ideas that govern its movement; that Jong is praised by some for mastery of language and criticized by others for having a tin ear?

There are other diametrically opposed responses to specific aspects of the novel. Are Jong's feminist witches a suggestive theoretical construct, or are they ludicrous, serving solely as evidence of her antimale viewpoint? Does Jong demonstrate understanding of the dynamics of social life in her depiction of the plight of the poor, of women and blacks, or is her portrayal superficial and ideological? Does Jong exploit the depiction of sexuality in a way that is pornographic, or does she enhance our understanding of human life by a candid portrayal of female sexuality? The answers to these questions depend on the ideological position from within which a reviewer experiences the novel.

A highly negative review of *Fanny* appeared in the *American Spectator*, one of the most conservative publications dealt with in these pages, rivaled only by the *National Review*. The *Spectator*, edited by conservative columnist R. Emmett Tyrrell, Jr., reviews few works of fiction, and thus it appears that Jong's novel was selected to make a point about trends in contemporary society. Both the *American Spectator* review and the similar review in the *Atlantic* appeared several months later than most of the reviews, suggesting that the novel was specially chosen for review by editors to make an ideological point. One can imagine that Jong is high on Editor Tyrrell's list of the enemies of culture. In his *New York Times* article, he accuses the feminist movement of a poverty of ideas: "When the last blood-curdling yell is loosed from the powder room, history will note that the ideology of the modern feminist is less prepossessing or challenging that the ideology of the modern nudist" (A17). Tyrrell states that "high intellectuals" have paid inadequate attention to feminist thought because

to question the tenets of women's liberation was to invite mayhem and be drawn into an orgy of idiocy.
What fleeting notice a feminist ideologue would attract was al-

ways owing to: a) the egalitarian perfumes of our time, b) the self-loathing that always seems to be licking at some of our cultural leaders, and c) outlandishness. This outlandishness, which characterizes almost every single feminist idea, was to be expected, for the whole movement was based on palpable fantasy. (A17)

The "fantasy" he has in mind is the belief, which he sees as characteristic of the movement, that women and men are no different from each other, a view he sees as contradicted by thousands of years of history. (Such an idea was not endorsed by the cultural feminists but had been seen as typical of the earlier radical feminists.)

One could say of critics like Tyrrell (and Allan Bloom a few years later) that if feminism had not existed, it would have had to be invented to serve as the focal point for rage against modern society. Feminism is perhaps rivaled only by rock and roll (another favorite target of Bloom's) as a convenient emblem of antihierarchical tendencies, permissiveness, and in short, all those things that threaten the worldview and the social, institutional, and cultural authority of people like Tyrrell.

Joshua Gilder,[6] a former editor for the *Saturday Review* and later a speech writer for President Reagan, was chosen to review Jong's novel for the *American Spectator*. Gilder criticized Jong's feminism and her use of the past. Assuming he is addressing a male readership, Gilder opens his review by advising his readers to resist the temptations of the garter-clad leg on the cover—"you'll be a happier man for it" (36). He sees Jong as putting forward a feminist program, but he is not touched by Jong's attempt to "spin a woeful tale of sexist tyranny" (37). He dismisses completely Jong's attempt to validate a woman's viewpoint. Jong's book illustrates for him that "the fantasies of women are bland and uninteresting, their ambitions trivial and their anger misdirected" (37). Like other authors of unfavorable reviews, Gilder sees the novel as a falling off from a previous, successful novel, in this case *Fear of Flying*. (One good way to damn a novel is to say that the author has lost her touch.) In Gilder's view Jong has been spoiled by success:

she has given up the promise of her beginnings for the comforts of being a Feminist Celebrity and not having to think. How much more simple it is to buy wholesale the pre-packaged thought of an ideology than to make up your own mind (as Isadora struggled so hard to do—with little success, to be sure—in *Fear of Flying*). (37)

Although Gilder appears to be saying that *Fear* was free from ideological intrusions, many reviewers who gave that novel unfavorable reviews contended that the novel was marred by an ideological purpose and hence a "tract" or "propaganda." Gilder pronounces Jong a "dumb blonde after all" (37) (albeit an ideological one).

Gilder finds Jong's feminism to be tinged with Marxism and Freudianism, which, in conjunction, he characterizes as "the prevailing ideological debris" (36) of our day. Feminism is described as a "holding action of the upper middle classes" with the wife sent out to work to add to the family income at the expense of family life. Trapped in her middle-class perspective, Jong is blind to issues of class.

Not only has Jong become for Gilder an example of most of the things that are wrong with the modern world, she has committed another offense. She has invaded a past Gilder wants to protect in order to maintain the view of history that undergirds his own ideology. In Gilder's eyes Jong has projected into the past ideas "cut after the fashion of contemporary cliché" (36). He believes it is a purpose of Jong's book to show that the present is superior to the past, and he questions this assumption.

Gilder prefers Cleland's *Fanny Hill*, having taken a liking to Cleland's "spirited" and "lustful" heroine and believing that Cleland's novel "demonstrates a much greater awareness of the dependent and vulnerable position of women in society" (37). The comment seems remarkably transparent: the sexuality of women is to be firmly attached to their role as the socially dominated. Jong's heroine, whom he sees as challenging society's values, is unattractive to him.

Finally Gilder views the book as an aesthetic failure. Besides being cliché-ridden, the action is implausible, the tone is passive, the erotic scenes aren't erotic, and finally, that most damning criticism in our day, the language is flat and uninteresting. Gilder writes: "Jong simply has a tin ear; she is deaf to all nuance in the language and has no feel for its rhythm" (36).

Sally Helgesen,[7] writing in *Harper's*, also criticizes Jong's treatment of the past. She is troubled by Jong's attempt to create "instant tradition," that is, to create tradition for a minority group. (She mentions

Alex Haley's *Roots* as another example.) Helgesen finds the novel "bogus," "phony," "a pastiche," and refers to "distortions" and "free-
form history" (81). She faults Jong for giving Fanny a "modern feminist
consciousness" (81). Such a consciousness, she asserts, is "predicated
on the primacy of the individual will and the inadequacy of traditional
Christian doctrine" (81). For Helgesen, the book's "atheism" is a fundamental reason for its failure. The "absence of the Christian context"
(81) and a central character who is not shown undergoing a struggle for
faith make the book implausible.

According to Helgesen, Jong's work is based on a "misunderstood
and poorly rendered past" (82). Clearly Helgesen has a view of the past
as something known and understood, a reservoir of truth. She deplores
public ignorance of past tradition and the fact that American society is
too "eclectic" and "diverse" to "make possible anything like European cultural cohesiveness" (82). Her view of cultural continuity is
reminiscent of that associated with the Swiss political philosopher Jacob Burckhardt, who spoke to his students of "all we owe to the past as
a spiritual *continuum* which forms part of our supreme spiritual heritage" (quoted in Surette 18). (We see why Jong's failure to incorporate
what Helgesen sees as an appropriate spiritual belief for Fanny is regarded as a severe lapse.) Jong and other contemporary innovators who
fail to value the past and maintain its life-giving continuities are putting society in spiritual jeopardy. Among these innovators (who are essentially barbarians), feminists are preeminent. Having created the
past in her own image and thus broken the spiritual continuity of past
and present, Jong is, in Helgesen's view, part of a movement of "profound historical ignorance" (82). Besides damaging our spiritual heritage, Jong has, according to Helgesen, written a novel that is both pornographic—because it renders sex mechanically—and lacking in wit
and humor.

One cannot fail to be struck by the deep distaste for the present expressed in these reviews. Jong's novels suggest for many an onslaught of
barbarism and a loss of the finer qualities of civilization. The fear that
western civilization has cast aside its birthright was, of course, expressed to great public applause by Allan Bloom and others in the late
eighties. The sense of something gone terribly wrong in American civilization, and, for some, in all of modern Western civilization, is called
forth in particular, it seems, by Jong's playful treatment of the past,

though we have seen other examples of such an attitude in Keith Mano's review of *How to Save Your Own Life* and in the reviews of Jong's first novel by Amis and Theroux.

In a similar vein, playwright James Goldman[8] sees in *Fanny* a feminist tract, and thus he cannot see a novel. He writes in the *Chicago Tribune Book World* that "Jong has not been able to bring the times to life" (1). Lists of eighteenth-century items are not authentic life, he asserts. Goldman reveals the basis for his own evaluation in what he says next (in a sentence that could stand as the epigraph for my study): "The essential reason why this novel refuses to work lies in its content, in what it is about. For in its bones, it is an earnest, deadly serious book about the Condition of Women, both in the 18th Century and today" (1). One can hardly imagine a more direct statement of the relation between literary evaluation and a reader's interests and beliefs. Goldman finds the book marred by "ideological passages" and criticizes the novel for being two books in one, "a bawdy novel and a think piece" (1). The novel "founders" because it does not work to have ideological passages "pasted on" to a bawdy novel. Goldman finds the ideas of Jong's novel "cloudy or wrongheaded" but asserts that not just wrong ideas but any ideas would have been inappropriate in the type of novel Jong was writing—bawdiness can't go side by side with ideas. Goldman would prefer that Jong discuss what is sometimes called sexual politics in a way that he finds congenial: "[Jong] has chosen a form and given us a heroine beautifully suited to an examination of our sexual attitudes, practices, beliefs, delusions, hang-ups, and dilemmas," but "this is not what is on her mind" (1). Other reviewers seem to think that exploring these things is what Jong is doing, but in Goldman's way of looking, Jong's examination of these attitudes is not true or meaningful.

Both American and British reviewers who don't like the novel are troubled by an intrusive feminism. Once again it is those who espouse an opposing ideology who call the novel ideological. Comments on feminism reveal an attitude of hostility to the women's movement. Some see feminism as an unjustified attack on men, finding in the novel "feminist ranting" (Evans 18) and "anti-male indictments" (Kemp 589). Others characterize feminism as a self-centered and even self-indulgent attempt to win mainly material gains, and still others seem to accuse the novel of a self-indulgent preoccupation with women's experience, especially childbearing, and a tendency on the part of feminists to glorify themselves as self-proclaimed exemplars of the life force. Thus we note Gilder's description of feminism as a ''holding action'' of the upper middle class and Kemp's impatience with what he sees as Jong's glorification of women's role in reproduction. These critics, who are cultural conservatives, also object to what they see as feminists' program for changing a traditional society by placing individual self-realization (what Helgesen calls the ''primacy of the individual will'') above social stability and continuity.

Several male reviewers also implicitly reveal a preference for conventional female sexuality (or female sexuality as it has usually been described by men), which plays a role in their assessment of the novel. Sometimes this attitude comes out in praise of *Fanny Hill* at the expense of *Fanny*.

The unfavorable British reviews reveal a similarity to the negative American reviews in that criticism of the novel for its feminist viewpoint is joined with the charge that Jong distorts the eighteenth century. In the British reviews, however, we see a more personal sense of ownership of British history and literary tradition and thus a greater sense of outrage at the liberties Jong takes with the giants of British literature, Fielding, Swift, and Pope.

Peter Kemp,[9] in a review entitled ''Moll Flounders'' in the *Listener*, sees the character Fanny as a ''feminist mouthpiece'' (589). Jong ''gets nowhere near a reasonable depiction'' of the eighteenth century (589). Kemp calls her attempt a travesty. He asserts that Jong ''chants the usual anti-male indictments'' (589). In a fairly brief review Kemp devotes well over half of his space to a discussion of the novel's concern with pregnancy and motherhood—''its maternity-ward cooings'' (589). With feminism seen as the carping of the disgruntled or the self-indulgent preoccupation with child-bearing and the extolling of ''the wisdom of the womb'' (589), Kemp finds little to interest him in the novel.

Lorna Sage,[10] a British academic and a prolific reviewer, wrote a negative review of *Fanny* for the *Observer*, making some of the same criticisms she made of Jong's previous novel in her review of that novel seven years earlier. Sage calls Jong ''feminism's most daunting advocate of self-indulgence'' (29) and also faults the novel for its ''cheery optimism'' (29). She emphasizes the ''salacious'' nature of the novel; like Cleland, Jong ''thinks the real reason for writing and reading is, after all, sex'' (29). According to Sage, Jong wrote the eighteenth-century novel for two reasons. The first is that through her character she vicariously enjoys impersonating men (Fanny spends a good share of the novel in male dress). The second is to play off ''contemporary Woman against eighteenth-century attitudes which just *happen*, it's suggested, to coincide with the attitudes of twentieth-century Man'' (29). Thus, for Sage, the novel represents a cluster of negative things: feminism, self-indulgence, optimism, pornography.

Novelist Judy Cooke's review seems oddly placed in the *New Statesman*, a decidedly left-wing journal of opinion, since it appears to be written from a highly traditional viewpoint, looking back toward an idealized past. I have commented previously on the conservatism of humanists, who must, it appears, stand for cultural continuity and the preservation or reproduction of the existing cultural values. Cooke entitles her review ''Who's Afraid of Erica Jong?'' Calling Jong ''a force to be reckoned with, all right, a Reagan among novelists'' (a derogatory allusion that suggests Cooke aligns herself with the left but otherwise appears to have little exact significance), Cooke confesses that she had been afraid of Jong before and is ''scared stiff now, having read *Fanny*'' (24). What frightens Cooke, it appears from the review, is a vision of a contemporary sensibility and a set of attitudes that make her very uncomfortable. She comments on Jong's lack of respect or appreciation for the eighteenth century and the novel's concomitant (and related, apparently, in Cooke's view) crudeness, with its ''consistent degradation of women, its gratuitous nastiness, its sadism'' (25). She asserts that Jong's description of sex—''cold, hygienic, an illustrated Kinsey'' (24)—is inferior to Cleland's in *Fanny Hill*. Jong is seen as representative of a crude modern sensibility, evidence of how far we are removed from a civilized age:

> I doubt that the book will have much success among admirers of Pope, Gay, Swift, Richardson, or Fielding. Wit, elegance, sentiment, charm; the tender evocation of Belinda's hair, Sophia's muff, even Pamela's cherry-trimmed cap; the irony; the tension between outer world and inner life; all these qualities seem to have annoyed Erica Jong almost without her knowing it.

Why, therefore, attack Pope and Fielding and everything they stand for while pretending to applaud? Because they pillory vice and folly, I suppose. (25)

We can only conclude that Cook and Jong represent a clash in literary taste and sensibility as well as in views of tradition and attitudes to modern life.

Another Briton who is put off by Jong's treatment of British cultural history is Stuart Evans, who wrote a review appropriately placed in that organ of the British establishment, the *Times*. Evans comments on the "offensive caricatures of Pope, Swift, and Cleland" and conjectures that Jong undertook the project to "set straight the appallingly lopsided record as laid down by Mr. Richardson, Mr. Fielding and Mr. Defoe, at whom (through her invention) she takes an early swipe" (14). Like other reviews that follow these same lines of response to the novel, Evans apparently finds it hard to believe that Jong's effort was motivated by affection for the eighteenth century. Evans finds the novel "long and tedious," full of "lurid sexual encounters," and punctuated by "feminist ranting" (14). In Evans's personal economy, Jong's novel has no value (except perhaps as an example of disvalue), and therefore Evans does not see it as a novel but experiences it as tedious and meaningless.

Clive James,[11] an important figure on the British cultural scene (who was, however, born in Sydney), wrote a review for the *New York Review of Books* entitled "Fannikins's Cunnikin," in which he succeeds in upholding the British reputation for lively review writing. Making use of the familiar book-reviewing convention of comparing the novel under review with other "similar" works, he signals his contempt for Jong by comparing her with a Jeffrey Farnol, a popular novelist who wrote period novels, "now entirely forgotten" (24). Farnol's books had the virtue of being "too short to bore you" (24). As compared to a good historical novelist who "[lights] up the past," Jong "makes the past darker" (24). James comments that "Jong deserves some credit for trying to bring back yesterday, but what she is really doing, inadvertently, is helping to make you feel even worse about today" (24). We see in the sentence immediately following this quotation why James feels worse about today—"[Jong] uses pornography to preach a feminist message" (24). In further comments about the novel's feminism, James sniffs at the idea that the witches portrayed in the novel could be prototype feminists. Like others in this group, James prefers Cleland. His explanation of his preference is revealing:

Cleland's *Fanny Hill* might not strike women as a book written from the woman's viewpoint, but it can easily strike men that way. The book's concern is with women's pleasure, not men's. Cleland's Fanny does a powerful job of evoking what a woman's pleasure is like, or at any rate what a man who likes women would like to think a woman's pleasure is like. She leaves a man sorry for not having met her. (25)

James's evaluation appears to be based on his preference for a type of description that promotes male fantasizing. He gives more credence to a male's imagination of what a woman's pleasure is like than to a woman's description of female pleasure, thus giving a rather clear indication of the biases on which he bases his evaluation of Jong's novel.

James finds no aesthetic value in the novel. First, he believes with Goldman that a bawdy novel cannot also be a novel of ideas—''at least Cleland had the grace to leave out the philosophizing'' (25). This response on the part of James and others reminds us how strong the mind/body dualism still is in Western thinking, where, from Aristotle through the Christian theologians and including Freud in *Civilization and Its Discontents*, sex is seen as totally separate from civilization and culture. Although he ''quite liked *Fear of Flying*, James pronounces the character Fanny ''a bore from page one'' (25). With no talent and no imagination, Jong's least forgivable characteristic is her verbosity. The reviewer finds no shape or coherence in the novel; it is just interminably long.

These reviews suggest that besides the fact of fundamental ideological differences, something about Jong's work is at odds with British sensibility. Jong's writing does not measure up to British standards for refinement and propriety. (Some exceptions to this general rule appear below.)

Some other reviewers encounter the same text but see a different work of literature, or, I should say, see a work of literature as opposed to what the negative reviewers generally see—merely an attempt at literature, a rambling, boring document, an unrealized fiction too solipsistic or propagandistic to qualify as a novel, or a crude work of pornography. Those who experience the novel as valuable because of experiential or ideological affinities or because the novel is in harmony with their literary tastes or because the novel appeals to their interest in the eighteenth century are able to see the text as a novel and praise it for its aesthetic qualities.

Among the favorable reviews is one by American academic Alan Friedman,[12] the author of critical works and also the author of a novel. Friedman begins his review, in the *New York Times Book Review*, by calling the novel a "literary prodigy" that "reaches back to an earlier century for its very life: language, spirit, and shape" (1). In his view Jong's affair with the past has produced a "surge of literary energy" (1). Unlike those who say Jong's work is flawed by an intrusive feminism, Friedman identifies the novel as a novel of ideas as well as an entertaining novel. The novel has not earned its status as a novel of ideas, he suggests, merely by allusions to eighteenth-century writers or other superficial means. Rather, ideas are the basis of its profoundest structure: "There are two related arguments which govern the movement of the book. The first of these is a defense of witchcraft, and the second is an oracular feminism" (20). Friedman gives a hint that helps to account for his valuing of the novel's matrix in his statement that he harbors a "sneaking affection" for the theory of witchcraft as an embodiment of matriarchal power proposed by "scholar Margaret A. Murray" (20) and utilized by Jong. The use of this material enables Jong to give mythic dimensions to her novel, Friedman believes. The other element of the novel's superstructure, Fanny's "up-to-date" feminism, is more of a potential problem, he believes. But "somehow, incredibly, this strategy works" (20). Friedman asserts that "it would be naive to insist that an 18th-century heroine who is in confident command of the entire arsenal of 20th-century feminism is a heroine who defies belief. The atavistic novel knows its true audience" (20).

While Friedman finds that Fanny's intellectualism lacks credibility, he is on the whole a fan of the character, whose "power lies in her voice. She can speak to us with the feeling simplicity of Richardson's Pamela, she can speak with the passionate clarity of his Clarissa" (20). He summarizes by saying that in *Fanny* Jong has taken a "quantum leap" beyond her two previous novels, *Fear of Flying* and *How to Save Your Own Life*. That he considers Jong's novel an unmistakable aesthetic success is demonstrated beyond a doubt when he awards her that last and most precious laurel—praise for her language: "The beauty of her language, for one thing, assures us that *Fanny* is a work of love, a fiction created for its own sake and for love of the 18th century" (20).

Jong's novel also got a favorable review from British academic Pat Rogers,[13] writing in *TLS* with the authority of an eighteenth-century scholar. In Rogers's judgment the novel is a success: "One has to say it: Erica Jong has succeeded remarkably well" (1190). Rogers continues, "The most surprising thing about *Fanny* is that it really does concern the eighteenth century" (1190). Rogers sees continuity with eighteenth-century literary forms: "stylistic mannerisms by Fielding; plot rather by Smollett" (1190). He accepts Jong's credentials as a researcher, mentioning the scholars she worked with. He too mentions the lists— "lists to delight Panurge's heart"—but comments that "the elaborate research seldom intrudes" (1190). Rogers praises Jong's faithful picture of London poverty, a feature of the novel that is highly praised by a favorable reviewer and severely criticized by an unfavorable one. See the comments of Joshua Gilder, above, for criticism of Jong's handling of class and poverty.

Rogers has no quarrel with an imitation eighteenth-century novel with a feminist theme. The novel has "strong feminist overtones," but the author has successfully integrated the feminist viewpoint with eighteenth-century reality. The type of oppression portrayed is in keeping with eighteenth-century life in which Fanny, who as a woman in this era faces severe oppression as a legal entity, has more in common with eighteenth-century blacks (also portrayed in the novel) than with the modern middle-class woman. Rogers, whose review is entitled "Blood, Milk and Tears," finds a coherent feminist metaphysic of the cultural feminist variety at the center of the novel, which seems to "align reason, enlightenment and cruelty with the 'dry' masculine powers" while associating female relation to the "ancient instinctual forces" with fluidity. He asserts, however, that Fanny has an identity beyond the sexual.

Rogers makes an extensive commentary on Jong's eighteenth-century language, which he praises as authentic (while using his prerogative as an eighteenth-century scholar to point out a few lapses). The language is suited to comedy, the mode Rogers identifies as characterizing the novel.

Rogers's review also exhibits the pattern of correlation between a favorable response to the novel and a preference for Jong's *Fanny* over Cleland's: "*Fanny* is at all events a much better book than Cleland's original *Memoirs*, with their rootless London and repetitive devices" (1190). The British novelist Anthony Burgess[14] wrote a highly favorable review of *Fanny* for the *Saturday Review*. The fact that Burgess's views differ from those of so many of his countrymen is not surprising, given his alienation from the British establishment. In a review of a history of American literature, Burgess alludes to his qualifications for reviewing such a book. He first asserts that "with the coming of Mark Twain and Walt Whitman it became impossible for an Englishman to write like an American, though an American had no reciprocal problem. A colonial literature encloses that of the mother country" (90). He continues with a personal statement: "So I, British born, though in European exile and once an adoptive New Yorker, look at literature that has modified my sensibility quite as much as that of my native country—in some ways more so, since I consider myself a kind of rebel against the British establishment" (90).

In the *Fanny* review Burgess alludes in his opening paragraph to some of the arguments he has had with women about women's fiction. His response is to assert that novelists "are really hermaphrodites, that the whole of human life is their province" (54). (He says that this claim is disputed by women who say that fiction has either a male or female sensibility.) Burgess calls *Fanny* an "authentic picaresque novel with a female protagonist" (54) and praises the novel as "genuinely original creation," not a pastiche or a parody (54). For Burgess, the character Fanny is an effective imaginative creation, and the story is a convincing eighteenth-century tale—there is "no whiff of offended hindsight: Fanny is not a woman of our age riding a time machine" (55).

As he informs the reader about the novel's content, he appears to find the material engaging and to be sympathetic to the situation of the female protagonist. He introduces Fanny by referring to the "situation of a woman in a male-dominated society even more priggish than our own" (55). By this remark, he, of course, distances himself from the flaw of his age—priggishness—and it is clear that he is not shocked by the novel's candid sexuality. His plot summary illustrates the truth that one cannot describe without also interpreting and evaluating, as he summarizes the story as the "trials of a high-spirited woman who in our day would be running an advertising agency or sitting on the High Court bench and taking pills and analysis in her spare time" (55). He finds Fanny's predicament always interesting and important and the reconstruction of the eighteenth century "imaginative and always convincing" (55). Burgess refers to Jong as a "literary scholar and a specialist in the 18th century [who] has transmuted her learning into literature" (55). Here Burgess contrasts sharply with the negative reviewers, who often characterize Jong as an amateur or dilettante scholar who once took a course in the eighteenth century.

Perhaps Burgess's liking for the novel has something to do with his characterization of the eighteenth century as "a civilization better than ours" (55). Burgess, who is known to take a dim view of the contemporary English scene, may well be intrigued by Jong's recreation of a past world of vitality and color, a world in which, incidentally, "able women could prevail" (55). Thus, in his evaluation of the novel, Burgess also seems to be saying that he goes beyond the narrow canons of the "female liberationists" (55). He is more truly "feminist" than the feminists, he would seem to say, or in his concept of the human, he is free of prejudice against the female gender. In the moment of feminism's hegemony, Burgess is not at all troubled by the spectacle of women as CEOs or judges in the highest court of law.

A theme that runs throughout Burgess's review is praise for Jong's language. He writes:

This brings me to an aspect of Ms. Jong's work rarely considered by her admirers or her detractors—its stylistic distinction. Style, indeed, must be regarded not as an aspect of a book but its totality: The intention, or pretention, to produce literature—as opposed to the book of a possible film—depends on verbal competence more than knowledge of "life," whatever that is. Ms. Jong's first two books are highly literate: They show mastery, or mistressy, of language; they depend for their effects on verbal exactitude and the disposition of rhythm. (54)

In keeping with his emphasis on her language, he identifies her—and praises her—as a poet. Unlike some other reviewers who characterized Jong's eighteenth-century language as created by simply adding a few capitals and "prithee's," and hence unskillful and tiresome, Burgess praises Jong's language, giving high praise indeed by stating that she has "gone further than Joyce," (54) who only attempted brief passages in an antique language in one chapter of *Ulysses*.

Several reviews by women who implicitly identify themselves as feminists illustrate a continuity of feminist response to Jong since her first novel.

Judith Martin,[15] author of the syndicated "Miss Manners" column and also author of comic novels, wrote a review in the *Washington Post* in which she imitates Jong's pseudoauthentic language. Martin betrays her feminist sympathies when she states that although Jong is indebted to various wits of the eighteenth century, "still 'tis they who owe their thanks to her. For by relating the true history of one Fanny . . . Mrs. Erica has filled a most lamentable Gap left by these Liter'ry Gentlemen and duly noted by many an English Major of the Female Sex" (4). In an allusion to the simplistic female characters created by the eighteenth-century (male) imagination, Martin asserts that it is only reasonable that Tom Jones should have a female counterpart who is something more than either a "wicked" or a "simpering" stereotype. Much of Martin's review focuses on the character of Fanny, which Martin finds complex and pleasing. Fanny has a "lusty Appetite," but " 'tis not the Whole of her" (4). She is also shown to be a person of "Learning, Courage, Curiosity, Kindness, Wit, and good Chear" (4). Martin praises Jong's handling of the eighteenth century and her creation of an eighteenth-century idiom. Preferring *Fanny* to Jong's earlier novels, Martin comments, "But 'tis a true heroine she hath made this Time, no mean and modern Creature whose search for Happiness is confin'd to her own Personage and certain of its Parts" (4). Here Martin reveals a sneaking admiration for the eighteenth century, a time when it would have been more likely, she believes, for "Persons of Intellect to savor the World in all its Richness . . . than to ply the Straits of Self Analysis" (4).

Julia M. Klein, reporter for the *Philadelphia Inquirer* who reviewed the novel in the *New Republic*, agrees with Martin that Jong's eighteenth-century imitation made possible a better novel than the previous two. Fanny, as a female seeking happiness and identity in a man-centered world, is a direct descendant of Jong's previous heroines, Klein asserts, but Jong's eighteenth-century setting helps her "steer clear of the shoals of solipsism, giving her distance on familiar feminist concerns'' (39). The resulting novel is a ''funny, lusty, charmingly didactic work that plunders eclectically eighteenth-century sources en route to a gleeful originality'' (39). Klein finds Fanny to be a thoroughly modern woman but does not appear to think this fact seriously flaws the novel, pointing out that some aspects of a woman's experience are ancient and modern at the same time. Klein finds coherence in the novel, first as a picaresque work, with the heroine encountering various examples of male treachery, and also as the story of a quest for identity, with Fanny attaining success at the end of the novel in the fulfillments of art and motherhood.

A review that appeared in an alternative press publication, *New Directions for Women*, shares much of the viewpoint of the previous two reviews. Reviewer Joanne Duval finds *Fanny* consistently amusing and ''often simply uproarious'' (14). She praises Jong's reconstruction of the eighteenth century and assumes that familiarity with and admiration for eighteenth-century literature will add value to the work for many readers, commenting, for example, ''The chapter on Swift, detailing his earnest attempt to rouse a stallion to amorous play with Fanny, will leave any lover of *Gulliver's Travels* weeping with laughter'' (14). Most noteworthy about Duval's review is her praise for Jong's evocation of ''a very powerful sense of the body'' (14), particularly appropriate, Duval thinks, in an eighteenth-century world with primitive conditions and little privacy. It pleases Duval that instead of giving us a male valuation of virtue—virginity—Jong gives us a woman who ''understands and joyfully accepts her own sexual pleasure'' (14).

Susan Dworkin,[16] a playwright, novelist, and editor of *Ms.*, reviewing the novel in *Ms.*, doesn't share the previous reviewers' admiration for Jong's eighteenth-century imitation. Not pleased herself by Jong's efforts, she speculates that Jong, having become a major novelist, could afford to please herself in the writing of *Fanny*. Dworkin welcomes the ideas, ''which remain stalwartly feminist,'' and the sensibility— ''witty and honest''—but prefers Jong in the contemporary mode of her other novels, in which she can project her own idiom and sense of humor. This lengthy work in eighteenth-century prose is hard to take, Dworkin explains, to one ''who hath ne'er taken that Self-Same Course in Swift and Fielding lo these Many Years ago'' (45). Thus one factor in Dworkin's evaluation is clearly stated here—she is not engaged by the evocation of the historical milieu. She likes Fanny best when she ''tells us (her daughters in truth) what a fool life has made of her," because "in these instances, the wise self-mockery of the true author shone through" (45). This feminist would prefer a more direct treatment of the modern woman's dilemmas.

The reviewers who like the novel are generally open to a playful re-creation of the past and the use of the past to explore twentieth-century ideas. Some prefer *Fanny* to Jong's previous novels, possibly because of their own interest in the eighteenth century or because they prefer Jong's Fanny to the modern Isadora, obsessed with self-analysis. A valorization of the comic mode contributes something to the enjoyment of the novel by some reviewers, sometimes themselves comic novelists, although a comic approach alone would probably not be enough to make them discount ideological conflict. Feminist reviewers are strongly attracted to the ideology of the novel. We note, however, that a feminist ideology is not enough to produce a rave review if the reviewer finds other things objectionable, as Dworkin does. Some other reviewers reveal reasons for responding positively to the content of the novel: for Friedman a liking for the theories of Margaret Murray, for Burgess an attraction to the book's vitality and sexual candor.

It is worthwhile noting here that responses to Jong's portrayal of the body attain a particular clarity in the reception of *Fanny*. I mentioned earlier in this chapter that some reviewers thought Jong willfully turned away from the spiritual truths that could be attained by a reverent attitude toward the past. These same reviewers characteristically see Jong's portrayal of sexual experience as merely physical, and sometimes Jong's sex is specifically called mechanistic and hence pornographic. However, the positive reviewers, usually female, can find a deeper, affirmative message in Jong's treatment of the body. The character Fanny has much more varied and sustained sexual experience than Jong's Isadora character of the first two novels, for whom sex was often only in the head in the form of fantasies. In the Fanny character, Jong explores more fully what "spiritual" truths can be glimpsed through sexual experience—as well as through the "bodily" experience of child-bearing. The power of sexuality and child-bearing as self-affirmation and life-affirmation is noted with approval by the favorable reviewers, but those who view the novel negatively often seem to want to contain sexuality. Joanne Duval, for example, comments positively on the power of themes of the body in the novel, but Judy Cooke and others see sexual candor about some fairly unsavory sexual experiences as simply "nasty." It is very important to some male reviewers, such as Clive James, that Jong's portrayal of female sexuality fits into categories that are operative in their own personal worldview.

Although the reviews I discuss in this chapter are almost evenly divided between highly positive and highly negative, a consensus emerged that *Fanny* was a success. In the light of previous responses to Jong's work, it was probably expected by everyone that Jong would get some highly negative reviews. (Indeed, if she did not, people might think that she had renounced her métier.) The ratio of good to bad reviews was high in comparison to reviews of previous novels, and the good reviews came from influential people and appeared in important journals, including *TLS* and the *New York Times Book Review* (with page-one exposure in the latter). For many, it made more sense to award laurels to a novel that was clearly a work of the imagination, with a historical setting and a complicated structure.

Analysis of journalistic coverage of Jong in the early eighties suggests that in the wake of *Fanny*, Jong was viewed with a new respect. Jong is often linked with writers of recognized merit, and her comments are included in the kind of stories that make implicit claims of cultural import. Linkages with other important figures had occurred before, especially in 1975–1976, but a significant cluster of linkages occurred in the popular press and in scholarly articles after the release of *Fanny*. In a *New York Times* story about authors' workrooms, Jong is linked with Maxine Hong Kingston, Joseph Heller, Mary Lee Settle, William Styron, and Joyce Carol Oates (Weissman C1). An interview with Jong appeared in the *Writer's Digest* for June 1981, with Jong's picture appearing on the cover. The interview is entitled "Erica: Being the True History of the Adventures of Isadora Wing, Fanny Hackabout-Jones, and Erica Jong." The reader is invited to "join the author of *Fear of Flying* and *Fanny* on a conversational romp through success, hostile critics, the labor of writing, bizarre mail, and Fielding's 18th-century England" (20). In April 1981 Jong was invited to join an otherwise all-male cast including Studs Terkel and Roy Blount, Jr., to comment, in *Horizon*, on relationships with editors (Rosen). She was selected by *Omni* as one of a group that included Dr. Albert Sabin, Art Buchwald, and Neil Simon to "peer at the world ahead and comment on problems and potentials they see there" ("Future Views" 124). In *Glamour* Grace

Lichtenstein named her one of the "Daring Woman of the Eighties," along with Golda Meir, Ella Grasso, Beverly Sills, Bella Abzug, and Goldie Hawn. She was interviewed by Anatole Broyard in the *New York Times Book Review*, along with Jill Robinson, on the subject "Men, Women, and Art"—now a legitimate subject for a distinguished literary journalist to write about in a major publication. In 1983, an interview with Jong appeared in the collection *Women Writers Talking*, edited by Janet Todd. Others interviewed were May Sarton, Grace Paley, Maya Angelou, Marilyn French, Alison Lurie, Diane Johnson, Margaret Drabble, and Luce Irigaray.

Jong's reputation was back on an upward trajectory in the early eighties, but, as we see in the next chapter, that trend was halted by the reappearance of Isadora Wing in the postfeminist years that quickly followed feminism's hegemonic moment.

5 / Jong in a Postfeminist Age: The Last Three Novels

Jong's success in both art and life in the early eighties was short lived, the mere "summer of a dormouse," to quote the epigraph from Byron that adorned Jong's *Parachutes & Kisses*. By late 1984, the time of publication of Jong's fourth novel, successful marriage, happy family life, and literary accolades were replaced with divorce, single parenthood, and bad reviews. This excursion into biography is not irrelevant in a study of literary reputation: Jong's example in these years again suggests pointedly the ways in which literary reputation follows personal reputation—for women, at least.

The good reviews that Jong was getting for art and life ended after 1982, when Jong's divorce became the most newsworthy item in her life and she published another Isadora novel—about a modern woman whose life outwardly mirrors her own. A *New York Times* feature story in October of 1984 points out that divorce had figured prominently in three books Jong had published in the previous year (Luzzi). These included—in addition to *Parachutes & Kisses*—*Ordinary Miracles*, Jong's fifth book of poetry; and *Megan's Book of Divorce*, a children's book with the subtitle "A Kid's Book for Adults as Told to Erica Jong." The *Times* story deals with the emotional difficulties Jong experienced after the divorce and quotes Jong on the problems of a woman whose career is a high priority in finding a man who will provide emotional support (Luzzi 21). Jong's problems had also made the *New York Times* on March 8, 1984, in a story about a four-million-dollar lawsuit Jong filed against her estranged husband, charging him with interfering with publication of the children's book by sending a letter to her publisher stating that Jong's use of her daughter's name in the book was in violation of the divorce decree ("Erica Jong Suit Accuses Ex-Husband on Book"

C20). (Jong subsequently changed the name to Megan.) The story was taken up by popular magazines with *People Weekly* running the headline "Mommy and Daddy Are Fighting Again since Erica Jong Used Her Daughter's Name in a Children's Guide to Divorce" (Kahn 51).

Jong made television appearances to promote both the children's book and *Ordinary Miracles* in the year preceding publication of *Parachutes & Kisses*, and in that same year she was featured in television interviews and magazine stories in connection with the ten-year anniversary of *Fear of Flying* (*CBS Morning News* on April 30, 1984, and November 7, 1983). In a story in the August 1983 issue of *Harper's Bazaar* entitled "Erica Jong the Survivor" Jamie Laughridge suggests that Jong's shifting marital status was "an item" for media exploitation: "Columnists fed us—and admittedly, we hungrily consumed—news about the less-than-pleasant split between Jong and her third husband Jonathan Fast, a science fiction writer. As ever, we wanted a post-mortem of love gone wrong among the talented and successful" (197).

More media headlines resulted from an article in *Glamour*. In October 1983 *Glamour* printed a poem from the forthcoming volume along with a sidebar profile under the headline: "Erica Jong's Solution to the Man Shortage" (Krupp 83). In a discussion of the difficulties of a woman's role in the 1980s, Jong was quoted by the magazine as saying that the next generation of women might decide that it is in their interests to withhold sex until marriage, to wait until they are "taken care of" (319). The story was picked up by CBS, and Forrest Sawyer interviewed Jong under the news peg: "Erica Jong denies that she's a born-again virgin" (48). In the CBS appearance Jong says the *Glamour* interviewer got her remarks somewhat askew and redirects the emphasis to the difficulties that accompany the attempt of career women to "have it all" in the eighties (*CBS Morning News*, September 28, 1983).

In many ways the situation in 1984 was similar to that in 1977, when *How to Save Your Own Life* got such a negative reception. In both instances Jong was going through a divorce, had been the subject of extensive media coverage, and then published novels about Isadora, a woman whose experiences had parallels to her own. Jong's example suggests that such circumstances are not propitious for literary reputation. Separating the woman author from the book is often not easy, as many examples from past history demonstrate. If the author is not a "proper woman" living a conventional life, the book can be more harshly criticized. Reminiscent of the reception of *How to Save Your Own Life* is the tendency of reviewers of *Parachutes & Kisses* to criticize the author as harshly as the book. They also dwell on the autobiographical nature of *Parachutes & Kisses* and categorize the novel as pop culture.

Some reviews suggest that sex is even more disapproved of in the forty-year-old Isadora than it was in the younger woman. (*Fear of Flying* and the younger Isadora are still often praised.) Clancy Sigal writes in the *Chicago Tribune*: "Isadora Wing, Erica Jong's self-identified heroine from 'Fear of Flying' is getting older and randier" (39). Herbert Mitgang writes, "Miss Wing . . . is pushing 40 years old. No matter: she is still engaged in a dozen random romances" (C23). Many reviewers quote Jong's description of Isadora in her post-divorce phase—"possessed of a demoniacal sexuality" (39). Reviewers dwell on the many lovers Isadora had after the divorce and also on the fact that she finally settles down with a lover fourteen years younger than she.

Male reviewers comment particularly on Isadora's plentiful orgasms and her appreciation of younger lovers. There is a hint, in some comments, of a very personal response to what is seen as a sexually demanding woman. Mitgang comments that "at age 39, Miss Wing has discovered men in their mid-twenties with energy levels to match or, with luck, surpass her own" (C23). C. D. B. Bryan speaks explicitly for middle-aged men when he praises Jong's description of "nature's cruel paradox, which has women reaching their sexual peak just when their men are being eviscerated by mid-life crises" (4) but asserts that Jong's solution—turning to younger men—is not adequate.

In some of the reviews, it is possible to detect the outline of the cultural stereotype of the Jewess, the woman defined by her physical nature, demanding and self-centered, living amidst great wealth but nonetheless prone to self-pity. There seems a note of personal attack in Clancy Sigal's comment: "In literary terms, Erica Jong has become an overindulgent fat woman, greedily and joylessly devouring anything on her plate. She should go on a strict diet, produce leaner books and stop writing about herself" (39).

Parachutes & Kisses arrived on the scene in what has come to be called a postfeminist age. Feminism did not disappear in the mid-eighties, as those of us who have remained staunchly feminist through the eighties and into the nineties would certainly testify, but feminism did change: it lost steam, partly because it ran into firm opposition and partly because many of its supporters and sympathizers came to believe its goals had been achieved. For a long time I resisted the term post-feminist because it seemed an acquiescence in the idea that feminism as a political movement had had its day, but I now see the usefulness of the term to designate a new chapter in the history of feminism.[1] "Post-feminism," say Deborah Rosenfelt and Judith Stacey, "demarcates an emerging culture and ideology that simultaneously incorporates, re-vises, and depoliticizes many of the fundamental issues advanced by Second Wave Feminism" (341). It implies the death of the activist phase of feminist movement and the end of the need for a feminist politics. Certainly one might point to the defeat of the ERA as a watershed. The Equal Rights Amendment, which had been a major focus of the femi-nist movement for ten years, was defeated on June 30, 1982. To many, the defeat was a signal that the activist phase had ended.

But postfeminism may also be seen as feminism under attack. In her history of the women's movement, Barbara Ryan points out that the antifeminism of the eighties was part of a nationalistic, conservative backlash that arose in response to the "Vietnam syndrome": the ques-tioning of our national goals and purposes in the aftermath of the Viet-nam War and the loss of confidence related to the economic decline that began in 1973 with the oil embargo. Perhaps predictably, the con-servative response was to call for a return to "traditional values." Once again, a finger was pointed at women as the cause of a breakdown of the family, and the breakdown was seen as the cause of disorder in the larger society. The later 1970s saw the advent of the Moral Majority with its profamily ideology. Fundamentalist religious groups gained strength in the 1980s, and a cornerstone of their ideology was a return to traditional roles for men and women (Ryan 101–2). In 1982 the Moral Majority called a conference to discuss ways of keeping women from working outside the home, and in the 1982 fall election campaign Re-publicans withdrew support for the ERA and began to emphasize issues having to do with family and children.[2] Feminists saw conservative de-mands as based in a vision of American founded in "a conveniently in-complete and romantic recollection of the United States in the 1950's" (Steinem et al. 38).

Writing in 1986, Nijole V. Benokraitis and Joe R. Feagin assert that a "majority of Americans are convinced that sex equality is no longer a high-priority problem" (2). Benokraitis and Feagin offer a list of crises of the late seventies and the eighties—including escalating terrorism, Three Mile Island, and Star Wars—suggesting that such threatening and acute problems overshadowed issues of sex discrimination. Also compelling is their point that in the picture of reality purveyed by the media in those years, sex discrimination was seen as a problem that had been conquered. In news coverage, "firsts" by women were played up; and in television programming, the woman news anchor or the glamorous professional in television drama were offered as evidence that sexual equality had been achieved. As their title indicates, Benokraitis and Feagin wrote their book to demonstrate that sex discrimination was alive and well in the 1980s.[3]

Feminists themselves began to retreat from sexual politics, becoming less critical of men and more apt to find positive values in heterosexual love and the family structure they had been so critical of in earlier years. In "Feminism, Postfeminism, and Contemporary Women's Fiction," Deborah Silverton Rosenfelt finds that postfeminist novels are more apt to express "skepticism and doubt" and an awareness of limits in place of the "revolutionary optimism" of feminist novels (*Modern Sexism* 282). Postfeminism questions the values of individual self-development—at least as those values were uncompromisingly advanced in the early days of feminism—and it intimates that the expectations of feminism were too high.

Of special significance was the response of the younger generation of women to the feminism of their mothers or older sisters. In an article in the *New York Times* (in what was probably the first use of the word "postfeminist," a few months after the defeat of the ERA) Susan Bolotin announced the arrival of the "post-feminist generation." The *New York Times Magazine* story, based on interviews with several young women in their twenties (the "Voices from the Post-Feminist Generation," according to the title of the article) revealed that anger—now described as "bitterness" and "bellyaching"—was outmoded and that acceptance and "pragmatism" were in. " 'Feminism' had become a dirty word" (30), according to Bolotin. The characterizations of feminism that were the basis of its rejection differ widely. Bolotin reports that some young women feel that "feminism is a radical theory of separatism, a special identification with women of those things that are distinctly feminine" (30); some make explicit associations between feminism and lesbianism. Some say that, in its promotion of women as men's equals, feminism is responsible for killing chivalry and romance. While there seems to be some confusion about the precise nature of the feminism that is being repudiated, there is general agreement among these successful young women, in many ways the beneficiaries of the movement of the 1970s, that careers are open to the talented: "It's the individual woman's responsibility to prove her worth. Then she can demand equal pay" (31).

Citing a number of recent studies, Barbara Ryan documents the wish of younger women in this era to "have it all" while believing they can accomplish such a feat on their own. Younger women typically anticipate a successful career, a substantial salary, and no significant problems combining a career and family. Ryan points out that there is a notable agreement with feminist goals while at the same time little understanding that achieving these goals has anything to do with a social movement. A belief in individualism has always been a strong ideology in America, and the younger generation easily forgot (or never noticed) that a political movement was responsible for the increased opportunities available to women who came after the activists of the sixties and seventies.

Some men, outspoken in their opposition to women's gains, made names for themselves by opposing the increased power of women. The book of Dr. Edgar Berman, *The Compleat Chauvinist: A Survival Guide for the Bedeviled Male*, got a lot of attention in 1982. Berman, part of the backlash against the increased power of women, asserted that women were unfit for leadership positions because of hormonal instability. Berman's book had been refused by four publishers before it was published by Macmillan. In 1984 Sidney Siller founded the National Organization for Men, to counter the "skyrocketing" power of women.[4] (At the same time some thought the defeat of the ERA was the beginning of an era of female passivity in politics because women would have no issue to organize around.)

Opposition to the women's movement began to speak with a loud voice. The most common themes were the violence feminist programs did to women's nature and the need to preserve traditional arrangements regarding gender and the family. William Chafe has observed that "the consistency of anti-feminist arguments constitutes one of the most striking facts of the entire debate in American over women's place" (quoted in Buechler 174). Arguments that feminism poses a threat to women because it undermines and destroys those institutions in which women's true nature has the opportunity to flourish were heard from those opposing suffrage in the nineteenth and twentieth centuries and again in the campaign against the ERA.

These are exactly Benjamin R. Barber's themes in an article in the *New Republic.* Barber attributes the defeat of the ERA to the discovery on the part of women that "radical feminism was to be a revolution carried out in the name of Woman against women" (26). The Barber piece was the feature article for the July 11, 1983, issue, advertised on the cover with the words "The New Feminist Ideal." According to Barber, the ideology of feminism, which had been so successful just a few years before, became discredited when women repudiated a movement that "called for androgyny—the eradication of sexual differences as the condition for political equality between the sexes" (26). Women who valued their family roles as wives and mothers, or the old-fashioned definition of their roles as men's sexual partners, turned away from the feminism of the previous years. In Barber's essentialistic formulation: "To liberate women could only be to extirpate the woman, leaving behind an androgynous shell of abstract personhood" (27). Women were not ready to give up their womanhood: "If accepting sisterhood meant abjuring womanhood—husbands, generativity, love, babies, nurturing—then they would do without sisters" (27).

Not surprisingly, feminists who had supported the amendment did not see it this way. Caryl Rivers speculated that defeat amounted to an expression of fear on the part of men "about what would happen to the world if women changed" (D19). American society might suffer if women ceased to put the major portion of their energy into the "helping and caring, which is the 'glue' that holds society together" (D19). Barbara Ehrenreich, whose book *The Hearts of Men: American Dreams and the Flight from Commitment* was widely reviewed in 1983 (and discussed in the Barber article), asserted that it was women who were having second thoughts, not men. Women who had presumably viewed feminism favorably in its period of greatest ascendancy had withdrawn support because of a fear that was at bottom economic. Succumbing to antifeminist arguments that wives would lose the economic security they currently possessed and distrusting the feminist promise of eventual economic equality, women withdrew their support. Ehrenreich comments, "In the ideology of American antifeminism, it is almost impossible to separate the distrust of men from the hatred of feminists, or to determine with certainty which is the prior impulse'' (147). Repudiation of feminist ideology was tied to the fear that if men were not forced to support women, they would not.

In these years American magazines were strewn with articles questioning the wisdom of the women's movement, not only in the conservative press where it was nothing new, but also in middle-of-the-road and even liberal publications (such as the Barber article in the *New Republic* referred to above, which appeared under the title ''Beyond the Feminist Mystique''). In the periodical literature of the time we find ''The Feminist Mistake,'' by Mona Charen, in the *National Review*; ''How the Feminists Hurt Women,'' by Barbara Amiel, in *Maclean's*; ''Feminist Myths Reconsidered,'' by Mary Mainland, in *America*. On the other side of the debate we find ''Feminism—A Lost Cause?'' by Mary Kay Blakely, in *Vogue*; and ''When a Good Word Takes on a Bad Meaning,'' by Tammy K. Daley, in *U.S. News and World Report*.

British publications echo the same sentiments. In the conservative *Encounter*, E. J. Mishan asks, ''Was the Women's Movement Really Necessary?'' and concludes that ''the persona of the new liberated woman is persistently and acutely opposed by instinctual patterns indelibly imprinted on her psychic plasm'' (8). In the more liberal *Guardian*, Chinyelu Onwurah laments that ''Sixties and Seventies Lib Hasn't Done Much for the Modern Ms.'' Especially suggestive are a pair of articles in the *Observer*. Echoing Barber in the *New Republic*, Roger Scruton argues on May 22, 1983, that feminism, an ideology of irrational extremists, is the enemy of women. To Scruton ''it is an inescapable, and also profoundly beneficial, part of the human condition that the sexes not only are socially distinct, but also perceive each other differently'' (27). The intrinsic differences between men and women are especially evident in sexual inclination and behavior. A woman's life is ''centered upon the bearing of children: this is what it *means* to be a woman,'' and her ''sexual inclinations grow from this biological condition and minutely reflect it'' (27). It is the nature of female desire to ''subdue, overcome, and pacify the unbridled ambition of the phallus'' (27), and in so doing to make civilization possible.

The following week Blake Morrison takes Scruton to task. Noting that Scruton is ''an intellectual of some repute,'' Morrison identifies Scruton's case against feminism as ''symptomatic of a new kind of *tra-*

hison des clercs: the betrayal of a 1980s intelligentsia ready to compromise its intellectual standards in order to score cheap points or provide lively 'copy' '' (27). Morrison says that such attacks—"intent on re-creating that cozy 1950's never-never-land of the stay-at-home mother and wife'' (27)—have acquired intellectual respectability in the days of flourishing Thatcherism. Morrison's article pinpoints very explicitly the disappearance of feminism's hegemony and relates it to the abandonment of the feminist cause by an intellectual class.

The transition to postfeminism seemed abrupt, but the seeds of disenchantment were evident even before 1982. An article appearing in 1980 gives an indication of what is to come and also provides hints toward an analysis of feminism's abrupt decline. In a speech to the Associated Merchandising Corporation's sales conference, advertising executive Lois Wyse made the following prediction: "We are fast approaching the time when women's issues are becoming boring, and boredom precipitates change'' (14). Wyse's words may serve to remind us how social movements take place in a wide context, including, in capitalist society, powerful commercial interests. Feminism was partly a media phenomenon, and, as such, it also became a commercial phenomenon. Its success owed something to the media, and its media decline came about when it was no longer good copy. The engine that drives the media is the search for novelty, and it is perhaps inevitable that the success of feminism must be followed by the death of feminism: both stories will sell newspapers and magazines and provide subjects for discussion on television talk shows. In the world where change is the law of existence, the moment of success is also the moment boredom sets in. Commercial and media interests impinge on social movements, affecting the success of those movements and the form they take and also mediating them to the public at large.

In the postfeminist climate, *Parachutes & Kisses* attracted less attention than Jong's previous novels. Of the eight journals Ohmann considers influential, it received a substantive review only in the *New York Times Book Review*, and in Great Britain it received only two reviews in British journals of comparable standing—*TLS* and the *Observer*. The individual reviewers in the American publications were not particularly well known. Although the reviews contain much outspoken criticism—and, in a few cases, kind words—one gets the sense that there is less passion, less engagement, than in the reviews of earlier novels.

Parachutes & Kisses features the Isadora character, who had been considered a feminist mouthpiece in 1973. Isadora, a sexually active woman, a writer—and in this novel also a single parent—struggles to find fulfillment in various areas of her life. A frenzy of sexual affairs follows the separation from her husband, and in subsequent months Isadora tries to juggle motherhood, lovers, and writing. Other events intervene—tax problems and a trip to Russia to search for her roots. Her story finds a resolution when she meets a young actor, Bean, and falls in love.

It is clear from the reviews that the character is not going over well in 1984. The story of a thirty-nine-year-old Isadora struggling with life after her husband walks out does not provoke the flurry of enthusiastic recognitions that a younger Isadora elicited in a different age. (The review by Grace Lichtenstein makes this point.) It was easier to identify with the young Isadora striking out on her own than with the struggles of the older woman. Several reviews mention the picture, drawn in the novel, of the abandoned wife, left alone to deal with the iced-over driveway and broken furnace, obliged to negotiate complicated visitation arrangements while comforting a child who misses her father, and, without a man of her own, reduced to dependence on a series of unsatisfactory lovers. Isadora's life is in some ways the nightmare of postfeminism, as portrayed by Ehrenreich and others. Isadora might be the woman who has set her expectations too high, as the postfeminists were claiming was the case with many. She asked for too much—from her mate and from society in general—and, in a postfeminist world, she is an eligible target of criticism by reviewers who accuse her of narcissism, of being unfair to her husband, of being greedy and self-indulgent. Isadora is condemned as the wrong kind of woman, and there is, in the reviews of *Parachutes & Kisses*, little sense that the novel is doing the cultural work of facilitating change. For most reviewers, the Jong heroine is constructed as a feminist of the old school, with major emphasis placed on her sexual activities. Hermione Lee refers sarcastically to a character she calls "Wing/Jong" as a "self-styled feminist heroine, sexual priestess and great writer" (25). Anita Susan Grossman similarly calls Isadora a "feminist heroine," and "a guru to her many followers" (88). Jong may write about the joys and sorrows of motherhood, about the difficulties of a single mother, and even other themes, such as the search for her roots in Russia, but her reviewers identify her with the issue of sexual politics of an earlier feminism. The favorable reviews find some basis to praise Jong, who is described as "still [speaking] some home truths to women" (Leber 62), but often implicitly suggest that Jong's "message" had more value in a previous era.

As one reads the reviews, one has the impression that the negative reviewers (who are in the majority) are repeating charges from the old reviews of Jong novels. The same things have been said about Jong so often—particularly in connection with the Isadora novels—that for many people they have become part of a general cultural understanding of Jong. Indeed, one could write a review of a Jong novel—certainly an Isadora novel—without reading the book. In the postfeminist days of the early eighties, however, these charges were made with a new, or renewed, authority.

Some of the criticisms of Isadora seem related to the changing view of women prompted by the postfeminist zeitgeist. It is nothing new for Isadora to be called self-indulgent, but when Peter Kemp says that Isadora's "breathy way with disclosures about her sex-life make her resemble some over-excited college girl" (1302), and Merle Rubin questions whether we can approve of "a heroine whose life is devoted to ego-gratification and thrill-seeking" (22), we may ask whether reviewers' impatience with an unreconstructed Isadora is not related to the fact that a postfeminist woman is expected to be more nurturing, more concerned with others' needs than with her own.

A number of reviewers fault Isadora for her failures in family life. Elaine Kendall wonders, tongue-in-cheek, why a man would leave a paragon like Isadora. Her answer is in keeping with a mood of renewed sympathy for men: "Though Isadora describes herself as the most generous and 'giving' of women, when the philanthropist role grows tiresome she lets out all the stops, sounding like a shrew, eminently leavable despite her fantastic sexual abilities, or perhaps even because of them" (3). Kendall's sympathy goes out to Josh, the husband. A "truly sensitive woman" (3) would have had a better understanding of his needs. Clancy Sigal is even more outspoken in his sympathy for the wronged husband: "Jong is intent on doing a job on Josh, the former husband" (39). C. D. B. Bryan also finds Isadora lacking in sympathy for men going through a mid-life crisis, as we noted above. In some publications, Jong's novel is paired with *Machine Dreams* by Jayne Anne Phillips, which came out at the same time. Phillips's novel is identified as dealing with a family theme and is praised above Jong's. Jong failed to treat the family theme in way that satisfied these reviewers.

The negative reviewers dislike Isadora intensely, citing several reasons, but usually reacting strongly to the sexual explicitness of the novel. The emotional response to the sexual content of Jong's novels was still very apparent in 1984. When I was in England in 1986 and read a number of British papers regularly, I noted in the British press a discussion that went on intermittently on the question of who is more puritanical, the British or the Americans. As one reads Jong's reviews, one may well agree that this is a good question. Those reviewers who have responded positively to Jong's novels over the years, such as John Updike, Anthony Burgess, and Molly Haskell, have approved of Jong's treatment of sex. Others have been deeply troubled, horrified, or enraged. Surely some of these do not believe it is in good taste for anyone to write about sex in the way Jong does, while for others it is *women* who should not write about sex openly. Hermione Lee, one of the reviewers of *Parachutes & Kisses*, makes criticisms of the sexual aspects of Jong's novel. However, she has also written a book about Philip Roth and is not troubled by Roth's sexual candor in *Portnoy*, which she recounts at length. For some reviewers, the foregrounding of the sexual aspects of Jong's novel is of such paramount importance that everything else is insignificant by comparison. These reviewers do not read any of Isadora's experiences, sexual or otherwise, as comic. Only the favorable reviewers, discussed at the end of this chapter, respond to the novel as comedy. As in the responses to Jong's previous novels, the evaluation of the novel as an aesthetic object is related to the content. Those who see Jong's content as trivial or obscene see failings in the novel's style and structure.

References in the reviews to Jong the public figure suggest that for some reviewers her media celebrity has not helped her literary reputation. In her review of *Parachutes & Kisses*, Anita Susan Grossman refers to the fact that Jong was regularly in the news: ''The autobiographical saga of Erica Jong, begun in *Fear of Flying* (1973) and *How to Save Your Own Life* (1977), continues for those who have not kept up with it via the gossip magazines'' (28). In a similar comment Clancy Sigal remarks in his review that ''it is always boring to listen to celebrities moan about the perils of fame'' (39), and Elaine Kendall refers ironically to the fact that Jong is ''a frequent and honored guest on TV talk shows'' (3). It is, parenthetically, a noteworthy point that almost every review I have found of this novel appeared in a daily or Sunday newspaper. Even the prestige publications that reviewed the novel are newspapers—the *New York Times Book Review*, *TLS*, and the *Observer*. In a review of *Cat's Eye* in the *Women's Review of Books*, Helen Yglesias remarks that some people believe that prolific writers like Margaret Atwood or Joyce Carol Oates cannot also be serious artists (3). A position as a celebrity is an even more serious handicap. A media figure as familiar as a movie star, a popular singer, or a political figure cannot be a legitimate writer, at least when she is female and the facts about her protagonist's life resemble her own life.

I have emphasized the role of a literary elite in forming reputation, but this elite makes its judgments in the widest possible social context and is inevitably influenced by media images. As Morrison's article points out, an intellectual elite also contributes to the creation of media images. Jong's example suggests that images and reputations are created in the complex interaction between an intellectual class, media hype, and the influence of a larger group of public voices and institutions. Erica Jong's literary reputation has been particularly influenced by media exposure because she has been a media celebrity ever since the success of *Fear of Flying*. It is true, however, that the literary reputations of every living writer—and to some extent even the reputations of those who have been deceased for decades or centuries (notorious examples are Mark Twain and Shakespeare)—are affected by the nature and frequency of media references.

The response to *Parachutes & Kisses* presents a view of Jong that is still the predominant cultural image of Jong. It is a view that quite possibly also militates against a more positive response to Jong in the academic world. Her works are seen as part of an system of commodification in which she is a willing participant. Her work, autobiographical in nature and sexual is content, is not art. The matrix of her morally shallow art is indicated by the constant references to her narcissism. The theory of the commodification of art allows no possibility that her readers can construct their own meanings. There is a hint of misogyny in the ease with which a morally shallow nature is attributed to readers who are assumed to be female. Merle Rubin, for example, surely sees as female those readers "who identify with her and who want to believe in her romantic fantasies" (22).

The media image Jong had in 1984 had an effect on the way evaluative communities took form. The reviews, mostly confined to popular publications, presented the journalist's view of Jong, so to speak. Often similar evaluations are made by male and female reviewers and also by British and American reviewers. Most reviews are united around the view that Jong's novel is pop culture and therefore in some way a cultural threat. There are some gender differences in that some male reviewers are put off by Isadora's sexuality in a way that is different from the negative female reviewers, with the women stressing the crudity and vulgarity and the men responding more directly to the middle-aged sexual woman of undiminished libido projected by the novel. Only a small minority of the reviews are reminiscent of the feminist reviews of some earlier novels.

The first group of negative reviewers discussed below are women writing in American publications. As they read the text, they constitute a novel about a kind of woman they evidently despise. They then distance themselves from this individual. By characterizing the book as popular fiction, they appear to be saying that although there are many women of this type, they themselves are in another category or class.

Providing an interesting contrast to some negative reviews of *Fear of Flying* and *Fanny* in which Jong appeared to be an important force on the cultural scene, able by her novel-writing efforts to give substantial aid to the forces of cultural decline, the unfavorable reviews of *Parachutes* suggest that Jong's ideas are merely trivial, trite, and outmoded, or obscene. In the first review discussed below, the writer goes to great lengths to insist that Jong has no importance as a cultural leader. Far from being "amanuensis to the zeitgeist," as Jong described Isadora in *How to Save Your Own Life*, she is now the boring echo of outmoded ideas.

For Merle Rubin,[5] writing in the *Christian Science Monitor*, Jong does not qualify as a serious artist. Careful to deny Jong any role as a cultural innovator, Rubin sees her as having the limitations of a popular writer. According to Rubin, Erica Jong's readers as well as Jong herself "on some level" think she founded the sexual revolution. However, in Rubin's view Jong didn't found anything but merely reflects the values and interests of her audience. A popular writer is one who tells people "what they want to hear—what they already know" (21). Jong's novel is "literary junk food that tries to pass itself off as artistic *haute cuisine*" (21). Jong shares with her audience the propensity to absorption in self: "Her self-immersion mirrors the narcissism of readers who identify with her and who want to believe in her romantic fantasies" (22). Jong deserves criticism because while she is clearly one thing, a mere popular writer, she asks, by means of her extensive literary quotations and her discussions of the role of the artist, to be taken for something else, a serious writer. Rubin presents one of the more interesting metaphors to describe the writer who is not an artist. For her, Jong's is a vacuum cleaner art. Like a vacuum cleaner to a Persian carpet, "her novels indiscriminately suck up all the flotsam and jetsam—astrology, Reichian orgones, every undigested platitude and prefabricated controversy ever batted about on a television talk show—leaving the intricate patterns and complexities of real life untouched in their wake" (22).

Laura Shapiro, writing in *Newsweek*, shares Rubin's view that Jong is following taste rather than creating it. She sees a book strictly about sex: "Erica Jong is still having a fine old time writing novels about sex, and although she has never embellished her theme with an insight beyond her first and famous one—that women like it—sheer repetition has now enabled her to complete an entire trilogy" (88). Shapiro can't understand the acclaim Jong's work has received from able critics. She herself thinks *Parachutes* would be appropriate for reading at the beach, presumably not a place to make a book an occasion for meditation and contemplation. She finds in the novel "all the breathy, portentous mannerisms of a cover story in *Cosmopolitan*" (88). The literary quotations do not succeed in conferring literary distinction on the novel.

Elaine Kendall,[6] writing in the *Los Angeles Times*, finds the novel pedantic—"[larded] with references to the ancient and modern greats" (3)—but hopelessly trivial because of the character and pursuits of Isadora. Kendall mocks Isadora as she summarizes the novel, characterizing her as boastful and emphasizing her sexual exploits. She sides with Josh, the husband Isadora breaks up with in the course of the novel and seems to think that Isadora would be better off in a more traditional role, cooking dinner, perhaps, like the girlfriend Josh takes up with after Isadora. For Kendall the novel is "entertaining, even affecting" when Jong deals with nonsexual matters, such as the trip to Russia and the portrait of the narrator's grandfather. Jong "could write another sort of book if she set her mind to it" (3). Thus Kendall sees the possibility of a different, more significant, and better novel in some of the novel's episodes.

Anita Susan Grossman, writing in the *Wall Street Journal*, also expresses a dislike for Jong's protagonist, who she is convinced is Jong herself: "We seem to have autobiography in the thinnest of disguises, with the only real fiction being the publisher's disclaimer that any resemblance to persons living or dead is purely coincidental" (28). The only fictional element within in the novel is the exaggeration by the boastful, self-centered protagonist of her own accomplishments. But Grossman will not dignify the novel by calling it a *roman à clef*—that "term presupposes too much original plot-making by the author" (28). Grossman does, however, have praise for a few parts of the novel, especially Jong's description of "Isadora's eulogy at her grandfather's funeral, a mixture of eloquence and savage wit as good as anything Ms. Jong has ever written" (28).

Three of these reviewers express the view that Jong is a better writer than this work reveals. Grossman says that "Jong is too intelligent a writer not to have higher ambitions for her work," (28) and Kendall sees evidence that "Jong could write another sort of book if she set her mind to it" (3). Rubin asserts that "Jong herself knows the difference between a celebrity . . . and a true artist" (22). Thus Jong has some residual reputation that these writers recognize even while damning her most recent effort. She has talent she is not using. The negative male reviewers below, and all the British reviewers, are less convinced of this. The best thing they can say about Jong is that the younger Jong had some ability.

The negative remarks of three male reviewers writing in American publications reveal the influence of gender in some of their evaluative comments. Clancy Sigal,[7] writing in the *Chicago Tribune Book World*, faults Jong for literary pretentiousness. While the early Jong had a degree of wit, the Isadora of *Parachutes & Kisses* is presented as an "Important Cultural Figure whose every thought and utterance have to be rendered as if on stone tablets" (39). Isadora is, furthermore, Jong herself. Much of the review, entitled "Jong's Ego Overwhelms Small, Sharp, Nasty Comedy," deals with domination in the novel of a note of vengeance toward the former husband. Jong's vengefulness, making her a "bully with words" (39), emanates ultimately from her own self-loathing, Sigal surmises, resulting in a novel that is an exercise in the banal. Self-justification and self-glorification make for "bad writing" as opposed to "truthfulness." Sigal, in sympathy with Isadora's former husband, forms a negative judgment of the novel based on his response to Jong's treatment of the aftermath of the marriage.

Herbert Mitgang,[8] writing in the *New York Times*, emphasizes Isadora's sexual activities, calling her a "priapean Central Park West princess" and "borderline nymphomaniac" (C23). He points out that these words, however, would never occur to her because she "considers herself to be a role model for the liberated woman" (C23). Mitgang then turns to Jong's literary allusions, listing by name thirty-one authors cited by Jong. Mitgang sees the story of Isadora's adventures in "free-lance beds" as the heart of the novel. For him the search for her grandfather's spirit in Russia, the "philosophizing," as he calls it, the trip to Venice described in the novel "all seem to be extraneous to the story" (C23). The "Wing the reader knows and loves" is the "raunchy" persona. When the character sticks to her priapean metier, she is "a wonderfully humorous Central Park West character"(C23). Mitgang ends by quoting S. J. Perelman, who once said "in admiration": "*A dirty mind never sleeps*" (C23). If successful, the novel is a success in what Mitgang considers a minor genre—the humorous raunchy novel. Such praise comes off as condescending, and, in effect, finally not a valuing but a devaluing of the novel. In Mitgang's reading of the novel, it is necessary to exclude the "extraneous," which turns out to be all Jong's attempts to explore dimensions of life beyond sexual expression, in order to uncover the true novel. The novel, like the woman, should know its place. It is bounded by the sexual and should not move beyond that.

While Mitgang can appreciate the humorous raunchy novel, *Playboy*, in 1984 at least, cannot. An anonymous reviewer in *Playboy* comments: "Jong writes rowdy, juicy, delicious sex—sometimes funny, sometimes agonizing, never, never, never, boring. But, like the mature Isadora, we need more than a good *schtup* [act of copulation] to stay tuned, and Jong is unable or unwilling to let Isadora wrestle with much more than the bedsheets" (33). The reviewer in *Playboy* says he wants more than just sex but, constrained by his own way of looking, constitutes a novel that is only about sex. If even *Playboy* doesn't like Jong's novels, we may conclude that her work is indeed an outmoded fashion for many.

The content of Jong's novel appears to arouse little interest for novelist C. D. B. Bryan,[9] writing in the *New York Times Book Review*. Bryan says he liked *Fear of Flying*: "Damn it, 'Fear of Flying' was fun! Isadora at 29 was fearless and vulnerable, garrulous and witty, self-mocking and guilt-ridden, tender and earthy" (14), almost a "young Wife of Bath." For Bryan, the Isadora of *Parachutes & Kisses*, however, is capable only of banality: "What are the truths of Isadora's life? The baby-boom generation is middle-aged; steep driveways are hell in the snow; children get hurt when parents divorce; and orgasms feel nice" (14). Bryan is particularly put off by the sexual content of the book, finding it an "endless recitation of sexual episodes" (14). In the last part of his review, Bryan reveals more fully why the novel fails to engage him. Although "Jong writes tellingly of nature's cruel paradox, which has women reaching their sexual peak just when their men are being eviscerated by midlife crises" (14), she fails in sympathy and insight in her treatment of this situation. Isadora merely avoids the problem by turning to younger men. In his own novel *Beautiful Women; Ugly Scenes* Bryan explores the situation of a man approaching middle age and sometimes troubled by impotence as he tries to become more sensitive to women's needs and to improve his relationships with them. For Bryan, Jong's novel is not sufficiently useful. It is interesting to compare Bryan's review to the review (below) of Grace Lichtenstein, herself a middle-aged woman, who relates to the novel in a very personal way and praises it for its truth to experience.

The British critics of *Parachutes & Kisses* are uniformly critical of the novel. Their criticisms do not sound so much different from the American reviewers, but, on the whole, are more consistently sarcastic and outspoken in their contempt. Almost all the reviewers remark on what they call the vulgarity of the novel and characterize the content as "smutty" or obscene. They also often comment on Jong's lack of ability as a writer.

Hermione Lee,[10] writing in the *Observer*, describes Jong's novel as an "epic of silliness, self-advertisement and execrable writing" (25). Her description of Isadora and her references to Isadora's sexual life reveal her contempt for the character she perceives—a self-obsessed, posturing, banal person: "Poor Isadora, greedy for love and happiness! . . . How is she to look after her darling cute little Amanda when the stream of nannies and cooks and cleaning ladies she hires are so unaccountably insensitive to her needs?" (25). Although Lee calls Jong's book "garbage" (25), she gives high praise to Jayne Anne Phillips's first novel, *Machine Dreams*, a "family story" (25). Noting that "Mrs. Phillips writes particularly well about male experience," Lee praises her for "the delicacy and opulence of her writing, and the subtlety of her structure" (25).

Peter Kemp,[11] who also wrote a highly negative review of *Fanny*, is as outspoken as other British critics of Jong. Wondering if the novel could be intended as a satire, he asks, in a review in *TLS*, if the author is mocking the protagonist instead of presenting her sympathetically. He finds Isadora disgusting because of her self-indulgence and narcissism and is particularly put off by her candor about her sexual affairs. She does little but "babble out bulletins about her crass states of mind and intimate sexual pleasures" (1302). In a word, the novel's content is "archsmut." Kemp presents a lengthy plot summary that reads like the satire he had speculated the novel might be. Describing Isadora's new lover, he says,

[Bean] is gratifyingly overawed by her literary fecundity and uninhibited in his response to her sexual ripeness.

His veneration of her writing is particularly essential since, inhabiting a yappingly literary menage—she has three dogs: Virginia Woof, Chekarf, and Dogstoyevsky—Isadora spends a great deal of time musing about her genius. (1302)

Kemp finds no aesthetic merit in the novel, which he describes as "336 emphatically ungifted pages" (1302).

In addition to Kemp's review in *TLS*, the London *Times* found three other opportunities to pan Jong's novel, one a review in the *Times*, one a review in the *Sunday Times*, and one a *Times* feature story, which also evaluates the novel.

In a review in the *Times* on October 24, 1984, Nicholas Shakespeare reviewed both Doris Lessing's *The Diaries of Jane Somers* and Jong's *Parachutes & Kisses*. Much of the article concerns his justification of his initial negative judgment of Lessing's *The Diary of a Good Neighbor* when it was published with the name Jane Somers. Shakespeare finds Lessing's central character narcissistic and her prose undisciplined. He is also unimpressed with Jong's novel, finding it "not particularly penetrating or erotic'' (16). Annoyed by Jong's self-indulgence and sexual explicitness, he comments: "One of the more self-indulgent novels to come my way, *Parachutes & Kisses* left me with the strong suspicion that it was written with a vibrator" (16). Isadora's sexual candor has merely exposed the fact that she is a "crashing bore." Finally, Shakespeare comments on Jong's proclivity for "learned reference" and concludes that "her most irritating quality is this attempt to wear blue stockings over her fishnets" (16).

Reviewer Victoria Glendinning, who reviewed *Parachutes & Kisses* in the *Sunday Times*,[12] also likes Jayne Anne Phillips's novel *Machine Dreams*, a "family web . . . woven backwards and forwards" (42). But Jong's novel, combining sexual passages and literary allusions, fails. She says that although Isadora notes that it isn't fashionable to write too much about sex anymore, she "has no other topic" (42). Glendinning calls attention to Jong's allusions, saying "Ms. Jong scatters the names of major authors across the pages like referees, with quotations from several more at the head of each chapter" (42). She believes, however, that "neither E. Jong nor I. Wing gain much from these associations" (42).

The objection to literary references in a novel about sex has come to be quite a regular refrain. If anything, there is, in the responses to the later novels, more annoyance at the literary allusions. There is also a firmer belief that a novel concerned with sexual matters is not serious literature—or possibly that a woman cannot write books in which sexual reminiscence and literary allusions are joined. Those who follow the debate about what subjects are appropriate for women writers could have found, in these years, a number of discussions in letters to the editors of book review journals, especially the *New York Times Book Review*. One finds complaints appearing with some regularity that the territory granted to women novelists is unnecessarily restricted. In 1987 Lynne Sharon Schwartz criticized Meredith Sue Wilson's review of Alix Kates Shulman's novel *In Every Woman's Life* . . . . Wilson had criticized the novel for being several books in one, referring to "poetic and philosophic passages," "illustrative fables," and "dialogues analyzing marriage" (56). Schwartz laments the "narrow territory granted to women writers, and the strict and conventional rules they are expected to obey" (36). Intertwining quotations from the review in question, she asks:

Would anyone dream of faulting John Barth's or Thomas Berger's work for being "powered by an authorial intelligence?" Of chiding Donald Barthelme or Philip Roth for demanding that the reader "keep the mind as well as the emotions alive?" Or of suggesting that Russell Banks or E. L. Doctorow "let go of the intellectual apparatus?" (36)

But there were those who took a very different position on the issue of female eroticism from the negative reviewers cited above. One of the most laudatory reviews of *Parachutes & Kisses* was written by Ken Franckling[13] for UPI. Franckling likes Isadora, commenting favorably on her "uninhibited eroticism, humor and hang-ups." Franckling acknowledges that Jong's novel is about a woman's situation: "Isadora is a post-feminist woman of the 1980's—mixing motherhood, career, and a lusty love life in a search for herself after a devastating divorce which ended marriage No. 3." He can, however, identify with the search for self, a discussion of which occupies most of the review. He concludes the review with high praise for Jong: "This is Jong at her best—perceptive, witty, passionate, understanding the need for confidence, self-expression and personal purpose in a complex society." Thus the story of the individual surviving, indeed conquering, with integrity and purpose, is one that Franckling finds interesting and meaningful, and although he does not spell out in detail the successful aesthetic qualities of the novel, he seems to judge it a success when he calls Jong a "gifted writer" and praises her wit and humor.

Another favorable review was written by Grace Lichtenstein[14] for the *Washington Post*, a paper that has given Jong a number of favorable reviews. Lichtenstein finds Isadora an appealing character, stating: "I like Isadora, even when she behaves foolishly, which happens often" (9). The basis of the liking is an ideological fit and an experiential relation. Lichtenstein comments that Isadora "continues to seek the feminist way of knowledge without abandoning pleasure, intellect, or honesty" (9). Her experiential connection is indicated clearly: "Like so many of us who are her age, she is caught between two generations—the baby-maker generation and the baby boomer one—on the cusp of liberation" (9). Lichtenstein does point out, however, that *Parachutes & Kisses* did not have the impact on her of *Fear of Flying*, which she says she read with aloud with her female friends, "howling with recognition'' (9). Jong's contribution in *Fear* was to describe sex from a woman's perspective in a serious novel, creating in her heroine a sexual woman who also has "intellectual respectability formerly allowed only male heroes of the Norman Mailer variety" (9). Lichtenstein accounts for her more subdued response to *Parachutes* by reminiscing that *Fear*, though probably not a better novel, "represented one giddy high in the first flush of liberation," and reasoning that it was more exciting to read, in *Fear*, about a woman rejecting her husband than, in *Parachutes*, about a woman whose husband leaves her. Despite her preference for Jong's earlier novel, Lichtenstein finds a message in the new novel: "women who have it all don't *really* have it all" (9). She looks forward to more sequels because "it will be instructive to watch Isadora Wing continue her struggle to grow up while she grows old" (9). Lichtenstein finds literary quality in the novel, praising the humor and also, significantly, exhibiting a positive response to the intellectual qualities of the novel, commenting that "Isadora balances four-letter words with five-syllable ones" (9).[15]

Among the reviewers of *Parachutes & Kisses* are some who value the novel because of experiential and ideological connections. Many reviewers, however, reveal deep hostility to Jong, mocking her for considering herself "an important Cultural Figure" (Sigal 39) when she ought to recognize she is just a dirty-minded woman. For some reviewers, anything the Jong who has reached her current status says is banal. If both feminism and Erica Jong are boring, powerful labels or presuppositions are at work mitigating the possibility that Jong's novel will be seen as having literary merit. For many Jong's status in 1984 was that of an old story, the assignment dreaded by the journalist because little can be done to give it the appearance of novelty that will make it a media success.

Some journalists felt that to create a story in such situation, the best course is to adopt the debunking mode. Such is the course taken by Gill Pyrah in the London *Times*, in an example which represents the media image of Jong at this time. In a feature story on Jong, Pyrah first comments at length about Jong's appearance, indicating quite explicitly that she is not as good-looking as her pictures: "Oh, but the camera does tell lies, you know, absolute whoppers" (11). Jong is a "rounded out lady" with "dumpy legs," who "appears wry, alert, and powerful," quite different from the "round-eyed and wide-mouthed" Jong of the publicity photos. To Pyrah, Jong's is an old tale: "Much of what she had to tell me had been warmed over many times on the publicity circuit" (11). Pyrah quotes Jong as saying she has found "stronger" powers of description, then adds:

> For "stronger" read "longer." Indeed, I had been prepared not to admire Ms. Jong because she makes her readers share interminable. . . . Well, the usual cliché is contemplation of her own navel, but it seems appropriate to pitch it a little lower here. Too thoughtful for the prurient reader, all others except—possibly even including—any current analyst must surely find it tediously self-indulgent. (11)

When the feature stories about an author sound remarkably close to many reviews—or when the reviews sound like the feature stories—we can conclude that the opinions expressed are highly mediated. Although the journalist's image of Jong is just one of several current in the various arenas of evaluation (including the academy), it is a powerful image that cannot be ignored by the other constituencies that create reputation.

Jong published two more novels after *Parachutes & Kisses—Serenissima: A Novel of Venice* in 1987 and *Any Woman's Blues* (Jong's most recent novel) in 1990. With some notable exceptions, reviewers continued to see Jong as a popular rather than a literary artist. The fact that she is viewed as a less significant property than she once was by the book reviewing establishment is indicated by the fact that reviewers for the two most recent novels are in general less well-known and that many of the journals identified by Ohmann as the most influential have failed to review the recent novels. *Serenissima* was reviewed in only four major reviewing organs, one American—the *New York Times Book Review*; and three British—the *Observer*, the *London Review of Books*, and the *Times Literary Supplement*. *Any Woman's Blues* was reviewed only in two of these—the *New York Times Book Review* and *TLS*. Other reviews for both novels appeared in newspapers and news and feature magazines. Reviews are absent from important periodicals that took notice of Jong's earlier work. But there are a few well-known names among reviewers of Jong's most recent novels. A British reviewer of stature who reviewed *Serinissima* was academic Valentine Cunningham; the novel was also reviewed by American novelists Carolyn See, Michael Malone, Joan Aiken, and Maureen Freely. Among the reviewers of *Blues*, the best-known (two British and two American) are academic Benjamin DeMott, former academic and now professional reviewer Peter Lewis, and novelists Andrew Sinclair (British) and Francine Prose (American).

The reviews of Jong's two most recent novels fall into three groups, with the largest group of reviewers categorizing Jong's novel as pop culture. These reviews exemplify the now familiar view of Jong's novels—money-making trash.

Another group of reviewers reads the novel in a totally different way, finding in it "criticism of life" and a stimulus for contemplation and moral and intellectual growth. These readers find the novel characterized by technical innovation and linguistic complexity. A third group is torn between these two views. They criticize Jong for the usual faults: pretentiousness, self-indulgence, trite ideas and language, but, believing that Jong has some gifts as a writer, they nonetheless assert that they find evidence in the novel that Jong could do better. The configuration of the contemporary responses to Jong's recent novels reveals how important is the mediation of a literary reputation by all the different cultural institutions that can figure in literary reputation. Ever since the publication, or rather, ever since the extraordinary reception, of *Fear of Flying*, Jong's work has been highly mediated. It has been impossible for a long time to approach a Jong novel except through complex layers of image, reputation, stereotype. The reviewers who seem to be of two minds about Jong know that she has been praised over the years by some important cultural spokespersons and has a literary reputation in some quarters. They also know that Jong has been identified by many with popular culture, that she continues to be a media figure, and that her work, especially recently, has had more characterizations as mass culture pap than as literary art.

At this stage in Jong's career, the nature of the evaluative communities has changed. In some ways evaluations now appear to cluster around more literary issues. Matters of ideology are more disguised or hidden, not foregrounded in the striking way we saw in the response to the earlier novels. Gender and responses to feminism still come into play, but communities are not so clearly united by gender or female life experience, nor in obvious ways by notions of cultural threat.[16] These developments probably relate to the fact that Jong's novels do not connect with cultural preoccupations as dramatically as they did twenty years ago and also to the fact that Jong is now well known as a writer and personality. The initial responses to a new writer have already been worked out; people have an opinion of her before they read the latest book. In the recent reviews distinctions between male and female reviewers are apt to be less apparent, as are distinctions between American and British reviewers.

The fact that the reception of women writers is not so much marked by gender foregrounding as in the 1970s may mean simply that a new set of cultural codes has been adopted. It is no longer socially or politically correct to be so explicit about gender, but this change in discourse does not necessarily mean that preoccupation with gender—or even the existence of misogyny—is no longer a significant factor in literary reception. If this were truly a postfeminist age—in the sense that sexual equality had been gained—the issue of gender would impact far differently on the cultural scene than it now does. My view is that Jong's gender, particularly in conjunction with her association with mass culture, is still a significant factor in responses to her work and the evolution of her literary reputation. It is also an interesting fact that the feminist reviews have dropped out. (There may, of course, be some that I have not found.) The absence of feminist reviews suggests, as do other measures, such as the lack of attention to Jong at the Modern Language Association and other professional conferences, that Jong has much less importance for feminists today than she did in the past.[17] (I discuss these matters more fully in the next chapter.)

Jong may still be identified with feminism in the popular imagination, but she is no longer the major symbol for feminism. She can still be brought forward as a media spokesperson for the progress of the women's movement, and she can still be referred to as ''an avid feminist'' in *USA Today* (Donahue D2), but she has been overshadowed by figures the public finds more shocking, such as Andrea Dworkin, whose *Intercourse* and *Ice and Fire* were reviewed about the same time as Jong's *Serenissima* and received the kind of abuse that is reserved for an idea that shocks the sensibilities of a large number of commentators. Jong and Dworkin appeared together on ''Donahue,'' an event that prompted Jong to write an appreciation of Dworkin for *Ms.*, ''Changing

My Mind about Andrea Dworkin,'' in which she characterized her attitude to Dworkin as that of a "respectful dissenter" (62), explaining that she does not agree with Dworkin's opinions on sex, but she respects her as a Thoreauvian nonconformist. When Jong's novel can be included under the rubric "Lazy, Hazy Summer Fare,'' as was *Serenissima* in a collective review in *Maclean's*, it is clear that she is no longer the enfant terrible she once was.

The first of the two novels under consideration here, *Serenissima: A Novel of Venice*,[18] reminds many reviewers of *Fanny*. In the novel Jong reconstructs a sixteenth-century Venice, superimposing it on a modern Venice, which the protagonist, a film star named Jessica Pruitt, visits for the Venice Film Festival. Anticipating starring as Jessica in Shakespeare's *Merchant of Venice*, she is transported to sixteenth-century Venice, becoming Shylock's daughter and living the role she has been obsessed with. Here she meets and makes love with William Shakespeare, who in Jong's imagination has traveled to Venice to avoid the plague. There ensues a zany plot of sexual adventure, fights and flights, rescue of a babe born in a convent to a nun, Christian villagers on the rampage against Jews, and, finally, Jessica's return to the twentieth century.

Reviewers who like the novel have a positive response to what they often refer to as a rich mixture of elements: the evocation of modern and ancient Venice, the Shakespearean quotations, the adventure plot with its time warp. These reviewers often enjoy the Shakespearean echoes. (Some reviewers like the novel only for these echoes.) Those who dislike *Serenissima* are not able to see the novel as a coherent whole, and, instead of a rich mixture, see a failed attempt, with Jong overwhelmed by the task, the victim of the ambition of her own design. Others who dislike the novel state the familiar criticism that the novel is lewd or that they dislike the heroine, whom they describe as vain or self-obsessed.

In several of the reviews we see a dramatization of a reviewer's attempt to constitute a novel he or she can relate to and thus view positively. Focusing on elements of the novel they find meaningful, reviewers speculate about what Jong should have done to complete the novel along the lines of a successful novel that has begun to take shape in their heads. Such tentative responses make an interesting contrast with responses to several of Jong's earlier novels. They also show that for a novel to be identified as an important work it must be seen as culturally significant. The reviewers in the first group are critical of Jong's new novel, but they also hold a residual view that Jong is a writer of merit.

American reviewer Michael Malone,[19] writing in the *New York Times Book Review*, begins his review of *Serenissima* by praising *Fanny*, in which, he says, Jong proved she could "write a historical novel that both honors its tradition with affectionate parody and creates its own full fictional reality" (12). Not satisfied with the new novel, however, he expresses the desire for another story, one different from the novel Jong wrote:

Perhaps had she really written the story implied by her premise, the story untold in "The Merchant of Venice" (of Shylock's daughter, who renounces her faith for a shallow suitor; who confesses, "Alack, what heinous sin is it in me! To be ashamed to be my father's child"), perhaps had she told Jessica's tale instead of following Shakespeare and Southampton from brothel to convent, Ms. Jong would have found the plot worthy of her careful research, her rich descriptive facility and her deep love of the period. (12)

Malone finds instead a mishmash of Shakespearean quotations and other literary allusions, Italian phrases, a zany plot, all of which create an "odd effect," a "mixture of Bartlett's index and Maxwell Anderson's pseudo-Elizabethan argot" (12). He implicitly mocks Jong's heroine, pronouncing her, with tongue in cheek, more of a scholar than the average Hollywood type and the mouthpiece for the literariness he finds so inauthentic. But Jong has only "one fictional heroine" (12), and she is not one whose story Malone is interested in.

The review by Diane Cole[20] in *USA Today* echoes other reviews of Jong's work, which note that Jong's pioneering efforts in claiming sexual description for the women's novel has made her more recent work seem derivative, albeit of her own earlier novels. Cole is disappointed in the novel, expecting more from Jong based on her past performance: "*Serenissima* disappoints on all counts" (4D). For Cole "Jong's prose lacks its customary edge; the sex scenes, once shocking, here seem formulaic in their raunchiness" (4D). Perhaps Jong was overwhelmed by the very richness of the materials her imagination called forth; she is unable to "juggle" successfully the disparate elements. Or "perhaps the presence of Shakespeare . . . simply daunted her" (4D). In any case, this reviewer, interacting with Jong's book, has begun to construct a different story, one she wishes Jong had written. Jong has set the scene for a "more serious examination of what it means to be an outsider in society—as a Jew, as a woman, as a poet, in the 16th century and in any century. Unfortunately, Jong does not give us this book" (4D).[21]

Reviews of *Serenissima* in British publications echo British reviews of earlier Jong novels, focusing on Jong's sexual explicitness, the heroine's self-absorption, and Jong's influence and the attention she receives.

The review in the *Observer* typifies that publication's disdain for whatever Jong represents for them, seemingly crudeness and commercialism. Reviewer Maureen Freely is annoyed by the attention Jong gets, especially since some of it comes from people with important status in the literary world. She mentions prepublication praise for the novel by D. M. Thomas, Fay Weldon, and Anthony Burgess. But Freely doesn't understand what these people see in the book:

What they find so exciting is not immediately apparent. The heroine, Jessica Pruitt, is depressingly conventional. A standard-issue famous actress with "hennaed" chestnut hair, "fabled" gold-brown eyes, and lips she is forever "reslicking" with pinkish lip gloss, she is full of right-on rhetoric she neither lives by nor understands. (27)

Freely's piece is a recapitulation of all the previous reviews of Jong's novels that have appeared in the *Observer*. The generic review can be summarized as follows: the novel is trivial, the heroine, while utterly conventional, is given some individuality by her extreme exhibitionism and prurience: "she spends the first 100 pages strutting around the Excelsior in Zandra Rhodes ballgown and futuristic Thierry Mugler jumpsuit 'absolutely festooned with zippers' " and "people who like their costume dramas without underwear will be titillated by this book" (27). The plot summary given in the review suggests that the book has no point for this reviewer.[22]

The overwhelming, if not totally complete, homogeneity of the British reviews is illustrated by two other reviews, one by Paul Binding[23] in the *Listener* and another by Suzannah Clapp[24] in the *London Review of Books*. Binding pronounces *Serenissima* to be ''drivel of a quite breathtaking kind. Who could read it without thinking so, indeed who could read it at all, are for me unanswerable questions'' (30). Clapp, who finds the heroine vapid, mocks her vanity and her intellectual pretensions: ''The beautiful Jessica gives quite a lot of thought to her appearance,'' but she is also ''a big reader'' and ''inclined to deepness'' (13). Nor is the reviewer engaged by Jong's picture of Venice or her Will Shakespeare, described as a moral and intellectual lightweight but an ''extremely energetic sexual partner'' (13).

But there is another British evaluation of Jong, and it is a positive one indeed. Joining Anthony Burgess and other British admirers of Jong is a reviewer with significant literary credentials writing for one of the most prestigious of British literary magazines. Valentine Cunningham,[25] who wrote a review of the novel in *TLS*, is an academic and author of several books on literature. Cunningham admired *Fanny* and believes that in *Serenissima* Jong ''deftly replays the hand'' (1025). He is intrigued by the ''doubleness'' the novel invokes: the old Venice, the modern Venice, the Hollywood actress, the daughter of Shakespeare. His description of the novel recreates something of the (for him) dazzling nature of Jong's creation: ''This is a novel full of masks, actors, costumes, performances. Persons and personae converge, intersect, get confused, at every turn, on and off stage, in public and private, in brothels, at balls, in the here and now, back then'' (1025). Cunningham also praises Jong's language, finding it one of the ''chief pleasures'' of her work: ''her command of the words, the names, the quotes, is sustained at such a stratospheric level'' (though he also comments that the novel sometimes ''[sounds] a bit too pleased with its own knowingness, social dexterity, literary aptness'') (1025). He comments further on the effectiveness of her story of life in the Elizabethan ghetto—both ''moving and arresting''—and is intrigued by the subtext of the aging starlet in a ''male-directed celluloid world'' (1025).

Joan Aiken's[26] review in the *Washington Post Book World* may serve to represent a group of reviews that praise the novel as an exciting amalgam of elements. Aiken, a British writer of children's books and historical romances, finds in the novel not only an elaborate plot—in which the ''action whizzes past''—and sexual adventure but also poetry and symbolism, all under Jong's control—''Jong's control of narrative is beautiful, floating, hypnotic" (5). As a writer of historical romances herself, Aiken no doubt sees herself as working in a similar mode and finds interesting and valuable the type of book Jong has created. She is predisposed to respond positively to the genre, not to devalue it or be bewildered by it. Speaking in the voice of authority as a historical novelist, she does make one criticism of Jong's novel: Jong hasn't quite solved the problem of dialogue in the historical novel.[27]

Jong's most recent novel, *Any Woman's Blues*, followed in 1990. Many reviewers of Jong's most recent novel express a dislike for her heroine, Leila Sand, a successful painter and mother of twin girls. A middle-aged woman, Leila is a self-described addict—of booze, drugs, and, most of all, of the sexual favors of Darton Donegal III, an aspiring painter and practicing parasite who is younger than she. Leila sets out to kick her various bad habits, joining AA, and weaning herself, with pain and difficulty, from her lover, determined to stand on her own two feet, an effort in which she has precarious success by the end of the novel.

In creating a heroine who embarks on a self-help regime, Jong is once again in tune with the times. Several newspaper articles document the self-help vogue that swept the country at the time the novel was written, resulting in the addition of whole new sections on addiction in bookstores. (See "In Land of Addictions, Shelves Full of Solace"). Although several reviewers remark on Jong's gift for spotting the timely subject, it is clear from the reception of *Blues* that in this novel Jong has not succeeded in tapping a movement of cultural significance powerful enough to give the novel significant visibility or, perhaps more to the point, that by many Jong can no longer be seen as the novelist who can speak for the culture.

A feature of *Any Woman's Blues* that has received a lot of attention from reviewers is the complex narrative structure. *Any Woman's Blues* is purportedly written by Isadora Wing, the novelist-protagonist of three of Jong's previous novels. Wing supposedly left the manuscript behind when the plane she was piloting went down, Amelia Earhart-like, over the Pacific. Wing's novel is presented by a feminist editor, and Wing herself, not dead after all, reappears to write an Afterword. Depending on the way they read the novel—either as a artifact of popular culture, simple-minded or at best gimmicky, or as a serious work of literature—reviewers either denounce the device as a ''cheap conceit'' (Rifkind A16) or praise the cleverness of the artifice and see it as a literary success, sometimes connecting Jong's experiments with postmodern literary style.

Not surprisingly, many reviews of *Any Woman's Blues* link a condemnation of the heroine as self-absorbed or shallow with an association of the novel with popular culture. Alessandra Stanley, writing in *Time* notes that Jong alludes to Colette but remarks that Cher and Norma Desmond of *Sunset Boulevard* would be more apt allusions. Stanley, totally out of sympathy with Jong and what she thinks Jong stands for, reads the text like a artifact of mass culture—flat, obvious, and simple. She is certain, for example, that it is ''with no irony intended'' that Jong ''creates as her heroine a sex addict who goes to AA meetings'' (68). Approaching the novel as mass culture, she also finds in it the flaws characteristically associated with mass culture—a lack of linguistic interest and distinction. She calls the novel poorly written, citing careless repetitions.

Four other reviews, all in the more popular of publications under consideration here—*Savvy Woman, Wall Street Journal, Maclean's,* and *People Weekly*—are practically interchangeable. In *Savvy Woman,* novelist Francine Prose[28] locates the novel squarely in the category mass culture. She is put off but not surprised by the ''sexual gymnastics'' and finds the novel shallow and ''less life-affirming than reductive'' (95). Such a production is ''not literature''; the complex narrative devices are mere ''literary gamesmanship,'' and the novel has ''no visible irony'' in those instances when it would be a saving grace. In the *Wall Street Journal* Donna Rifkind[29] notes Jong's preoccupation with sex: Leila is a ''heroine in an Erica Jong novel, which means she can barely get though breakfast without thinking about sex 700 times'' (A16). Rifkind applies all the mass culture stereotypes to Jong's work: Jong fails to present any serious wisdom for the reader; her depiction of Leila's experiences don't ''add up to a reflection of women's problems in today's society. They just add up to a determined effort to sell a lot of books'' (A16). As this reviewer expects from popular fiction, the lack of meaningful content is accompanied by bad writing—clichés and cheap conceits. Similarly, in *Maclean's,* Marni Jackson finds Jong doing ''what she clearly enjoys most, which is to write about old-fashioned, reckless sex'' (55). Again, she criticizes the novel for an ignoble subject,

no helpful or wise message, and bad writing: a "lackadaisical narrative," "sentimental veneer," "a literary device that does not work"
(55). Ralph Novak,[30] in *People Weekly*, calls Jong's novel "imbecilic
drivel" and notes that the book is about sex; Jong may "[meditate] on
art or philosophy for a phrase or two, but what she is mostly about is
orgasms" (26). Leila is a "woefully unconvincing and inconsistent creation" (26). Jong has a "fixation on women as whining victims" (26).

Criticism of the new novel coupled with residual respect for Jong is
illustrated in the *New York Times Book Review* by Benjamin DeMott,[31]
who also reviewed *Fear of Flying* in 1973 for the *Atlantic*. It is not his
own very cool and slightly puzzled response to the Jong of *Fear* that he
has in mind, however, in this comment: "Isadora Wing, Leila Sand's
forebear, was a figure of wit as well as appetite; her lively brain powered
'Fear of Flying' with a current of shrewd, funny observation on men,
women, marriage and physicality, male and female" (13); and in his
concluding statement: "What's missing [from *Any Women's Blues*] is
what won the author of 'Fear of Flying' a place among the true and un-
forgettable headliners of the late-20th-century literary vaudeville: gor-
geous, saving sass" (13). "Sass" is of course the word used by Updike in
the famous review of *Fear*, and the tone and character of DeMott's tribute strongly evoke Updike's comments, not his own basically negative
assessment. In the new novel, DeMott finds only "literary self-indulgence": Jong's writing is "cliché-strewn" and "soap-opera like."

There is a moralistic strain in DeMott's review explicit in several
comments as well as in the title of the review, "The Fruits of Sin." De-
Mott states an assumption that Leila is an Isadora seventeen years older
and then asks: "What happens to a female Portnoy, a supermerry, su-
perraunchy Wife of Bath who never looks back? If she becomes Leila
Sand, what happens is that she sometimes finds herself banging her
frustrated head on the floor, in a pool of her own blood, wailing in
wretched loneliness, no comfort left but prayer. Hedonists, attend"
(13). DeMott then distances himself from this view by turning to "readers as opposed to moralists" and pointing out that for the latter it's literary self-indulgence that is a problem.

What we might call the Puritan's view of Leila and her creator, which
DeMott invokes, should not, however, be passed over. DeMott's comments reveal that the ruminations of the moralist are on his mind, and
his explicit reference to moral questions illustrates that it is still true

in the present moment, for some readers, that books about sex can't be serious literature, at least not those written by an author of the female gender. DeMott does not resolve the contradiction between admiring a sexy young character and treating what he asserts to be the same character seventeen years later with disapproving pity. I would suggest that this contradiction cannot be resolved but that DeMott has simply adopted the consensus of opinion on *Fear of Flying*. DeMott's changed view of the first novel offers a striking example of a shift in literary reputation. And DeMott's near quotation of the Updike review of *Fear* makes possible an identification of the source of DeMott's revised view. As a result of Updike's literary authority and the wide dissemination of his opinion—which came about because of his prestige and because the book and Jong were highly visible—many adopted a new view of Jong's first novel even though they contradicted themselves. The cultural scene had also changed a great deal between DeMott's two reviews. It is no longer fashionable for sophisticated people to express the bewilderment, the skepticism, or the outright hostility to feminism that was common in 1973. As people have adjusted their attitudes and values to fit the modern day (a common and probably quite natural phenomenon), some have forgotten that they ever held the views they professed in the past.[32]

There are, however, highly favorable reviews of this novel. One such review appeared in an American magazine, *Elle*, written by Margaret Cezair Thompson. Thompson thinks Jong has written "a very timely and important book" and one which "is also a hilarious satire" (69). She admires Leila Sand—"to my mind, Jong's greatest heroine"—and sympathetically describes her entrapment in obsession and her "essentially spiritual" quest. For her, "Leila Sand is just the right age (in her prime as an artist, past her prime for childbearing) to look at sex, art, and society from a trustworthy angle" (69).

Of the five reviews published in British journals, three are hardly distinguishable from the negative American reviews (and one of the three is written by an American, Jean Hanff Korelitz, who was partly educated in Britain). The review by David Montrose in *TLS* accuses Jong of resorting to "easy sensationalism" instead of probing the themes she introduces. The review concludes: "The amazing thing is: Jong appears sincerely to believe that these platitudes will help other sufferers repair their lives" (7). Helen Birch, writing in the *Listener*, is equally unimpressed with the novel. She acknowledges that Jong deserves credit for initiating a new genre of novels about sexually liberated women, but the new novel has no more aesthetic distinction than one of the self-help manuals the novel alludes to. Avoiding complex issues, Jong has merely retreated into the self. In the third review, Jean Hanff Korelitz,[33] writing in the *Sunday Times*, makes an explicit characterization of Jong and her heroine as consumption-oriented denizens of pop culture: "The truth is that Leila (like Isadora, like Erica?) is so self-engrossed that popular culture has become her fodder and made her a kind of junk-food heroine. (Another Big Mac? Another lover?) The woman who learned to fly in the 1970's is still up there in the stratosphere, being propelled by various puffs of hot air" ("Books" 4).

Two other reviews by British men possessed of confident cultural capital make entirely opposite judgments of Jong's novel. Novelist Andrew Sinclair,[34] writing in the *Times*, believes that Jong's latest novel represents a return to literary viability. In a metaphoric description inspired by titles of Jong's novels, Sinclair posits a trajectory in which Jong the artist initially flew confidently, then "somewhere between her pretensions and her practices, she fell to earth" (20). With the publication of *Any Woman's Blues*, "she has found her silk parachute and her style of sky-diving" (20). Like most other reviewers, Sinclair's discussion of Jong's literary ability requires a narrative involving change—like all media reportage, we might add. Instead of a downward slide in literary achievement, Sinclair sees a recovery, calling the prose "sharp, witty, incisive, and engaging" (20). He also praises the larger structures of the novel, saying that "for the first time since *Fear of Flying*, Jong does turn particular experiences into general consequences" (20). He finds the novel "extremely stimulating and intriguing" (20).

A very positive review of *Any Woman's Blues* by Peter Lewis[35]—appearing in *Stand Magazine*, a literary magazine originating in Newcastle upon Tyne—demonstrates the mechanisms of construction of literary reputation. Peter Lewis is a worthy spokesman for the literary establishment. A university faculty member and the author of a number of scholarly books on British writers, he is also a frequent reviewer. His praise of Jong is underscored by the company in which he places Jong in the review itself, which treats a variety of novels and critical books, all having to do with the theme identified in the title of his review—"Of Bonds and Bondage." Paramount among the mechanisms for identifying and creating literary distinction found in Lewis's review is his creation of a literary pedigree for Jong. It's a very prestigious pedigree, as prestigious in its own way as Updike's location of Jong's literary ancestors in Philip Roth and Salinger. Lewis links Jong's work with a British tradition, remarking that "she does, for example, owe a clear debt to Fielding's comic epic conception of the novel, as well as to the Augustan persona" (83). Jong's comic epic takes her through the bizarre world of contemporary New York "in an attempt to reconcile the warring impulses within her and to reach some form of inner harmony" (83).

Lewis's serious and respectful reflection on the story Jong tells is facilitated in part by his ability to make literary connections, as indicated in his concluding comment: "she achieves a dialogic complexity by her disorientating and Fielding-like blend of involvement and detachment" (83). We must note, however, that his creation of literary ancestors comes along with his interest in the content of the novel. In Lewis's lengthy article-like review, he treats seven novelists, including Raymond Williams, and also discusses a critical book on Williams and one on feminism. Among the novelists is John McGahern, whom Lewis calls "one of Ireland's finest living writers" (83). Lewis focuses on the treatment in these books of various forms of bondage, including close family and social bonds and concomitant entrapment.

Lewis's review is also noteworthy for his thumbnail history of feminists' responses to Jong's novels and their role in the construction of its reputation. One could read his comments as indicating that his response to the novel as art came in spite of feminist distortions of Jong's work. He attributes the fact that Jong's books are often read as thinly veiled autobiography to the responses of early feminists, who "approached literature in far too naive and transparent a way as though it were a direct transcription of experience" (83). Readers of this study will be aware that the view that Jong was merely telling her life story was held most strongly by her detractors, often male critics. The female critics who made this charge were not feminists but rather those who echoed male viewpoints. Feminist readers did respond enthusiastically to the content of the novels, but by and large they responded to Jong's books as novels—realistic novels—not autobiography. Lewis's comment is reminiscent of the earlier comments we have seen that separate feminists from imagination.

The attitude toward Jong on the part of many reviewers could be summed up by the headline of a *Los Angeles Times* feature story (by Josh Getlin) that appeared after the publication of *Any Woman's Blues*: "No Fear of Flying: 'Bad Girl' Novelist Erica Jong Is Back with Steamy New Book." In other words, Erica Jong is a known quantity; she is producing what she is expected to produce.

For the journalistic scoop, it is no longer enough just to interview Erica Jong; it is necessary to produce something startling. As a public figure, Jong has reached that degree of familiarity that requires an intensification of journalistic rhetoric—more sensational revelations—to capture headlines. An article by Leslie Bennetts in the February 1990 issue of *Vanity Fair* is a case in point. Bennetts describes Jong's lifestyle, her character flaws, and the connections between her life and her fiction. In connection with a discussion of Jong's most recent book, *Any Woman's Blues*, Bennetts explores in some detail Jong's purported indulgence in alcohol—mirrored in her fictional heroine, Leila Sand—and says that Jong reportedly threw up on Robert Redford at a party, a charge Jong denies and that greatly provoked her ire (telephone interview, April 13, 1991).

Although Jong understandably dislikes reports that she threw up on Robert Redford, she has not been reluctant, in recent years any more than in previous years, to be the subject of publicity. She has appeared on television, not only in connection with the release of each new book, but on other occasions as well, such as her appearances with Margaret Atwood on WNET's "Bookmark" on March 5, 1989, and with Gloria Steinem on "Geraldo" on March 1, 1990. Magazine articles she produced for *Vogue*—"Is There Sexy after Forty?"—and *Glamour*—"Is There Life after Being a Good Girl?"—were in keeping with her image as the sexual woman, but she wrote other articles seemingly designed to modify or counteract associations with uninhibited sexuality.

In a 1986 article in *Vanity Fair* entitled "The Awful Truth about Women's Lib," Jong joined forces with some other postfeminist spokespersons, praising Sylvia Ann Hewlett's *A Lesser Life: The Myth of Women's Liberation in America*, a book that raised the hackles of feminists like Deborah Rosenfelt and Judith Stacey, who discussed it in *Feminist Studies*. Jong suggests that American feminism made a mistake in stressing equal rights above the needs of mothers and children:

"American feminism has been not only indifferent to the problems of mothers but downright hostile to children and childbearing" (118). Jong cites her own experience of being "booed off the stage by a feminist audience of the lesbian-separatist variety" when reading her poems on pregnancy and childbirth to a women's poetry festival in San Francisco in 1978. The article resulted in more television appearances, where she was pitted against feminist spokespersons such as *Ms.* editor Letty Cottin Pogrebin (*CBS Morning News*, November 4, 1986) and NOW's Eleanor Smeal (*Today*, July 31, 1986), who argued that Jong's statement was a misrepresentation of the movement. In 1989 Jong wrote an article for *Ms.* affirming meaningful sex. In "Ziplash: A Sexual Libertine Recants," she writes, "I never *advocated* the zipless fuck. I merely *chronicled* it" (49).[36]

Such articles as those noted above are Jong's attempts to exercise some control over her public image (though it appears that her efforts have not been very successful). Over the years she has written book reviews, introductions to editions of important writers, e.g., Colette, and appreciations of Nabokov and Miller. Such efforts have had little effect on the journalists' view of Jong, however, which is highly responsive to her celebrity status, an identity that is partly the product of her willing participation in a certain kind of journalistic enterprise—the production of feature stories whose major purpose is entertainment or commercial value.

In intervening to project or modify a public image, Jong is not different from other writers, of course. Some—like Norman Mailer and Truman Capote—are known for their efforts to make themselves known. Other writers have commented frankly on their efforts to enhance their careers and reputations. In an interview with Katherine Usher Henderson, novelist Carolyn See describes the difficulty she had in becoming known. Referring to her "ignorance" of the literary world at the time she began writing, she says, "I was on the wrong coast, I was the wrong age, the wrong sex at the time, and then I did nothing whatsoever to rectify that situation, so that my first novel, *The Rest Is Done with Mirrors* had a printing of 2,000 copies." She explains that she has since corrected the situation: "I'm on the National Book Award Committee; I'm on the board of the National Book Critics Circle; I do a lot of editorials now that get national attention. But I was a slow learner. I didn't know anything about how the world of lit worked'' (112). Jong's example may be an instructive one for contemporary writers: while it is necessary for a successful career as a writer to make oneself known, the writer must be careful to guard against crossing that line from known writer to celebrity.

6 / Jong among the Academics

We have been discussing Jong's standing in the "sphere of repute" that John Rodden calls popular or public reputation—the sphere that involves sales and public recognition. It is now time to look more carefully at Jong's reputation in another sphere, the academic, where lasting reputations are built through the integration of a literary work into the interpretive strategies of the academy.[1]

In this chapter I examine, through Jong's example, how a literary reputation is built (or not built) in the academy. Barbara Herrnstein Smith points out that although the academy is not the only institution within which the evaluation of texts takes place, "the activities of the academy certainly figure significantly in the production of literary value" (46). Academic authorities decide what counts as literary and therefore deserves a special kind of attention and the presumption of "lasting value." The constructed nature of literary value is clear in the story of the particular way the academy has appropriated (or not appropriated) Jong's work. Academic users can establish the mythic nature of a work and thus lift it above the mere pot-boiler; they can assimilate the work to genres, such as the picaresque or *Bildungsroman*; and they can link the work with other established authors and books. Even passing reference or citation is valuable in establishing literary quality, while inclusion in anthologies, bibliographies, and syllabi are gestures of prime importance.

What is Jong's literary reputation today among academics, feminist and otherwise? My purpose in trying to answer this question is not primarily to determine Jong's present-day rating on the literary stock market—although making such an estimate becomes a necessary part of the project—but rather to use Jong's example to gain knowledge about the dynamics of literary reputation. In this chapter I discuss scholarly articles on Jong as seen within the context of the mass media response and the response of the more "literary" or "academic" reviews. In trying to "sum up" Jong's reputation—taking into consideration both spheres of repute—I have become strongly aware of two distinct images of Jong. On the one hand, there is the image of a novelist who has received serious attention by some representatives of the literary elite, both from academics and members of the literary establishment outside the academy. Jong's is an important presence in, for example, Nancy A. Walker's *Feminist Alternatives: Irony and Fantasy in the Contemporary Novel by Women* (1990), and in other scholarly works, and striking tributes to Jong also appear among her contemporary reviews. But this literary image is shadowed by another powerful image— that of media celebrity and pop writer writ large, and in that manifestation, Jong suffers from the trivialization that seems an inevitable part of mass media exposure. Although it is of course impossible to "fix" Jong's reputation, which has the same potential to shift as all literary reputations, I will suggest that her present reputation is bifurcated. A community of feminist scholars (not *all* feminist scholars, of course) in the academy values her contribution. In the larger literary community she has other admirers: male scholars who have written journal articles and the more "literary" book reviewers, including some who reviewed the last two novels positively. On the other hand, a broader sampling of opinion, such as that presented by a survey of reviews of her most recent novels, suggests that an image created by media hype has stuck, perhaps permanently, to Jong—she is characterized by many as merely a popular writer, one who has gained attention through sensationalism and purple prose, a writer who produces what will sell and who reaps the profits, which are tallied up in dollars and in continued celebrity.

But perhaps a more accurate "take" on the current reviews is this: the media characterization has been such a powerful force in creating an image or media identity for Jong that it has effectively given permission for the indulgence of misogynist attitudes and the expression of misogynist viewpoints. Certainly the characterization of Jong in many reviews is misogynist. I'm speaking here of the portrait of Jong as self-absorbed, narcissistic, self-indulgent, self-obsessed, rich and famous but undeserving of fame and wealth. Such charges are consonant with the typing of Jong as a popular culture writer, since the author is presumed to be as shallow as her readers. Jong's reputation has suffered from the binary division of culture, along with the demonizing of a "female" low culture. For many Jong is firmly identified with pop culture because of her popularity and her media exposure. The identification with popular or mass culture is also facilitated by foregrounding of Jong's gender and that of her presumptive readers. It then follows that for those who wish to distance themselves from popular culture, Jong's fiction is "easy" and self-indulgent art. In this view both Jong and her work are seen as trivial. An elitism persists in the old school of cultural authorities and even among postmodernists, because the struggle over cultural authority persists.

The view of Jong that dominates the reviews of her recent novels has spilled over into the area of academic evaluation, as epitomized by a brief evaluation of *Any Woman's Blues* in the *Hudson Review*, a literary journal of note. Jong's novel is mentioned in a long review essay by William H. Pritchard, advisory editor of the journal. Although he gives extended treatment to the work of novelists Iris Murdoch, Ann Beattie, Gore Vidal, and others, Pritchard dismisses Jong in a brief paragraph, consisting of a quotation about lust from *Blues*, and the following comment: "The pathos of it all is that the composer of such lyric vibrations isn't content merely to have written a ten-million-copy bestseller (*Fear of Flying*) but wants to pass as a serious artist. And of course the monkeyshines of her latest production suggest the utter improbability of such a notion" (489). As I will suggest in this chapter, the fact that this view of Jong is held by many and known to all makes it difficult, first, for Jong to gain supporters in the academy and, second, for the supporters she does have to influence the academy's evaluation of her.

But Jong's reputation today is a complex matter, with evidence suggesting that a literary reputation is being built within some quarters of academia. A survey of scholarly books, articles, and dissertations[2] suggests that Jong's work has to some degree been adopted into the corpus of texts that are mined for scholarly output. *Fear of Flying* began to be cited within a few years of its publication.[3] Some of the earliest notice Jong received was from foreign scholars, according to the MLA bibliography, where articles by Dutch and Italian authors are among the first mentioned, starting in 1976 and 1977. Articles in other languages—Russian, German, French, and Danish—have followed, with articles originating in Europe appearing in almost equal numbers to articles in American journals. I have found no articles in British journals, but in his *Bestsellers: Popular Fiction of the 1970's*, British academic John Sutherland places Jong squarely in the tradition of pop culture. It is possible that Jong's most distinguished reputation may not be in English speaking countries at all, but in other parts of the world. One can speculate that European (not British) attitudes to sexuality would create a climate for a very different reception for Jong's work. There is clearly material for another study here, having to do with Jong's reputation beyond the United States and Britain.[4] The *Arts and Humanities Citation Index* lists numerous citations to foreign journals. Unfortunately, it is beyond the scope of my study to explore the precise nature of Jong's reputation and the mechanisms by which that reputation was created in such countries as Denmark, Belgium, Italy, East Germany, France, South Africa, and the Soviet Union, though indexes list articles about Jong from all these countries.

An examination of the *Arts and Humanities Citation Index* reveals numerous citations to Jong. Citations were heavy in 1976, the first year of the index, and citations in a diverse body of journals including the *Journal of the American Academy of Religion*, *Salmagundi*, the *Rocky Mountain Review*, *New Literary History* and many foreign journals indicate that Jong was read widely by an academic audience. Many of these articles merely name *Fear of Flying* as representing a certain kind of novel, but Frank W. Shelton's use of a passage from *Fear of Flying* as a starting point for an article about the treatment of the family in the novels of Willa Cather suggests both the readiness with which Jong's example came to mind in 1976 and its eligibility for citation, at least for some authors, in a scholarly context.

The first American scholars to be attentive to Jong in the early years were feminists, with the earliest articles appearing in feminist journals. These include Arlyn Diamond's "Flying from Work" in *Frontiers* (1977) and two articles in *Regionalism and the Female Imagination—* Emily Toth's "Dorothy Parker, Erica Jong, and New Feminist Humor" (1977) and E. M. Broner's "The Dirty Ladies: Earthly Writings of Contemporary American Women" (1979). (Both of these journals have ceased publication.) Diamond's article is critical of Jong, lamenting her failure to be realistic in her portrayal of women's frustrations in the world of work, but Toth and Broner pay tribute to Jong as creator of a new form of female humor. Toth emphasizes the courage of Jong's satire and the joy of her celebratory laughter, noting that "*Fear of Flying* handles sexual desires (but not performances) with the *joie de vivre* usually reserved for men" (77). Broner explores the candid sexual language of Jong and other contemporary American writers, stating, "Writing humor is a serious business. Writing dirty is a cleansing one" (34).

Soon feminist scholars began to elaborate on Jong's classical and literary allusions. In " 'Isadora-Icarus': The Mythic Unity of Erica Jong's *Fear of Flying*" (*Rice University Studies* 1978), Jane Chance Nitzsche mentions the savage attacks of reviewers who "frequently ignored" the novel's literary qualities. She herself has high praise for Jong's "very literary novel" (89) and undertakes an elaborate and detailed exploration of the unity conferred on the novel by the use of the Icarus myth. She finds the novel organically structured on the myth in all its elements: the minotaur, the labyrinth, the history of Theseus and Ariadne.

In introducing the theme of the *Bildungsroman*, a 1978 article by Joan Reardon in the *International Journal of Women's Studies* strikes the keynote for a couple of articles in various journals, both feminist and mainstream. Reardon alludes to the early reviews, mentioning Updike and Miller along with examples of the most negative assessments, Theroux and Crain. Reardon appears not to be aware of the positive feminist reviews, which were of course not published in widely known journals. She also refers to Lehmann-Haupt's passing comment about the need for writing "sensitive to the ambiguities of growing up intelligently female these days" (307), a theme that Reardon says was not explored by reviewers, who "did little to establish [the novel's] considerable literary value" (306). (Reardon makes no connection between the education novel and the Updike review.) Reardon goes on to make an elaborate analysis of *Fear* as an education novel, citing Jerome Buckley's outline in *Season of Youth* of the growth to maturity followed in the *Bildungsroman* and finding in Isadora's journey parallels to the journeys of Alice in Wonderland and Dante. Reardon argues that Isadora's rejection of Alice and Beatrice signifies her rejection of male definitions and that Jong employs the image of menstruation (Reardon notes that the novel consists of one twenty-eight day cycle) to convey Isadora's "inward journey into her own womanhood" (308).

Also focusing on Jong's *Fanny* as *Bildungsroman* is Mary Anne Ferguson's 1983 article, written for the collection *The Voyage In: Female Fictions of Development*, edited by Elizbeth Abel, Marianne Hirsh, and

Elizabeth Langland, and also appearing in the *Denver Quarterly*. In the article entitled "The Female Novel of Development and the Myth of Psyche," Ferguson deals with *Fanny* along with Eudora Welty's *At The Landing* and Lisa Alther's *Kinflicks*. Ferguson mentions *Fear of Flying* as among the novels that "[laid] the groundwork for expanding the notion of female development beyond purely sexual maturity" (59) but finds that in *Fanny* Jong has reached new heights of achievement: "Jong has gone beyond myth to a new image of human possibility in which male and female autonomously and uniquely achieve full development and freely join in mature love" (71–72).

Jong was also noticed by male scholars. A 1987 article by James Mandrell in *Novel*, "Questions of Genre and Gender: Contemporary American Versions of the Feminine Picaresque," uses *Fanny* along with Rita Mae Brown's *Rubyfruit Jungle* and Sharon Isabell's *Yesterday's Lesson* to consider whether the conservative picaresque genre, which tends to confirm the outsider status of the protagonist, can be adapted for feminist purposes. Mandrell concludes that in *Fanny*, which he praises for "cunning artifice" of narrative (167), Jong succeeds in transforming the picaresque, thus writing a "true woman's novel that advocates and articulates fully the woman's point of view, a novel that does not unwittingly partake of masculine models and thereby repeat or recapitulate the patriarchal domination of women" (169). It is clear that Mandrell, who makes many references to contemporary feminist criticism, has been influenced by the feminist presence in the academy.

Another article focuses on *Fear of Flying* and the American picaresque. In a 1987 article in the *Centennial Review* entitled "The Woman Writer as American Picaro: Open Journeying in Erica Jong's *Fear of Flying*," Robert J. Butler argues that Jong's novel fits squarely in the American tradition of the picaresque: "Isadora, like all American *picaros*, lights out for new frontiers which promise ceaseless motion, endless personal development" (316). Butler's references to other contemporary novels by women and to Jong's other novels are evidence that he has become acquainted with female literary culture.

Not surprisingly, Jong is given respectful attention in several books that deal with literary treatments of sex and the body. Maurice Charney includes a chapter on Jong in *Sexual Fiction* (1981). Charney sees Jong's novel as "conceived on the model of Philip Roth's *Portnoy's Complaint*" (113) and emphasizes the mind-body dualism—the connection of the erotic and the forbidden. Isadora, like Portnoy, views guilt as an aphrodisiac.

Especially important is Susan Rubin Suleiman's discussion of *Fear of Flying* in *The Female Body in Western Culture* (1985) and in *Subversive Intent: Gender, Politics, and the Avant-Garde*, where she reproduces the same material in another context. Although she says that *Fear of Flying* is not "a great novel" or even "a great feminist novel" (10), Suleiman, who remarks that the story of *Fear of Flying* is so well known she does not need to repeat it, sees Jong's work as a milestone in what she calls "sexual poetics" (9). It is "a self-conscious reversal of stereotypes, and in some sense a parody of the language of the tough guy narrator/heroes of Henry Miller or Norman Mailer" (9).

Suleiman quotes some of the negative reviews by women and comments that she finds it surprising "that no one noticed—or at any rate, no one gave its due to—the self-irony that accompanied the complaints and the vulgarity; nor did anyone give proper weight to the allusions that occasionally surfaced in the text, undercutting both the heroine and her male predecessors" (9). Suleiman asserts that "what is involved here is a reversal of roles *and* of language, in which the docile and/or bestial but always silent, objectified woman of male pornographic fiction suddenly usurps both the pornographer's language and his way of looking at the opposite sex" (9). Although Suleiman almost goes out of her way to make it understood that she is not making great claims for the literary value of Jong's novel, she actually does give it high praise, and the accolades she gives the novel for its cultural and literary innovation speak just as loudly as her disclaimers. In placing Jong in the context of the avant-garde, Suleiman not only locates Jong's work in the context of the provocative and the transgressive, she also classes her with figures who have been evaluated as important contemporary artists.

The gesture of distancing oneself from Jong has become almost automatic for feminists who want to be taken seriously, as we see in the examples of Suleiman, Joanna Russ, and others. However, Nancy A. Walker's notice of Jong is an exception to the rule of obligatory disclaimer. Although Jong's novels are not given the prominence in Walker's *Feminist Alternatives: Irony and Fantasy in the Contemporary Novel by Women* (1989) that is accorded the work of Doris Lessing, Margaret Drabble, and Margaret Atwood, her work is treated extensively and with respect, and it is linked with that of a number of respected writers including Gail Godwin and Toni Morrison, as well as Drabble, Lessing, and Atwood. Walker argues that Jong uses irony in both *Fear of Flying* and *Parachutes & Kisses* to challenge authority and also "to suggest that autonomy arises from the self rather than being conferred by an outside agency" (25). Jong is also treated briefly in Walker's *A Very Serious Thing: Women's Humor and American Culture* (1989), and she is represented (by several poems) in the anthology of the works of women creators of comedy compiled by Walker and Zita Dresner entitled *Redressing the Balance: American Women's Literary Humor from Colonial Times to the 1980's.*[5]

Jong is also an important figure in Gayle Greene's *Changing the Story: Feminist Fiction and the Tradition* (1991). Greene's book, like Walker's *Feminist Alternatives*, is a revaluation of recent feminist writers, but Greene comes to a very different conclusion about Jong. While she confesses to having liked *Fear of Flying* when it first came out, she now judges it to be basically reactionary. While politely and even deferentially acknowledging Suleiman's claim that Jong breaks new ground, Greene finally dismisses Jong's novel saying that Jong "confuses liberation with sexual liberation and confuses sexual liberation with the freedom to act and talk like a man" (91). Greene notes that she has quoted from Jong numerous times in the first chapters of her book but says that the quotations are "suspiciously excerptable, on the surface, as is the feminism of the novel. The novel does not finally change 'the old story' at the level of plot, language, or meaning" (91). (I discuss feminists' views of Jong again later in this chapter.)[6]

My history thus far suggests that Jong's work may have reached a tentative precanonical status. Mandrell's article in *Novel* illustrates that in 1987 popular contemporary women writers could be a legitimate subject for treatment in a prestigious journal. Her study, a very literary treatment of a gendered literary form and the possibilities for its appropriation by women, and especially Butler's article, which places Jong's novel in a tradition formerly regarded as belonging exclusively to male American writers (without dwelling on the novelty of adding a woman writer to such a company), are indications that Jong's work might possibly be gaining precanonical status. The articles by Nitzsche, Reardon, and Ferguson, integrating Jong's work into the structures of Western myth, point to the same conclusion. But a handful of articles do not a canonical author make, and it would be premature to predict such a result for Jong's work.

While Jong has received some noteworthy kudos, on the whole scholarly attention to Jong has not been overwhelming. There are no book-length studies of Jong's work, nor has she been singled out for the recognition that is implied in the dedication to her work of a special issue in such journals as *Contemporary Literature*, *Twentieth-Century Literature*, and the *Review of Contemporary Literature*. Indeed Jong appears to get little notice from such journals, which have given significant attention to such writers as Updike, Roth, and Mailer. Nor has Jong been awarded any literary prizes since she received awards for her poetry before the publication of *Fear of Flying*. Jong's work has received little attention at national conventions of the Modern Language Association, even though panels on her work have been proposed.[7]

It is clear from the summary of the scholarly reception of Jong's work that feminist critics played a crucial role in introducing Jong to the academy as a subject of critical attention. The articles about Jong appearing in the new feminist journals were probably not, however, widely read by those outside feminist circles. By the late seventies a few articles had appeared in mainstream journals, and in the mid-eighties we find several articles by male scholars. It is clear that Jong's work was mediated for male scholars by feminist critics, not necessarily just by those who had written on Jong, but by the presence in the academy of feminist scholars and by the new interest in women writers.

But what has been the relationship between the two evaluative stages—the book reviews and the academic evaluations? We are confronted here with something of a paradox. Although Jong's literary repute is in important ways the product of the growth of a feminist community in the academy, those who have written articles have displayed little knowledge of the feminist reviews. Favorable reviews cited in the first articles, by Reardon and Nitzsche, are those of Updike and Miller. We know that the comments of these two men were on the back of the paperback edition of *Fear*. The effect of their endorsements, while impossible to measure in any scientific way, must have been significant since many people's first reading of *Fear* was framed by these evaluations. Endorsements from feminist writer Elizabeth Janeway and novelist Hannah Green also appeared on the back cover of the paperback, and these also must have influenced some readers. Possibly the feminist reviews, which appeared in the *Village Voice*, *Spare Rib*, and the *Washington Post*, were not widely known, bearing out Ohmann's generalization about the greater value of some journals over others in the formation of opinion. (Of course, few if any Americans would have read the British *Spare Rib*.) A review from a feminist perspective also appeared in the *New Republic*, one of the journals Ohmann identifies as important, but this review was mixed, as we have seen.

One other response to the first reviews is something of an anomaly: those who wrote the first articles more often than not cited negative reviews, especially the review of Paul Theroux. The negative reviews had rhetorical value, to be sure. Negative reviews are often cited in scholarly articles after a work is seen as having achieved literary value, at which point they provide a rhetorical counterpoint to the more "mature" and "enlightened" understanding of those later commentators who have come to see the "value" of the work. But the great gusto with which the negative reviews of Jong's novel were quoted in the first scholarly articles suggests that they served the function of facilitating an oppositional stance. For some feminists, the angry denunciations of the novel by the *New Statesman*'s Paul Theroux, *Commentary*'s Jane Larkin Crain, and others appeared to be evidence that the novel did have literary value, or at least to prompt that supposition. Emily Toth writes:

> Theroux's is only the most vicious of many hostile reviews, all of which seem to be extremely angry: angry, apparently, that a woman could write a book with a character who has the same sexual urges that a man does; angry that a woman could use street words (like "fuck") instead of the more traditionally feminine words for sexual organs or making love.
>
> Moreover, Theroux seems to confuse Erica Jong and Isadora Wing—one author, one character—with all women, when he claims the novel pictures "woman as a hapless organ." (80)[8]

Joan Reardon spent more time on the hostile reviews by women reviewers, quoting Crain's "unforgiving dismissal" that "no feminist novel really rewards critical scrutiny" (306).

The reviews—the high praise, the outspoken attacks, and the sheer magnitude of attention—did much to position Jong's work favorably for scholarly study. We cannot, however, underestimate the importance of the novel's connection to an extraordinary social movement in creating the visibility that made it available to the critics—in the United States most often feminist critics—who first adopted it as literary prose. Of course we cannot separate the volume of the reviews and their appearance in important journals from the connection with feminism. Ohmann mentions both sales and attention from reviewers as a precondition for the notice from academics that marks a work as a candidate for precanonical status. The case of Jong's first novel is a special one, however, not only because of the magnitude but also the nature of the popular response. That the novel was identified as of particular cultural significance by large numbers of people is borne out by the media reports current at the time. Because of its tremendous visibility, the novel had less need for the approval of cultural authorities at the reviewing stage in order to become acceptable to (feminist) academics. For the feminist scholars, approval of mainstream reviewers may not have been so important. On the other hand, it seems a necessary precondition for scholarly approval that the novel should have been widely reviewed. The conventional way to start an article in a scholarly journal on a new or recent work of literature is by discussing the reviews, and with no reviews by known reviewers or in important journals, there is no easy way for a book to be introduced into the discussions that are an essential step in moving a work to canonical status.

We have seen the importance of feminist critics in the creation of Jong's literary reputation. If that reputation is languishing today, that development can, at least in part, be attributed to a diminution of interest on the part of present-day feminists. Although Jong has some support from feminists, as we see in the notice given her work by Nancy Walker and others, we must conclude that on the whole Jong does not rank particularly highly with contemporary feminists. It is not surprising that lesbian feminists do not choose to write about or promote Jong's work, but what about others? Elaine Showalter (and Carol Smith) interviewed Jong for the *Columbia Forum* in 1974, and Rozsika Parker and Eleanor Stephens interviewed Jong for *Spare Rib* in 1977, but Jong's work gets little attention from major feminist critics today. Even brief notice, such as that in volume 2 of Sandra Gilbert and Susan Gubar's *No Man's Land: The Place of the Woman Writer in the Twentieth Century*, where one paragraph is devoted to cross-dressing in

Fanny, is unusual among leading American feminist critics. Jong has been conspicuously absent in recent years, not only from general literary journals and MLA programs, but from feminist journals as well. One must conclude that there is some deliberateness in all this. Reviews of Jong's novels suggest that many men—at least in the past—have felt threatened by her, but are present-day feminists embarrassed by Jong?

There are several reasons why Jong is not very popular with feminist academics today. Admittedly her work exemplifies what I will call middle-class writing. Jong has gotten a poor evaluation, for example, from Elizabeth Fox-Genovese, who has been associated with a collectivist ideology. Fox-Genovese wrote in 1980 in the *Antioch Review*:

> [*Fear of Flying*] demonstrates how easily a reactionary—or at least socially complacent—road for women's liberation could branch off from feminism. For Jong, like others after her, retreats from the insight that personal solutions are socially rooted. Like the psychoanalysis of which she is, in so many respects, critical, she basically comes down on the side of adaptation and internal freedom. (207–8)

But those who espouse a collectivist viewpoint are something of a minority among feminists today, most of whom are quite middle-class and individualistic in orientation. The phrase ''socially complacent'' may be key, however. ''Race'' and ''class'' have become important watchwords in American feminism, even the middle-class version, and there is no way Jong's novels can be suitable for an agenda that privileges issues of race and class. Jong may be seen by some as representing an exhausted middle-class feminism, a historical form of feminism much under attack in recent times. Jong's very visibility increases her ineligibility as a politically correct feminist's novelist.

Jong's identification with sexuality and sexual politics may be working against her. While feminists embraced the sexual revolution at first, in later years they turned their scholarly attention increasingly to bonds between women and family relationships. And even though Jong has associated herself with the cause of families and children by pointing out the failings of the feminist movement in this regard, her remarks don't seem calculated to help her gain favor with most academic feminists.

For some time, it has not been considered politically correct among many feminists to promote heterosexual sex. Most dismissals of Jong have rested on her thoroughgoing and assertive heterosexuality. Jong has been charged with repeating the same "old story" of female fulfillment though relations (sexual and otherwise, but especially sexual) with men. Many feminists share Rosalind Coward's view, stated in the essay "Are Women's Novels Feminist Novels?" that "a preoccupation with sexuality is not in and of itself progressive" (233). According to this view, Jong and other novelists of a certain kind of heterosexual sexuality are contributing to a climate in which women will continue to be defined by their sexuality, or at least they are doing nothing to change a such a climate. Even those feminists who do not align themselves with Catherine MacKinnon and Andrea Dworkin in viewing heterosexual relations as universally oppressive have been loathe to connect a focus on heterosexual relations with feminism.

As I write the concluding portions of this chapter, in 1994, I notice more dialogue about the evils of allowing certain notions of political correctness to dominate in the movement. This dialogue is inspired in part by the challenges of a generation of younger feminists. Books by Katie Roiphe (*The Morning After: Sex, Fear, and Feminism on Campus*) and Naomi Wolf (*Fire with Fire: The New Female Power and How It Will Change the 21st Century*) have charged that feminists of the previous generation (billed by Roiphe's publishers as the "feminist establishment") have clung to narrow notions of political correctness. Roiphe charges that there has been a valorization of victimhood in campus talk about date rape and suggests that feminists need to rethink their views on sexuality. Wolf laments the exclusion of many different ways of being feminist by certain notions of ideologically pure feminism, which Wolf says embraces marginalization. If these books signal an openness to the extant varieties of feminist conviction, there may be hope that feminists such as Jong can be reevaluated.

In the present moment, however, although much is said in feminist criticism about literature being a site of meaning production or the formation of ideology, Jong's work is dismissed as not contributing to this cultural work. It is sometimes acknowledged that Jong's work may have played such a role early on, but it is maintained that now that certain ideas—such as the right of women to sexual pleasure—have been accepted, Jong's work no longer belongs in a feminist canon.

I will cite here the example of Rita Felski, who mentions Jong in a suggestive passage that offers a broad definition of feminism, but then pointedly excludes Jong:

> My definition of feminist literature is thus a relatively broad one, which is intended to encompass all those texts that reveal a critical awareness of women's subordinate position and of gender as a problematic category, however this is expressed. The decision as to which texts to include under this definition will necessarily involve a degree of subjective judgment. The novels of Erica Jong, for example, which have marketed as examples of feminist writing, do not seem to me to reveal any serious questioning of the existing basis of male-female relations or any sustained refusal of the values of a male-dominated society. (14–15)

Felski goes on to say that some ideas, once oppositional, have filtered down to a large population and thus can no longer be considered "consciously feminist or oppositional in any meaningful sense" (15). It is surely noteworthy that Felski notes a degree of subjectivity in her judgments about what is feminist. Why it is that some writers, such as Fay Weldon, Margaret Atwood, Toni Morrison, or Marilynne Robinson can be considered feminist while others, such as Erica Jong, can not? I submit that the element of "subjectivity" is an important one here. The whole history of the reception of Erica Jong's work has inevitably colored the way that her work is perceived.

The effect of Jong's media celebrity and her association with popular culture has been incalculable. That many people, including members of the academic establishment, find it easy to dismiss an author who has been enriched by a bestseller has been illustrated over and over again in these pages. Furthermore, Jong has in many ways cooperated with those who have kept her in the public eye. An author can be forgiven, even admired, for having the media swoop down on her and thrust her into the spotlight, but can she be forgiven for staying there? In a discussion with Jong in 1976, interviewer Mary Cantwell said to her, "I still think there's a contradiction here—between your desire to protect your writer-image and, say, your emergence as a talk-show personality'' (98). Jong responded:

I don't see it the way you do. Because of our advertising-oriented culture, writers, to get bought, get packaged. Becoming a part of the whole celebrity thing in American is not because one approves of it. It was sort of thrust upon me, truly. . . . I see it all as a kind of salesmanship. . . . I'm sorry I have to fight against that image [created by the paperback book covers] but it sells the books and that enables me to do my thing. It means freedom. (98)

Jong's case is indeed one of mediatization[9] of literary reputation. Media exposure surrounding the release of Jong's first novel gave the work—with subsequent novels following in its wake—an important boost, making it visible to the academics who had the authority to create literary reputation. But media exposure, the huge sales which followed, and continued media attention to Jong also created an image that works against literary reputation, making it possible to dismiss Jong for having nothing to tell but an ''old story,'' for having sold out, having failed to develop as an artist, and having become an echo of herself. Although Jong's reputation is hardly fixed at this point and there is indeed considerable evidence that her work may have achieved a tenuous precanonical status, it is undeniably true that the media image that has been created around Jong has had a negative effect on her bid for literary reputation.

Conclusion / Literary Reputation in the Real World

The extraordinary story of the reception of Erica Jong's work forces us to locate literary evaluation and reputation in the real world. With a vengeance, one might add. As one confronts the role in the formation of Jong's literary reputation of deep philosophical and political conflicts and beliefs, gender biases and prejudices, misogyny, anti-Semitism, and powerful commercial and media interests—not to mention the very personal motives of well-wishers, enemies, and, as Jong claims, rejected suitors in the role of reviewers—one can hardly view literature in the old way, as belonging to a refined, rarefied, esoteric, and self-contained cultural sphere.

Erica Jong's story begins with *Fear of Flying* and its enormous impact on the cultural scene of 1973. Jong's novel, written from the standpoint of the woman who experiences herself as sexual, provoked an exuberant sense of identification from women readers in particular, but was seen as flagrantly transgressive by many male readers and also by male-identified female readers. Jong's novel, flying in the face of a centuries-long male-constructed notion of female sexuality, caused an explosion. Cast as a spokesperson for women's new freedom, sexual and social, Jong became identified with feminism. It is perhaps not surprising that feminism's symbol became feminism's scapegoat. In a still deeply misogynistic culture, all the old scapegoating mechanisms surfaced again: the sexual woman as scapegoat, the assertive woman as scapegoat, the Jewish woman as scapegoat.

We should add to the list the celebrity as scapegoat, or rather, the female celebrity as scapegoat. Perhaps it was inevitable that in our media-dominated culture Jong should become a media celebrity. Every sphere of activity is perhaps susceptible to what Dana Polan calls mediatization or spectaclization (343), but what better than literature? Writers, along with artists, certainly rank fairly close behind film stars, politicians, and professional athletes as public figures. Erica Jong, thrust violently into the limelight after the publication of *Fear*, was a very useful commodity for the media requirement of "good show endlessly superseded by other good shows" (Polan 350). Good-looking, articulate, and associated with that titillating universal, sex, she was a TV producer's dream. Jong herself cooperated with the media in that she appears not to have been averse to being a part of a good show. She believed that she could turn the electronic media, in particular, to her use in two ways: to make her work known, in order to gain the sales and the financial security that would enable her to continue to do what she wanted to do; and to provide a platform for self-defense—an opportunity to counter the image of the monster engendered in the print media, by appearing the normal woman and speaking in her own voice on the television screen.

Before the television appearances came the print celebrity. Immediately after the great success of *Fear of Flying*, Jong was the subject of numerous news and feature stories and was inundated with requests for articles. She has of course continued to be a public figure, sought out for comments on topical matters, solicited for charitable appearances, and scrutinized by newspaper and TV reporters. Events in Jong's personal life scream at us from headlines: "Mommy and Daddy Are Fighting Again since Erica Jong Used Her Daughter's Name in a Children's Guide to Divorce," we read in *People Weekly*. Jong's sojourn in the limelight has sometimes been a voluntary interlude as in the charitable appearances for PEN and other groups. On one occasion, in a benefit for Poets and Writers, Inc., she appeared with Norman Mailer and Ken Follett. Jong rode an elephant, and was described by the *New York Times* as wearing a "revealing silver outfit" ("New York: Day by Day" December 7, 1985). (Jong reports [telephone interview, April 13, 1991] that she was fully clothed in a body stocking and costume.)

Jong's literary reputation is thus tied up with the phenomenon of fame. Our society requires a constant supply of people to fill the difficult, if envied, role of the famous. It is in the nature of American, or perhaps all modern, capitalist society that certain of our desires be projected onto the famous. In his study of the anatomy of fame, *The Frenzy of Renown: Fame and Its History*, Leo Braudy says, "In a society committed to progress, the seeking of fame, the climbing of the ladder of renown, expresses something essential in that society's nature" (5). Fame offers the opportunity to be liberated from the anonymity all citizens of a complex world are condemned to. Seeking fame and obsession with the famous "are connected to normal desires to be known for one's talents or oneself" (5). Jong herself has commented in an interview: "I used to fantasize that I would reach a point where I would be such a big celebrity that all my personal problems would vanish, but the truth is, you lose hope when you gain fame" (Hadad 206). Braudy believes that the preoccupation with fame in contemporary America, the country without a past, is unprecedented because fame "is the only way out of increasingly complex political and economic dependence" (8). As we all strive for success and fear failure, the famous epitomize our aspirations and our fears.

Fame, however, cannot be given to all of us and would be an illusory solution to life's problems if it were. Thus arises the complex dynamic that couples adulation with contempt. To be famous is to be entrapped by the definitions of others. Inevitably, hero worship must be followed by debunking, the lionized must be demythologized and ultimately despised. It is not difficult to think of examples of those who have been raised up to eminence and then cast down. Those who fit into the category of "other," notably women, are of course prime targets. I think of the merciless photographs of a bleary-eyed Rita Hayworth, the talk about Elizabeth Taylor's fat and her many husbands, and a more recent media festival of humiliation—Nancy Reagan as shown to us by Kitty Kelley. It is this phenomenon of the scapegoating of the famous that has played such an important role in Jong's public, and hence, by necessity, also her literary, reputation. Jonathan Swift may have sought contemporary fame, deliberately initiating one publicity stunt after another in an effort to start a fire of reputation that he hoped would blaze into futurity, as Ann Kelly argued ("Mutual Attraction: Jonathan Swift and Popular Culture") at the 1990 meeting of the Modern Language Association, but Swift didn't have to reckon with the problems of a late-twentieth-century female celebrity. Celebrity has made Jong a highly eligible target for misogyny. Hatred of women, and possibly also anti-Semitism (however disguised, perhaps even from the persons expressing it), is socially acceptable, or can at least be expressed in a socially acceptable way—in the book review—if it is directed at a rich, success-ful, female celebrity, particularly one associated with female sexuality. Jong, certainly something of an authority herself on fame, has drawn on her own experience to comment on the phenomenon of celebrity. In a 1975 article in *Vogue*, Jong wrote:

In a society that recognizes only three ways of treating people— routine contempt (this is reserved for most of us, the unfamous), fawning adulation alternating with savage attacks (these two treat-ments are applied to the famous, in turn, like hot and cold com-presses)—being famous requires the hide of a elephant, the studied indifference of a Zen master, and the inner determination of a life-long failure facing still another rejection slip. In fact, I hate both words "success" *and* "failure," because both states come down to precisely the same thing in the end and are virtually interchange-able. (216)

Jong herself has experienced the alternation of "hot and cold com-presses," sometimes applied almost simultaneously. In September 1975 Jong was interviewed by *Playboy*, an attention normally regarded as a tribute (Joseph Heller was the subject of the *Playboy* interview the pre-vious month). In Jong's case, the lengthy and informative interview, discussing both literary issues and very personal matters, was juxta-posed with a cover blurb that was an unmistakable insult. The *Playboy* cover for the issue pictured a model with bare bottom thrust out toward the camera, accompanied by the words, "Erica Jong Bares Her Mind." No wonder Jong's literary reputation remains contested territory.

And how does the academic critic, who bears the heavy burden of serving as intermediary between the living author and posterity, re-spond to such a public figure? The first answer to the question is that academics have played an important role in creating the image. There have been a number of professors among Jong's reviewers, and many others—perhaps all to some degree—carry with them values imbibed at the academy. Although the academy is by no means monovocal, it con-tains a powerful community that speaks for high culture and tradi-tional literary values and that places little value on the body, the sexual woman, or a comedy of sexuality.

For most members of the academy, belief in the distinction between the consumption of books and the critical appropriation of books is still strongly held. Consumption is seen as not only easy but so damaging to the mind and soul of the consumer as possibly to merit intellectual and moral health warnings on dust jackets of popular books. However, responses to Jong's work suggest that pleasurable consumption and critical use are not poles apart. The feminist reviewers and critics (and others who would not necessarily be called feminist) of *Fear of Flying* and Jong's other novels certainly experience pleasurable consumption, but they also clearly make critical responses in the way such responses are defined—by employing the honorable academic practices of analyzing, discriminating, and close reading, by calling attention to formal elements, by placing the book in a literary historical context and by pointing to significant themes.

However, it is in the interests of a gendered and patriarchal academy to maintain the traditional distinctions regarding the use of cultural objects. The reputations of Jong and other women writers have been affected by a heavy-handed use of cultural authority. In truth, in Jong's case, in which media influences, assumptions about cultural categories, gender biases, and the wild card of sexuality are thrown together, a negative response to her work seems almost inevitable—"overdetermined," to use a word popular today in critical circles. Of course there is the other side to the story. Jong continues to get very favorable reviews that categorize her work as highly literary. The contradictions in the responses to her work is what makes her example so useful for those interested in the construction of literary value.

And Jong still has supporters among feminists (and others) in the academy. Very possibly, however, some who admire or enjoy Jong would hesitate to champion her under the present circumstances. A feminist can advance her career more readily by connecting herself with some other woman writer, living or dead, more likely to be acceptable in feminist circles or in wider academic circles. For many, Jong's work is not seen as suitable for current academic fashions.

Jong's story, the narrative of the triumphs and vicissitudes of one writer's reputation, is unique but highly instructive. It illustrates not only the contingencies that govern individual literary judgments and the importance of the intersection of the literary work with the cultural moment but also the remarkable role the media can play in contemporary literary reputation. Although Jong's story is unique (and suggests that every reputation story is so), insofar as it is a woman writ-er's story, it is also representative. Jong's striking example has served to highlight and clarify certain cultural responses to writing by women. In some ways Jong is Woman writ large, made so by her identification with sexuality and feminism along with her status as a public figure. The story of her literary reputation may serve to illustrate that deeply held cultural values and beliefs about women have enormous influence in how writing by women is received.

Notes

CHAPTER I. CAN IT BE GOOD LITERATURE IF IT'S
FUNNY, SEXY, AND WRITTEN BY A WOMAN?

1. I have in mind here mainly journalistic articles, but even in a scholarly universe that prides itself on detachment, journal articles sometimes participate in the same *ad feminam* mode (see Chapter 6).

2. See pages 45–46 of *Contingencies of Value* for a fuller discussion of the complex and numerous ways value is created.

3. Andrea Dworkin finds the review of her books *Ice and Fire* and *Intercourse* by Carol Sternhall (May 3, 1987) "contemptuous beyond belief" (4). She then comments, "Thirteen years after its publication, your reviewer comments that 'Woman Hating' is brilliant—thanks. And only four years after the publication of 'Right-Wing Women,' it too is called brilliant. Don't get ahead of yourselves. Neither book, by the way, was reviewed in the *New York Times*." Dworkin promises to "check back in a decade to see what you all think" (4).

4. Thomson says that he got out a lot of old reviews when he was writing his autobiography in the 1960s and commented to Aaron Copland (with whom he gave concerts when the two composers were young), "I've just been reading a lot of terrible reviews." Copland said in response, "Virgil, don't you remember? We always got terrible reviews." Thomson then comments, "All of a sudden, we got better ones" (8E).

CHAPTER 2. EVALUATIVE COMMUNITIES IN THE
RECEPTION OF *FEAR OF FLYING*

1. Except for passages cited from other sources, the account presented here is based on a telephone interview with Erica Jong on April 13, 1991. Interpretive comments are, of course, my own.

2. Although my study deals with Jong's reception in the United States and Great Britain, I do present some information about her worldwide reputation in Chapter 6.

3. The figures are from Jong.

4. See Steven Buechler's *Women's Movements in the United States: Woman Suffrage, Equal Rights, and Beyond* for a discussion of opposition to the women's movement in the United States.

5. This conference, billed as the first major conference to concentrate on "physical consciousness raising," "physical liberation," and "sexual pleasure" (Johnson 10), attracted both male and female participants. Male participants mentioned the woman's movement as instrumental in causing them to question assumptions about female sexuality and about their own.

6. See also discussion of the concept of surplus visibility in Patai's "The View from Elsewhere: Utopian Construction of Difference" in *"Turning the Century": Feminist Theory in the 1990s*, edited by Glynis Carr.

7. In addition to the characteristics mentioned here, the Jewish American Princess is usually described as sexually withholding. This characteristic does not fit the Jong persona.

8. My understanding of the dynamics of interpersonal relations within a community of novelist-reviewers and of utilization of ethnic and gender stereotypes in reviewing was greatly enhanced by my conversations with Erica Jong on April 13, 1991, and July 11, 1991.

9. Harré and Davies present the concept of positioning as more useful than the older concept of role because it focuses on dynamic aspects of encounters, in contrast to role, which implies a static and unchanging approach to identity. Positioning, produced through discursive interaction, allows one to explore the act of taking up new subject positions. The feminist practice of consciousness raising could serve as an example of positioning through discursive practice. The reading of feminist novels and other literature comprised a discursive practice that enabled many women to assume new subject positions.

10. Ehrenreich et al. discuss Anne Koedt's "The Myth of the Vaginal Organism," Barbara Seaman's *Free and Female*, and Alix Shulman's "Organs and Organisms" in pages 70-72.

11. Susan Suleiman has called *Fear of Flying* a fictional counterpart of *Our Bodies Our Selves*, published the same year as Jong's novel by the Boston Women's Collective.

12. Jane Larkin Crain (b. 1947; B.A. Swarthmore, M.A. Columbia) now works as an editor.

13. Ellen Hope Meyer has written for the *Washington Post* and is one of the founders of the *Mediterranean Review*, which appeared from 1970 to 1973.

14. Millicent Dillon (b. 1925; B.A. Hunter College, M.A. San Francisco State University) is a fiction writer. She has written for *Ascent*, the *Threepenny Review*, *Encounter*, and *Inquiry*. Dillon has also addressed the question of feminism in her fiction. The short story "All the Pelageyas" features a narrator who is troubled and even enraged at the anger expressed by Adrienne Rich in a lecture. She is further distressed by the responses to her own criticisms of Rich presented to an academic audience.

15. Both Patrick Brantlinger in *Bread and Circuses: Theories of Mass Culture and Social Decay* (222–48) and Herbert Gans in *Popular Culture and High Culture: An Analysis and Evaluation of Taste* (43–64) discuss the similarities of critiques of society made from the left and the right. Critics from the left generally blame the problem on the harmful effects of mass society, and the critics from the right on the defects of people.

16. See pages 125–34 of *Contingencies of Value.*

17. Patricia Meyer Spacks (b. 1929; B.A. Rollins College, Ph.D. University of California, Berkeley) is currently Edgar F. Shannon Professor of English and Chair of the English Department at the University of Virginia. She is the author of many books including *The Female Imagination* (1972). *The Female Imagination* has been found lacking by Elizabeth Janeway, who said, "Overall, Spacks is uncertain about major themes to be explored and major questions to be asked in approaching the work of women writers" (391).

18. Alfred Kazin (b. 1915; B.A. City College of New York, M.A. Columbia) is Distinguished Professor Emeritus at the graduate center of the University of New York. He is well known for his many books and essays on American literature.

19. Benjamin DeMott (b. 1924; B.A. Johns Hopkins, Ph.D. Harvard) has written many essays on modern society's tendency to undervalue the old truths. He is professor emeritus of English at Amherst College.

20. Three other reviews by male reviewers are not entirely negative, but they are not positive either. None of the three reviewers can really get a handle on the book and give mixed, rather incoherent and therefore lackluster reviews that neither praise the novel nor completely damn it. Jong's novel did not provide the impetus for them to take up subject positions with any enthusiasm or find any significant use for the novel. In the *New York Times* review, Christopher Lehmann-Haupt (b. 1934; B.A. Swarthmore, M.F.A. Yale) reviews Jong's novel along with Jane Howard's nonfictional *A Different Woman* in a review entitled "Nuances of Women's Liberation." Lehmann-Haupt welcomes both, books, saying he has been "hoping for books that would explore the subtlety and variety of the woman's liberation movement, and for writing that would be sensitive to the ambiguities of growing up intelligently female these days" (35). Although he finds things to admire about Jong's novel and can identify strongly with the protagonist, he finds the novel "disappointing"; predictably familiar in the portrayal of Jewish middle-class urban experience, it "doesn't bite very deep" (35).

The reviews by Terry Stokes and Michael Wood (b. 1932; B.A. Cambridge; professor at the University of Exeter) are of interest largely because they appeared in influential journals. Writing in the *New York Times Book Review*, Terry Stokes's summary of the novel suggests that he fails to find in it the coherence of successful art, and he also states that the novel fails because of the flaws of the characters: "Isadora is as passive in the end as she was at the beginning. Oddly, the narrator denigrates all women by casting them in her mold; people who don't know what they want" (40). Michael Wood, writing in the *New York Review of Books*, finds Jong's novel "self-indulgent," with "far too much maudlin or portentous self-examination which it seems we are meant to take seriously" (20). He does not find any overriding comic character to the novel, even though the words of praise he finds for the novel have to do with its jokes—"there are some very good jokes in this novel" (20).

21. Paul Theroux (b. 1941; B.A. University of Massachusetts, further study, Syracuse) is the author of numerous novels, stories, and nonfiction works.

22. Martin Amis (b. 1949; B.A. Oxford) is a novelist and a prolific reviewer. He was selected by the British Press Association as runner-up for the Critic of the Year Award in 1986.

23. According to Devon and Hodges, these male cultural critics postulate that the changes have been so drastic as to bring about a feminization of the modern individual. With the loss of traditional institutions and forms of authority, the formerly male qualities of self-control and personal integrity fall by the wayside. A consumer ethic—seen as female—of hedonistic morality and a constant search for novelty and sexual and creative fulfillment reigns.

24. John Updike (b. 1932; B.A. Harvard), the novelist, frequently writes reviews.

25. In *His Other Half: Men Looking at Women through Art*, Wendy Lesser also finds fault with Updike's portraits of women. She calls Updike (and Milan Kundera) "thorough misogynists" but adds, "If pressed, I would probably say that the offense lies in their insufficiency as artists rather than just in their attitudes to women" (6).

26. Henry Miller (1891–1980) is best known for *Tropic of Cancer* and *Tropic of Capricorn*, which suffered thirty years of censorship in the U.S.

27. Benjamin Stein (b. 1944; B.A. Columbia, L.L.B. Yale) has been a speech writer, journalist, and author of fiction and nonfiction works.

28. Although Felski speaks only slightingly of *Fear of Flying*, I do believe her comments describe Jong's novel.

29. When I discussed Jong's book with women who read it in 1973, I found many women who responded to the novel much as the feminist reviewers did. I cite the transcript of an airing of "Pandora's Box" on March 17, 1993, on the Montgomery College (Baltimore, Md.) Channel 3/51. In this discussion, which took place on the twentieth anniversary of the publication of *Fear of Flying*, Norma Berkeley, Gail Forman, Brianne Friel, Myrna Goldenberg, and Percy North agree that in 1973 a heroine who was "both sexy and smart and having a good time" appealed to them.

30. Molly Haskell (B.A. Sweet Briar, further study, the University of London, the Sorbonne), a reviewer and author, currently reviews films for *Vogue*.

31. Rosie (Rozsika) Parker (Courtauld Institute) is an art historian and has published several books of feminist art history. She is a founding member of the Women's Art History Collective in England and one of the original members of the collective that publishes *Spare Rib*.

32. Ghislaine Boulenger is identified by her publication as an editor and translator.

33. Elaine Reuben (b. 1941; B.A., Brandeis, M.A., Ph.D., Stanford) was director of Women's Studies at George Washington University.

CHAPTER 3. HOW TO SAVE YOUR OWN LIFE

1. In asserting that the attacks on the Book-of-the-Month Club over ostensibly aesthetic matters really had to do with conflict over the exercise of cultural authority, Janice Radway makes an argument similar to the one I make here. In "Mail-Order Culture and Its Critics: The Book-of-the-Month Club, Commodification and Consumption, and the Problem of Authority," Radway says that even under the aegis of cultural studies, assumptions about a gendered subject remain alive because "the legitimacy of our authority depends significantly on our continuing ability to naturalize *that* subject as the norm in opposition to others" (514).

2. Phillips has told her version of the story in *You'll Never Eat Lunch in This Town Again*.

3. Jong appeared as a guest on many television shows during the early years, but few transcripts (and fewer tapes) are available. References in newspaper stories indicate significant television exposure. See the Shales story ("Erica Jong's 'Albatross' ") in the *Washington Post* on January 8, 1975, alluding to television appearances on successive days in the Washington area with Kate Millett and *Washington Post* reporter Sally Quinn. The researcher who attempts to get transcripts or tapes of TV shows from the 1970s or early 1980s finds that it is virtually an impossible task, especially in the area of "soft news." CBS has an index of news programs (including *Sixty Minutes*) from 1975 to 1986 (with transcripts); ABC has an index for hard news only from 1970 (with no citations on Jong); NBC has no index. Neither the UCLA Film and Television Archive nor the Vanderbilt Television News Archive was able to access additional material on Jong (the Vanderbilt archive contains only evening news). Some transcripts are available from the networks: NBC has no transcripts before 1983, and ABC has no transcripts before 1986. NBC will search its database for dates of interviews since 1983, but the researcher must be prepared for long delays. It took me two months and many phone calls to get the information I needed to purchase the four transcripts available of Jong's NBC appearances since 1983. Some new services exist, but these provide little retrospective searching. Burrelle's Broadcast Database provides full text searching of network news programs to subscribers but is retrospective only to 1990. Journal Graphics can provide transcripts for current programs, has a 1990 index and an index (not very complete) going back to 1968.

4. Although becoming an instant celebrity is exciting, it is also traumatic,

as Jong has often discussed. See ''Erica Jong: Learning to Cope with Her 'Fear of Flying,' '' by Sally Quinn.

5. Author interviews have always been a feature of television programming, but novelists are not among the preferred guests. An article by novelist Dan Wakefield, which appeared in the regular feature ''The Guest Word'' in the *New York Times Book Review* in January of 1975, illustrates that novelists were rarely seen on television at that time. Wakefield suggests that talk show hosts look to novelists as interesting guests and names several that he would like to see on television, including Joyce Carol Oates, Joan Didion, Harry Crews, and Erica Jong. Wakefield very soon got his wish regarding Erica Jong. In a 1979 story in *Publisher's Weekly*, Hilary Kale, assistant to the book coordinator for NBC's *Today*, describes the process by which authors are chosen for *Today*. Kale says that novelists ''are difficult to sell to us and to our executive producer'' and therefore ''rarely appear'' (58). Best-sellers are in another category, however. If the author ''speaks well and can do more than just describe the book's plot, there is a chance that he or she will appear on the *Today* program'' (58). Publishers today make every attempt to arrange television appearances as part of promotional tours. See, for example, the *New York Times* news story ''Coaches Help Authors Talk Well to Sell Well,'' which shows how publishers test prospective authors for effectiveness in front of the camera *before* offering contracts. Novelists are usually exempt from such tests, however, and only one novelist is named as having been coached by the paid consultants who are the subject of the story (McDowell).

6. She was joined in the circus appearance by Norman Mailer and Ken Follett, and at the Algonquin Hotel by James Dickey and John Guare. See ''New York Day by Day'' on December 7, 1985, and the story by Leslie Bennetts on October 14, 1982.

7. In the *Sixty Minutes* appearance with Henry Miller, Jong said that ''a lot of husbands hold me responsible'' (19) for their wives leaving them, and on the *CBS Morning News* on September 28, 1983, Jong complained that ''whenever I'm interviewed, I'm always the spokesperson for the women of today'' (48).

8. I differ with Collins in that I still see a firmer cultural hierarchy in place. Literary intellectuals and academics still have vast authority to move works to canonical status. The advent of postmodern theory has not substantially altered the traditionally elitist values of the academy, especially not where women are concerned.

9. Jong says that Burgess first came to her attention when he included *How to Save Your Own Life* in his *99 Novels*. Subsequently, the two corresponded intermittently (telephone interview, July 11, 1991).

10. The case of Gershwin is an interesting one in this context. At the time of the observance of the fiftieth anniversary of his death, in 1987, it was clear that his status had shifted markedly in the direction of high culture. I remember being told by a music history professor in 1960 that Gershwin had no importance as a modern composer—he merely wrote tunes.

11. Nor is placement of a work of art necessarily under the control of the artist, as an Indianapolis poster artist found. Nancy Noel was appalled when her work became an artifact of popular culture sold in discount stores. Fred Cavinder reports that when she found her posters being distributed in discount stores without her authorization, she filed to obtain a restraining order, seizure and destruction of the contraband, and punitive damages. She was upset that her work was in the discount stores at all, saying, "When I went into the poster business, I never expected to see myself in the discount stores. I always kept my quality and appeal high" (B4).

12. For a history of the shifting and artificial nature of cultural categories in America, see Lawrence W. Levine's *Highbrow, Lowbrow: The Emergence of Cultural Hierarchy in America.*

13. In "The Book-of-the-Month-Club and the General Reader: On the Uses of 'Serious' Fiction," Janice Radway discusses the "middlebrow" function of BOMC editors, who choose books that provide for their readers "a model for contemporary living and even practical advice about appropriate behavior in a changing world" (535). Their view of their function is close to that of many book reviewers.

14. Penelope Mesic (b. 1949; B.A., M.A. University of Chicago) is identified by her publication as a writer, teacher, and illustrator.

15. D. Keith Mano (b. 1942; B.A. Columbia, fellow, Cambridge) is a novelist and a contributing editor to the *National Review.* Frank Day writes in the *Dictionary of Literary Biography* that his novels—which are characterized by violence and sexual explicitness—present events from the point of view of a conservative Christian and reveal "his hatred for much of the life of his time" (214).

16. Mano's impatience and disgust with feminists has been expressed often in various articles written for his publication. See "Lib on the Rocks," in which he characterizes NOW members as lesbian and overweight—"I think there's some glandular hookup between gay and fat. . . . It's hard to be a successful heterosexual when Charles Atlas would herniate himself carrying you over the threshold" (326)—and suggests that as a consequence of these flaws of its members, NOW will fail.

17. In an appearance (with Erica Jong) on *Bookmark* (WNET) on March 5, 1989, Atwood comments extensively on this issue and tells her "favorite story" about the matter: "I wrote a book called *Lady Oracle* in which the central character weighed 250 pounds. And I gave a public reading and prefaced it by saying I've never weighed 250 pounds. This is not autobiography, and I'm not the central character of this book. Then I read, read the passage, and the first question from the audience was 'How did you lose all that weight?'"

18. See especially "The Life We Live and the Life We Write" in the *New York Times Book Review* on February 10, 1985.

19. Christopher Lehmann-Haupt (b. 1934; B.A. Swarthmore, M.F.A. Yale) has

worked for the *New York Times* since 1965 and has been senior book reviewer since 1969.

20. Lance Morrow (b. 1939; B.A. Harvard) has worked for *Time* magazine since 1965. He won a National Magazine Award in 1981 for his *Time* essays.

21. Isa Kapp is a literary editor for the *New Leader*.

22. Janet Maslin is identified as an associate editor of *Newsweek* in the issue in which her review appears.

23. John Leonard (b. 1939; attended Harvard, B.A. University of California, Berkeley) was with the *New York Times* from 1967 to 1983, first as chief book review editor, then as chief cultural critic. He is also a novelist.

24. Diane Johnson (b. 1934; attended Stephens College, B.A. University of Utah, M.A., Ph.D. University of California) teaches at the University of California at Davis.

25. In a brief review in the *Saturday Review*, one of the prestigious journals mentioned by Ohmann, reviewer Linda Kuehl finds nothing to admire in the novel. Jong "has mistaken risque for risk" and displayed concerns too "petty," "personal," and "solipsistic" to be the basis for significant literature. Kuehl nonetheless suggests that Jong is capable of something better: "Jong is too canny and full of life to settle for this whistle in the dark. One hopes she will regain distance (by which I do not mean indifference) and write her next novel with less concern about how people see her" (27).

I argue that the almost universally negative reception of Jong's second novel had a lot to do with Jong's popular success. When we remember that Jong's first novel also had critical success, we can gain further insight into the reception given to the second novel by reviewers such as Kuehl, who seem to have residual admiration for Jong despite their negative view of the second novel. I am reminded of a comment made by Pulitzer Prize–winning playwright Marsha Norman in a radio interview on the negative reception customarily given to the play written *after* the one that wins the Pulitzer. Her facetious suggestion was to hire someone else to write the play and get it over with.

26. I am indebted to Ross's *No Respect* for my understanding of the issues discussed in this paragraph. See especially pages 123–34.

27. Jeremy Treglown (B. Litt. Oxford) was formerly a lecturer at Oxford and University College, London University, and is now on the staff of *TLS*.

28. Peter Keating is a lecturer in English at the University of Edinburgh.

29. Peter Ackroyd (b. 1949; Cambridge, Yale) is managing editor of the *Spectator*. He is a poet, novelist, and essayist.

30. Lorna Sage (b. 1943; B.A. University of Durham, Ph.D. University of Birmingham) is senior lecturer in English and dean of the School of English and American Studies at the University of East Anglia. She has extensive publications as a reviewer and as a literary critic.

31. Auberon Waugh (b. 1939; Oxford) is the author of essays, novels, and short stories and a frequent reviewer. He received awards from the British Press Association in 1976 and 1978.

32. Ronald Harwood (b. 1934 in Capetown, S.A.; Royal Academy of Dramatic Art) is the author of novels and of plays that have appeared on the British stage in recent years.

33. Jean Radford is identified as a member of the collective that publishes *Spare Rib*.

34. Marcia Fuchs (b. 1950; B.A. State University of New York, Buffalo, M.S. Drexel University) is a librarian. She writes reviews and critical essays on popular fiction and children's literature.

35. Craig Fisher (b. 1947; B.S.J. [Journalism] Northwestern University; further study, University of Texas, Austin) is a journalist and writer.

36. There is anecdotal evidence (the only kind available, as far as I know) that Jong has had many male readers, but Jong's reviewers, and especially the reviewers of this novel, tend to characterize her readers as female.

CHAPTER 4. FANNY

1. See the articles by Ferguson and Mandrell. Susan Gubar and Sandra Gilbert also include discussion of *Fanny* in volume 2 of *No Man's Land*.

2. See the articles by Klemesrud and Bennetts in the *New York Times*.

3. Gail Sheehy wrote a series of articles based on interviews with well-known feminists, such as Gloria Steinem, and discussing other subjects of general interest, such as the childhoods of American women leaders.

4. Jong later did an art book on witches (1981), a work of prose and poetry illustrated by Joseph A. Smith.

5. White identifies those on the other side of the debate as "pan-textualists," for whom "any representation of history has to be considered a construction of language, thought, and imagination rather than a report of a structure of meaning presumed to exist in historical events themselves" (483).

6. Joshua Gilder (b. 1954; B.A. Sarah Lawrence College) was associate editor of the *Saturday Review* at the time he wrote the review of *Fanny*.

7. Sally Helgesen (b. 1948; B.A. Hunter College) is an author and contributing editor of *Harper's*.

8. James Goldman (b. 1927; B.A. University of Chicago, M.A. Columbia) is the author of novels and plays.

9. Peter Kemp (b. 1942; B.A. Honors University of London, M.Phil. University of London) was senior lecturer in English at Middlesex Polytechnic. He is now a full-time reviewer. He has written books on several twentieth-century figures.

10. Lorna Sage (b. 1943; B.A. University of Durham, Ph.D. University of Birmingham) is senior lecturer in English and dean of the School of English and American Studies at the University of East Anglia. She has extensive publications as a reviewer and a literary critic.

11. Clive James (B.A. University of Sydney, M.A. Oxford) is a critic, essayist, and novelist.

12. Alan Friedman (b. 1918; B.A. Harvard, M.A. Columbia, Ph.D. University of California, Berkeley) was director of writing programs for the University of Illinois, Chicago, at the time he wrote the review.

13. Pat Rogers (B.A., M.A., Ph.D., Cambridge) is the author of numerous books on the eighteenth century. Formerly a professor at the University of Bristol, he is now DeBartolo Professor of Liberal Arts at the University of South Florida.

14. Anthony Burgess (1917–1993; B.A. University of Manchester) has had a stormy relationship with feminists. He was designated one of the sexists of the year for 1980 and awarded a pink marzipan pig by Women in Publishing. He believes it was for his objection to the name Virago Press. He has criticized what he terms the absurdities of the militant feminist movement but portrays himself as a friend and admirer of women. He insists in "Grunts from a Sexist Pig" that in art judgments have nothing to do with sex. In his generous review of *Fanny*, he projects an image of himself along the lines suggested above.

15. Judith Martin (b. 1938; B.A. Wellesley).

16. Susan Dworkin (b. 1941; B.A. Wellesley).

CHAPTER 5. JONG IN A POSTFEMINIST AGE

1. I acknowledge the influence of Deborah Rosenfelt and Judith Stacey on my understanding of the usefulness of the term postfeminist.

2. See the *New York Times* stories by Brozan and Clymer.

3. Benokraitis and Feagin point out that while women make up over half of the labor force, women's employment patterns have not changed. In terms of federal programs, many of the gains that women made in the 1970s were wiped out in the 1980s under Reagan. Furthermore, violence against women is escalating. The authors also point to a resurgence of femininity in the 1980s, possibly as a reaction to continued obstacles to success in the work world, where women's efforts are hampered by the fact that they are still the primary caregivers for children. The authors identify the failure of women to make greater gains as, most importantly, owing to male resistance to sex role changes.

4. Berman's book is discussed in the story by Judy Klemesrud; the story about the National Association for Men appeared in the regular *New York Times* feature "New York: Day By Day" on February 28, 1983.

5. Merle Rubin (b. 1949; B.A. Smith, Ph.D. University of Virginia) contributes regularly to the *Christian Science Monitor* and also contributes to the *Los Angeles Times* and the *New York Times Book Review*.

6. Elaine Kendall (b. 1929; B.A. Mount Holyoke College), a professional writer, has written a book about men, *The Upper Hand*, in response to the many books on women. Her book presents an unflattering history of male actions and values from the Middle Ages to the present.

7. Clancy Sigal (b. 1926; B.A. UCLA) is an American novelist living in England and a regular contributor to the *New Statesman*, *Encounter*, and *Time and Tide*.

8. Herbert Mitgang (b. 1920; B.A. St. John's University, Jamaica, N.Y.) is a member of the New York bar. The author of a number of novels and other books, he has been with the *New York Times* since 1945.

9. C. D. B. Bryan (b.1936; B.A. Yale) is a writer of fiction and nonfiction. Like Jong's, Bryan's novels have been characterized as autobiographical.

10. Hermione Lee (B.Phil. Oxford) teaches at the University of York. Her works include books on Virginia Woolf and Philip Roth. She writes in the book on Woolf that her intention is to write about Woolf's work as "literature" and not about extraneous things such as the author or the social setting. Lee writes of Woolf, "As fuel for the woman's movement, or as fictionalized versions of the ethos of Bloomsbury, her novels are of very limited significance, though, paradoxically, their recent popularity arises largely from those two centers of interest" (25).

11. Peter Kemp (b. 1942; B.A. University of London, M.Phil. University of London), formerly senior lecturer in English at Middlesex Polytechnic, now reviews full time. He has written books on several twentieth-century authors.

12. Victoria Glendinning (b. 1927) is a British educator, journalist, and author, especially of biographies. She was formerly an editorial assistant for *TLS*.

13. I can find no information on Ken Franckling beyond the fact that he writes for UPI. UPI supplied the review at my request, but I do not know what papers it was published in (UPI file PUT AZNO522, n.p.).

14. Grace Lichtenstein (b. 1941; B.A. Brooklyn College), journalist, is the author of *Machisma: Women and Daring*, among other books, and a professor of journalism at Columbia.

15. In several brief, favorable reviews, some of these same themes are repeated. In a review in the *Library Journal*, Michele Leber notes that "feminist Isadora [is] still speaking some home truths to women" (1862). She praises the novel for "energy, wit, candor" and is pleased that "Isadora manages to exit upbeat; humor and wit prevail" (1862). In the review section called "Briefly Noted," the *New Yorker* turns what at first appears to be a criticism into a compliment by observing that the fact that "that Erica Jong's . . . novel seems somewhat dated, with all its tongue-in-cheek intimacies, may be a measure of her impact upon her fellow writers' ambitions and upon her readers' memories" (190).

16. We must remember, of course, that one or two similar reviews can suggest a much larger community of evaluators. It is probably only in the case of a work like *Fear of Flying* that one can expect to get a response from a full range of well-populated evaluative communities in the reviews. *Fear of Flying* struck an ideological nerve that had been newly exposed, and it was written by a relatively unknown author, one whose reputation had not already been thoroughly mediated.

17. See the article by Karen FitzGerald in *Ms.* for one expression of opinion by a feminist of the younger generation. FitzGerald states that Jong's work has only historical interest for her.

18. *Serenissima* has sold the least well of all Jong's novels—only about five-hundred-thousand copies. All the others have qualified as best-sellers, appearing on best-seller lists.

19. Michael Malone (b. 1942; B.A., M.A. University of North Carolina, further study, Harvard) is a novelist and college instructor.

20. Diane Cole is identified by her publication as a writer in New York.

21. Two other reviews, both by women novelists, find nothing engaging about the novel. Carolyn See, writing for the *Los Angeles Times*, doesn't like Jong's heroine, whose vanity and exhibitionism offend her. Her plot summary suggests an inept novel, failing in every dimension, including the characterization of Shakespeare: "some dim pudding you'd meet in a second rate singles bar" (4). Susan Jacoby, writing for the *Chicago Tribune*, finds the verbal play of the quotations tedious and is bored by the plot. She can respond positively to the novel only insofar as it becomes the occasion for meditations on Shakespeare's play.

22. It is surely apparent by now that the *Observer* doesn't care for Erica Jong. The reviewer, Maureen Freely (b. 1952; B.A. Radcliffe), is, however, a young American novelist, a member of what has been called the postfeminist generation. Her novel, *Mother's Helper*, highly praised by reviewer Hermione Lee in the *Observer*, presents a satirical picture of a family putting into practice the "self-indulgent" values of the sixties, including feminism, which Freely herself has said (in the *Observer* article mentioned below) she cannot identify with. A review in the *New Statesman* says of Freely's novel that "like so much social satire, *Mother's Helper* is written from a profoundly conservative point of view" (Shrimpton 643). Freely, who was living in Hampstead at the time, is the subject of a feature story in the *Observer*, written by Sally Vincent, in which Vincent describes the older generation of feminists as having "turned its collective back, unwilling to recognize that along with female consciousness they have also raised a generation of young women who share neither their anger nor their intrinsic righteousness" (64). Freely, one of the younger generation, is highly critical of what she calls "knee-jerk feminists," who "justify all their actions on the grounds of once having been oppressed" (64).

23. Paul Binding is identified by his publication as a poet, novelist, and critic.

24. Susannah Clapp writes regularly for the *London Review of Books*.

25. Valentine Cunningham is a lecturer in English at Oxford and an author of several books of literary criticism.

26. Joan Aiken (b. 1924 in Rye, Sussex, of American parents) is a British writer of children's books and historical romances.

27. Several other reviewers also see the novel as a serious and significant work of fiction. The reviewer in the *West Coast Review of Books* awards

Serenissima four stars for excellence, considering it a ''meaty culmination of her earlier works'' (21). Jong has ''continued her growth as a novelist but lost little of 'pizazz' in the doing'' (21). He praises her evocation of Venice, the ''very soul'' of the novel, and recounts the plot as a tale of rich adventure. He finds the time-travel device effective—''Why should recent 'time travel' films be more believable than this?'' (21). Jong has done such a good job of re-creating sixteenth-century Venice that ''our imaginations are rapt rather than stretched'' (21). Similarly, Canadian Darlene James (Margaret Darlene James, b. 1950; B. A. University of Toronto, M.S. W. McGill University; social worker, free lance writer), in a review in *Maclean's* also responds positively to the rich materials of the novel, which she sees as arising from Jong's ''own crazy quilt of identities—poet, crafter of outrageous erotic fantasies . . . serious literary scholar, lionized jet-setter'' (50). James implies praise for Jong's language in her mention of Jong's ''lyrical pen'' for the love scenes and her ''wickedly sharp'' satirical pen.

28. Francine Prose (b. 1947; B.A. Radcliffe, M.A. Harvard) is a novelist. She has taught at Harvard, the University of Arizona, and the Breadloaf Writers' Conference.

29. Donna Rifkind's reviews have appeared in three quite conservative publications: the *Wall Street Journal*, the *American Scholar*, and the *New Criterion*.

30. Ralph Novak (b. 1943; B.S. Northwestern University, M.S., Journalism, Northwestern University) is book review editor of *People Weekly*. He has been with *People* since 1974.

31. Benjamin DeMott (b. 1924; B.A. Johns Hopkins, Ph.D. Harvard) is professor emeritus of English at Amherst College.

32. Two other reviews mix praise and outspoken criticism. Joseph Coates says in his review in the *Chicago Tribune* that Jong's novel gave him ''the blues—aesthetic, moral, cultural, any kind there is'' (7). Nonetheless he calls the novel ''a remarkably good book''—though one ''fighting to free itself from the pretentious gabble it's written in'' (7). But, simultaneously, it's ''not . . . a good novel''; Isadora Wing, the nominal author ''can't write.'' There is ''something worthwhile'' in Jong's depiction of alcoholism, sex addiction, etc., but ''the writing is often so bad we can't believe any professional writer could be responsible for it'' (7). He conjectures that the whole thing may be an experiment—Jong may mean for Isadora to be a bad writer. Similarly novelist Ann Hood, writing in the *Washington Post*, finds much of Jong's novel ''vibrant and witty and honest'' (3). Hood has reservations about the narrative devices and believes the plot ''falls on the wrong side of the line of believability,'' even verging on melodrama. Jong's novel shows ''occasional insights that could have made Jong a spokeswoman for women once again,'' but Jong has no solutions for women ''who must face the 1990's without the benefit'' of rich friends, money, and success (7).

33. Jean Hanff Korelitz (b. 1961; B.A. Dartmouth College, M.A. Cambridge) is

a writer who has published poetry and reviews in American and British journals.

34. Andrew Sinclair (b. 1935; B.A. Cambridge, Ph.D. Cambridge) is a writer of fiction and nonfiction and a lecturer in history at the University of London.

35. Peter Lewis (B.A. University of Wales, M.Phil. University of Leeds) teaches English at the University of Durham.

36. In most cases, Jong wrote the articles at the request of the editors. Editors control content and headlines. Jong said in 1991 that in the last two years she had stopped writing for glossy magazines, not wishing to write on the trivial topics she was often asked to write about. She said that early in her career she was pleased to be asked and would usually write the article requested, trying to write "intelligent" articles and sometimes being successful in having them "squeak through" (telephone interview, July 11, 1991).

CHAPTER 6. JONG AMONG THE ACADEMICS

1. Rodden mentions one other sphere of repute, the intellectual or avant garde, which he says precedes academic reputation in some cases. This sphere does not figure in Jong's reputation. Jong has never been the favorite of an avant garde, described by Rodden as those who write for "non-specialist 'intellectual' quarterlies or 'advanced' magazines" (69), often promoting a writer who is a direct challenge to the Establishment. I discuss a leadership cohort of feminists who introduced Jong to a wider academic audience, but they were themselves academics and do not fill the requirements for an advance guard, which is usually gendered male.

2. I have found references to over a half dozen dissertations in various countries. There may be others as well.

3. I deal here with the responses to Jong's novels, though it should be noted that before the publication of her first novel, she had gained recognition as a poet, with two published books of poetry. For a review of Jong's career as a poet, see my interview with her in the Boston Review. Her poetry has been highly praised and, like her novels, also harshly criticized. The success of her novels increased sales and visibility of her poetry, but Jong says that "from the time that Fear of Flying became a great succès de scandale, and then sort of settled into its place as a novel about growing up, it has never been possible for me to rejoin the poetry world. . . . never again, after Fear of Flying was I reviewed as a poet, with my poetry reviewed as poetry" (29).

4. I have done research in Jong's French reception, and although I have found only a limited number of reviews (the first in 1976), those I have found are uniformly warm. French reviewers have been less shocked by Jong's sexual content than American and British reviewers and have praised her wit. (See, for example, Dominique Acker's review of Fear of Flying in La Quinzaine Littéraire.) It appears that Jong's sexual novels, falling within French notions of permitted

sexual joking and play, were seen as less threatening in France. (See Philippe Raynaud's "Feminism and the *Ancien Régime*" for a comparison of cultural attitudes about female sexuality in the French and Anglo Saxon traditions.)

5. Jong's poetry appears in a number of anthologies, including the *Norton Anthology of Literature by Women*.

6. That there are also several articles whose sole purpose is to severely criticize Jong is something of an anomaly in modern literary criticism, because most academic authors set out to establish the importance of their chosen subjects. Given the controversial nature of Jong's reputation, however, such articles should come as no surprise. Besides the Arlyn Diamond article noted previously, I will mention two others. In 1980 Evelyn Gross Avery published an article in *MELUS* entitled "Tradition and Independence in Jewish American Novels," in which she argues that Jong's heroine has a self-destructive tendency: she blames her family and heritage for her inadequacies and cannot overcome her self-love. In the *University of Dayton Review* (Winter 1985–1986), Francis Baumli subjects Jong to all the criticisms she received in her unfavorable reviews: her novels are simply autobiography, she is driven by her ego, she exhibits aggressive tendencies, and she values men mainly for their sexual prowess. In *Maledicta* John R. Clark argues that "zipless fuck" is a linguistic absurdity.

7. Before the publication of *Fear of Flying*, Jong was awarded prizes by the Poetry Society of America and *Poetry* magazine. A special session on Jong's work was to be held at the 1994 MLA convention, with Jong serving as respondent.

8. Jong herself has cited the Theroux review frequently, in the *Esquire* article mentioned in Chapter 2, in "Writing a First Novel" (where she quoted most of the review), in a *New Statesman* interview with Ros Coward, in *How to Save Your Own Life* (without naming Theroux). (See my "Sources for the 'Aging Midget-cum-Literary Critic' in Erica Jong's *How to Save Your Own Life*" in *Notes on Twentieth-Century Literature*.)

9. I have adopted the term "mediatization," from Dana Polan, who has written about the mediatization of intellectuals.

Bibliography

WORKS BY ERICA JONG

Any Woman's Blues. New York: Harper and Row, 1990.
At the Edge of the Body. New York: Holt, Rinehart and Winston, 1979.
"The Awful Truth about Women's Lib." *Vanity Fair* (April 1986): 92–93, 118–19.
Becoming Light: New and Selected Poems. New York: Harper, 1991.
"Changing My Mind about Andrea Dworkin." *Ms.* (June 1988): 60–64.
"Colette—Connoisseur of Clutter, Chatter." *Los Angeles Times Book Review,*
   December 14, 1975, 3.
"Daughters." *Ladies' Home Journal* (May 1975): 60–65.
The Devil at Large: Erica Jong on Henry Miller. New York: Random House
   (TurtleBay), 1993.
Fanny: Being the True History of the Adventures of Fanny Hackabout-Jones.
   New York: New American Library, 1980.
Fear of Fifty: A Midlife Memoir. New York: HarperCollins, 1994.
Fear of Flying. New York: Holt, Rinehart and Winston, 1973.
Fruits & Vegetables. New York: Holt, Rinehart and Winston, 1971.
Half-Lives. New York: Holt, Rinehart and Winston, 1973.
Here Comes and Other Poems. New York: Signet, 1975.
How to Save Your Own Life. New York: Holt, Rinehart and Winston, 1977.
"Introduction: *Fear of Flying* Fifteen Years Later." New York: Signet-NAL Pen-
   guin, 1988: xi–xv.
"Is There Life after Being a Good Girl?" *Glamour* (August 1987): 268–69, 320.
"Is There Sexy after Forty? Erica Jong Unzips the Last Taboo." *Vogue* (May
   1987): 304–5.
"Jong Triumphant: In which the renoun'd Author of *Fear of Flying*—who has
   stunned All & Sundry by writing a huge, bawdy, historical Novel—here con-
   fesses her ulterior Motives and the Pleasure of the Endeavor." *Vogue* (August
   1980): 229–30, 279–80 (printed with an excerpt from *Fanny*).
"The Life We Live and the Life We Write." *New York Times Book Review,* February 10, 1985, 26.
Loveroot. New York: Holt, Rinehart and Winston, 1975.
"Marriage: Rational and Irrational." *Vogue* (June 1975): 94–95.

Megan's Book of Divorce: A Kid's Book for Adults as Told to Erica Jong. Illus. Freya Tanz. New York: New American Library, 1984.
"A New Feminist Manifesto." Review of *The Second Stage* by Betty Friedan. *Saturday Review* (October 1981): 66–68.
"Notes on Five Men." *Esquire* (May 1975): 69–73.
Ordinary Miracles. New York: New American Library, 1983.
Parachutes & Kisses. New York: New American Library, 1984.
"Revenge Symposium." *Esquire* (May 1983): 89 (Jong's contribution appears along with those of many other authors).
Serenissima: A Novel of Venice. Boston: Houghton Mifflin, 1987.
"17th Century Women: The Stronger Sex." Review of *The Weaker Vessel* by Antonia Fraser. *Chicago Tribune Book World*, September 30, 1984, 26, 31.
"Speaking of Love." *Newsweek*, February 21, 1977, 11.
"Succeed at Your Own Risk." *Vogue* (October 1975): 216–17.
"Time Has Been Kind to the Nymphet: 'Lolita' 30 Years Later." *New York Times Book Review*, June 5, 1988, 3, 46.
Witches. Illus. Joseph A. Smith. New York: Harry N. Abrams, 1981.
"Writer Who 'Flew' to Sexy Fame Talks about Being a Woman." *Vogue* (March 1977): 158, 160.
"Writing a First Novel." *Twentieth-Century Literature* 20:4 (1974): 263–69.
"Ziplash: A Sexual Libertine Recants." *Ms.* (May 1989): 49.

INTERVIEWS WITH ERICA JONG

"Contemporary Authors Interview." With Jean W. Ross. In *Contemporary Authors*, New Revision Series, vol. 26, 189–92. Detroit: Gale Research, 1989.
"Erica: Being the True History of Isadora Wing, Fanny Hackabout-Jones, and Erica Jong." With John Kern. *Writer's Digest* (June 1981): 20–25.
"Erica Jong: 'Can You Think of a Good Reason to Get Married?'" Interview with Mary Cantwell. *Mademoiselle* (June 1976): 125, 96, 98 (part of a longer article entitled "Three American Women: Three Surprising Interviews").
Interview. With Gretchen McNeese. *Playboy* (September 1975): 61–78, 202.
Interview. With Karen Burke. *Interview* (June 1987): 95–96.
Interview. With Philip Fleishman. *Maclean's*, August 21, 1978, 4–6.
Interview. With Ralph Gardner. In *Writers Talk to Ralph Gardner*, 190–201. New York: Metuchen, 1989.
Interview. With Rozsika Parker and Eleanor Stephens. *Spare Rib* (July 1977): 15–17.
Interview. With Wendy Martin. In *Women Writers Talking*, ed. Janet Todd, 21–32. New York: Holmes and Meier, 1983.
"An Interview with Erica Jong." With Elaine Showalter and Carol Smith. *Columbia Forum* (Winter 1975): 12–17.
Telephone interviews, April 13 and July 11, 1991.

"That Mispronounced Poet: An Interview with Erica Jong." With Charlotte Templin. *Boston Review* (March/April 1992): 5–8, 23, 29.
"Two Women: Liv Ullman and Erica Jong, an Intimate Conversation." *Redbook*, August 19, 1977, 104–5, 147–48.
"Women and Men and Art." With Anatole Broyard. *New York Times Book Review*, December 27, 1981, 23 (joint interview with Jill Robinson).

TELEVISION APPEARANCES BY ERICA JONG

"Bookmark." WNET, New York. March 5, 1989 (with Margaret Atwood).
"Geraldo." WGN, New York. March 1, 1990.
"Morning News." CBS, New York. November 7, 1983; September 28, 1983; April 30, 1984; November 4, 1986.
"Sixty Minutes." CBS, New York. August 17, 1975.
"Today." NBC, New York. July 31, 1986.

WORKS BY OTHER AUTHORS

Abel, Elizabeth, Marianne Hirsch, and Elizabeth Langland. *The Voyage In: Fictions of Female Development*. Hanover, N.H.: University Press of New England, 1983.
Acker, Dominique. "Une Naissance à Soi-même par-delà un Voyage Initiatique Burlesque et Sensuel." *La Quinzaine Littéraire*, November 16, 1976, 14.
Ackroyd, Peter. "Born Twee." Review of *How to Save Your Own Life*. *Spectator*, 7 May 1987, 24.
Aiken, Joan. "Erica Jong's Carnival of Venice." Review of *Serenissima*. *Washington Post Book World*, April 19, 1987, 4–5.
"Altitude Sickness." Review of *Fear of Flying*. *Times Literary Supplement*, July 26, 1974, 813.
Amiel, Barbara. "How the Feminists Hurt Women." *Maclean's*, October 1, 1984, 13.
Amis, Martin, "Isadora's Complaint." Review of *Fear of Flying*. *Observer Review*, April 21, 1974, 37.
Atwood, Margaret. "Bookmark." WNET, New York. March 5, 1989.
———. "Playing Around." Interview with J. R. (Tim) Struthers. In *Margaret Atwood: Conversations*, ed. Earl G. Ingersoll, 58–68. Princeton: Ontario Review Press, 1990.
Avery, Evelyn Gross. "Tradition and Independence in Jewish Feminist Novels." *MELUS* 7:4 (1980): 49–55.
Barber, Benjamin R. "Beyond the Feminist Mystique." *New Republic*, July 11, 1983, 26–32.
Baumli, Francis. "Erica Jong Revisited; (or) No Wonder We Men Had Trouble

Understanding Feminism." *University of Dayton Review* 17:3 (Winter 1985–1986): 91–95.

Bennetts, Leslie. "Forever Jong." *Vanity Fair* (February 1991): 64–76.

_____. "On Aggression in Politics: Are Women Judged by a Double Standard?" *New York Times*, February 12, 1979, B13.

_____. "Singing and Dancing Debut, of Sorts." *New York Times*, October 14, 1982, C18.

Benokraitis, Nijole V., and Joe R. Feagin. *Modern Sexism: Blatant, Subtle, and Covert Discrimination*. Englewood Cliffs, N.J.: Prentice Hall, 1986.

Binding, Paul. "Italy!" Review of *Serenissima*. *Listener*, September 24, 1987, 29–30.

Birch, Helen. "From the Pulpit." Review of *Any Woman's Blues*. *Listener*, August 23, 1990, 28.

Blakely, Mary Kay. "Feminism—A Lost Cause?" *Vogue* (October 1983): 402, 404–5.

Bolotin, Susan. "Voices from the Post-Feminist Generation." *New York Times Magazine*, October 17, 1982, 29–31, 103, 106, 116–17.

Boulenger, Ghislaine. "Afraid to Be She." Review of *Fear of Flying*. *Washington Post*, December 13, 1973, D13.

Bourdieu, Pierre. *Distinction: A Social Critique of the Judgement of Taste*. Trans. Richard Nice. Cambridge: Harvard University Press, 1984.

Brantlinger, Patrick. *Bread and Circuses: Theories of Mass Culture as Social Decay*. Ithaca: Cornell University Press, 1983.

Braudy, Leo. *The Frenzy of Renown: Fame and Its History*. Oxford: Oxford University Press, 1986.

Broner, E. M. "The Dirty Ladies: Earthy Writings of Contemporary American Women—Paley, Jong, Schor, and Lerman." *Regionalism and the Female Imagination* 4:3 (1979): 34–43.

Brown, Tina. "Can a Million Americans Be Wrong?" *Sunday Times*, January 26, 1975, A35.

Brozan, Nadine. "Swapping Strategies at Forum on Family." *New York Times*, August 2, 1982, 13.

Bryan, C. D. B. *Beautiful Women, Ugly Scenes*. New York: Doubleday, 1983.

_____. "The Loves of Isadora, Continued: Is Marriage Impossible?" Review of *Parachutes & Kisses*. *New York Times Book Review*, October 21, 1984, 14.

Buechler, Steven M. *Women's Movements in the United States: Woman Suffrage, Equal Rights, and Beyond*. New Brunswick: Rutgers University Press, 1990.

Burgess, Anthony. "Grunts from a Sexist Pig." In *But Do Blondes Prefer Gentlemen?* 1–4. New York: McGraw Hill, 1986.

_____. "Jong in Triumph." Review of *Fanny*. *Saturday Review* (August 1980): 54–55.

_____. "Native Ground." Review of *Columbia Literary History of the United States*, ed. Emory Elliott. *Atlantic* (January 1988): 89–91.

_____. *99 Novels: The Best in English since* 1939, *A Personal Choice.* New York: Summit, 1984.

Butler, Robert J. "The Woman Writer as American Picaro: Open Journeying in Erica Jong's *Fear of Flying.*" *Centennial Review* 31:3 (Summer 1987): 308–29.

Campbell, Mary. "Miss Mutter Prefers Dior—and Stradivarius." Associated Press. *Indianapolis Star,* January 1, 1989, E6.

_____. "Virgil Thomson Still Composing Music at 90." Associated Press. *Indianapolis Star,* November 23, 1986, 8E.

Cavinder, Fred. "Artist Sues to Halt Unauthorized Sales." *Indianapolis Star,* June 18, 1988, B5.

Charen, Mona. "The Feminist Mistake." *National Review,* March 23, 1984, 24–27.

Charney, Maurice. *Sexual Fiction.* London: Methuen, 1981.

Clapp, Suzannah. "Dark and Buzzing Looks." Review of *Serenissima. London Review of Books,* October 1, 1987, 13.

Clark, John R. "A Humble Predacity upon the Corpus of Erica Jong." *Maledicta* 1 (1977): 211–13.

Clymer, Adam. "Subtle Shifts in GOP Appeals Aimed at Women." *New York Times,* August 5, 1982, 16.

Coates, Joseph. "An Artist Spray-Painted with Thick, Purple Prose." Review of *Any Woman's Blues. Chicago Tribune Book World,* January 7, 1990, 7.

Colander, Pat. "Erica Jong Won't Play Cult Game as Instant Sexpert." *Chicago Tribune,* June 1, 1975, E10.

Cole, Diane. "Jong's 'Serenessima': Brushing Off Shakespeare." Review of *Serenissima. USA Today,* May 15, 1987, 4D.

Collins, Jim. *Uncommon Cultures: Popular Culture and Post-Modernism.* New York: Routledge, 1989.

Cooke, Judy. "You Name It." Review of *Fanny. New Statesman,* October 24, 1980, 24.

Cooter, Margaret, et al. *Reviewing the Reviews: A Woman's Place on the Book Page.* Written and edited by Women in Publishing. London: Journeyman, 1987.

Coward, Rosalind. "Are Women's Novels Feminist Novels?" In *Feminist Criticism: Essays on Women, Literature, Theory,* ed. Elaine Showalter, 225–39. New York: Pantheon, 1985.

_____. "Coming Down." *New Statesman and Society,* August 10, 1990, 12–13.

Coyne, Patricia S. "Woman's Lit." Review of *Fear of Flying. National Review,* May 24, 1974, 604.

Crain, Jane Larkin. "Feminist Fiction." Review of *Fear of Flying* (and other novels). *Commentary* (December 1974): 58–62.

Cunningham, Valentine. "Back to Shiftwork." Review of *Serenissima. Times Literary Supplement,* September 18, 1987, 1025.

Daley, Tammy. "When a Good Word Takes on a Bad Meaning." *U.S. News and World Report,* January 12, 1987, 9.

Darling, Lynn. "Jong: Erica and Erotica in Connecticut."*Washington Post*, September 25, 1980, D1, D15.

Davies, Bronwyn, and Rom Harré. "Positioning: The Discursive Production of Selves." *Journal for the Theory of Social Behavior* 20:1 (March 1990): 43–63.

Day, Frank. "D. Keith Mano." in *American Novelists since World War II*, ed. James L. Kibler, 208–14. Vol. 6, *Dictionary of Literary Biography*. Detroit: Gale Research, 1980.

DeMott, Benjamin. "Couple Trouble: Mod and Trad." *Atlantic* (December 1973): 122–27.

———. "The Fruits of Sin." Review of *Any Woman's Blues*. *New York Times Book Review*, January 28, 1990, 13.

Diamond, Arlyn. "Flying from Work" *Frontiers* 2:3 (1977): 18–23.

Dillon, Millicent. "All the Pelegeyas." *Ascent* 4:3 (1979): 49–62.

———. "Literature and the New Bawd." Review of *Fear of Flying* (and other novels). *Nation*, February 22, 1975, 219–21.

Doane, Janice, and Devon Hodges. *Nostalgia and Sexual Difference: The Resistance to Contemporary Feminism*. New York: Methuen, 1987.

Donahue, Deirdre. "She Sings a New Verse in 'Blues.' " *USA Today*, February 6, 1990, D1.

Dudovitz, Resa L. *The Myth of the Superwoman: Women's Bestsellers in France and the United States*. New York: Routledge, 1990.

Duval, Joanne. "A Jubilant Celebration of Spirit." Review of *Fanny*. *New Directions for Women* (November/December 1980): 14.

Dworkin, Andrea. Letter. *New York Times Book Review*, May 24, 1987, 4.

Dworkin, Susan. "In Which the Author Hides under the Skirts of an 18th-Century Wench, Thereby Indulging Herself and Us." Review of *Fanny*. *Ms.* (November 1980): 45.

Echols, Alice. *Daring to Be Bad: Radical Feminism in America 1967–1975*. Minneapolis: University of Minnesota Press, 1989.

Ehrenreich, Barbara. *The Hearts of Men: American Dreams and the Flight from Commitment*. New York: Anchor/Doubleday, 1983.

Ehrenreich, Barbara, Elizabeth Hess, and Gloria Jacobs. *Re-Making Love: The Feminization of Sex*. New York: Doubleday, 1986.

Eliot, George. *Middlemarch*. Boston: Houghton Mifflin (Riverside), 1956.

"Erica Jong Suit Accuses Ex-Husband on Book." *New York Times*, March 8, 1984, C20.

Evans, Stuart. "Fiction." Review of *Fanny* (and other novels). (London) *Times*, November 27, 1980, 14.

Evans, Timothy J. "Paul Theroux." In *American Novelists since World War II*, ed. Jeffrey Helterman and Richard Layman, 478–83. Vol. 2, *Dictionary of Literary Biography*. Detroit: Gale, 1978.

"Executive Sees Boredom in Women's Issues." *New York Times*, December 11, 1980, D14.

Felski, Rita. *Beyond Feminist Aesthetics: Feminist Literature and Social Change*. Cambridge: Harvard University Press, 1989.

Ferguson, Mary Anne. "The Female Novel of Development and the Myth of Psyche." *Denver Quarterly* 17:4 (Winter 1983): 58–74.

Firestone, Shulamith. *The Dialectic of Sex: The Case for Feminist Revolution.* New York: Bantam, 1970.

Fish, Stanley. *Is There a Text in This Class? The Authority of Interpretive Communities.* Cambridge: Harvard University Press, 1980.

Fisher, Craig. " 'Fear of Flying' Heroine Flies a New Flight Plan." Review of *How to Save Your Own Life. Los Angeles Times Book Review,* March 20, 1977, I, 13.

———. Telephone interview. May 18, 1991.

FitzGerald, Karen. "What Do the '60s and '70s Say to the '80s?" *Ms.* (July 1986): 56, 84–85.

Fox-Genovese, Elizabeth. *Feminism without Illusions: A Critique of Individualism.* Chapel Hill: University of North Carolina Press, 1991.

———. "The New Female Literary Culture." *Antioch Review* 38:2 (Spring 1980): 193–218.

Francke, Linda. "Mother Confessor." *Newsweek,* December 16, 1974, 65–66.

Franckling, Ken. "Radical Novelist Erica Jong Meets Time Work." UPI. *Indianapolis Star,* May 10, 1987, 11E.

———. Review of *Parachutes & Kisses.* UPI. File PUT AZNO522 OC TO NKH.

Freely, Maureen. "Unzipping Shakespeare." Review of *Serenissima. Observer Review,* September 13, 1987, 27.

"Freshman Survey Finds New Trends." *New York Times,* January 11, 1976, A45.

Friedman, Alan. "Erica Jong Circa 1750." Review of *Fanny. New York Times Book Review,* August 17, 1980, I, 20.

Frye, Northrup. *Anatomy of Criticism.* New York: Atheneum, 1968.

Fuchs, Marcia. Review of *How to Save Your Own Life. Library Journal,* January 15, 1977, 218.

"Future Views: Enduring Individuals." *Omni* (October 1980): 124, 147.

Gans, Herbert J. *Popular Culture and High Culture: An Analysis and Evaluation of Taste.* New York: Basic, 1974.

Geng, Victoria. "Requiem for the Women's Movement." *Harper's* (November 1976): 49–56.

Getlin, Josh. "No Fear of Flying: 'Bad Girl' Novelist Erica Jong Is Back with a Steamy, New Book." *Los Angeles Times,* January 22, 1990, E1–2.

Gilbert, Sandra M., and Susan Gubar. *No Man's Land: The Place of the Woman Writer in the Twentieth Century.* Vol. 2, *Sexchanges.* New Haven: Yale University Press, 1989.

Gilbert, Sandra M., and Susan Gubar, eds. *The Norton Anthology of Literature by Women: The Tradition in English.* New York: Norton, 1985.

Gilder, Joshua. "Fanny." Review of *Fanny. American Spectator* (March 1981): 36–37.

Glendinning, Victoria. "Dreams of Fair Women." Review of *Parachutes & Kisses* (and other novels). *Sunday Times,* November 25, 1984, 42.

Goldman, James. "Jong's Fanny: A Heroine Too Far Ahead of Her Time." Review of *Fanny. Chicago Tribune Book World*, August 10, 1980, 1.

Graeber, Laurel. "An Opinion: The Woman's Movement: Too Much of a Good Thing?" *Mademoiselle* (August 1975): 42–47.

Greene, Gayle, *Changing the Story: Feminist Fiction and the Tradition*. Bloomington: Indiana University Press, 1991.

Gribben, Alan. "The Importance of Mark Twain." In *American Humor*, ed. Arthur Power Dudden, 24–49. New York: Oxford University Press, 1987.

Grossman, Anita Susan. "Sorry, Jong Number Three." Review of *Parachutes & Kisses. Wall Street Journal*, November 21, 1984, 28.

Hadad, M. George. "Erica Jong." *Mademoiselle* (August 1975): 206.

Harwood, Ronald. "Confessions of a Transexual Lover." Review of *How to Save Your Own Life* (and other novels). *Sunday Times* (London), May 1, 1977, 41.

Haskell, Molly. *From Reverence to Rape: The Treatment of Woman in the Movies*. 2d ed. Chicago: Chicago University Press, 1987.

————. Review of *Fear of Flying. Village Voice Literary Supplement*, November 22, 1973, 27.

Helgesen, Sally. "Instant Tradition." Review of *Fanny. Harper's* (January 1981): 81–82.

Hite, Molly. "Writing—and Reading—The Body: Female Sexuality and Recent Feminist Fiction." *Feminist Studies* 14:1 (Spring 1988): 121–42.

Hood, Ann. "Addictions of a 90's Woman." Review of *Any Woman's Blues. Washington Post Book World*, January 23, 1990, 3.

Huyssen, Andreas. "Mass Culture as Woman: Modernism's Other." In *After the Great Divide*, 44–62. Bloomington: Indiana University Press, 1986.

"In Land of Addictions, Shelves Full of Solace." *New York Times*, June 21, 1989, D1.

Jackson, Marni. "Crash Landing." Review of *Any Woman's Blues. Maclean's*, February 19, 1990, 55.

Jacoby, Susan. "The Bawdy Bard." Review of *Serenissima. Chicago Tribune Book World*, April 5, 1987, 7.

————. "A Generation Gap of Our Own." *Vogue* (April 1981): 291, 328–29.

James, Clive, "Fannikin's Cunnikin." Review of *Fanny. New York Review of Books*, November 6, 1980, 25.

James, Darlene, "Lazy, Hazy Summer Fare." Review of *Serenissima. Maclean's*, July 20, 1987, 50–51.

Janeway, Elizabeth. "Women's Literature." In *Harvard Guide to Contemporary American Writing*, ed. Daniel Hoffman, 342–95. Cambridge: Harvard University Press, 1979.

Jelanik, George. "The Vocal Scene." Produced by WQXR, New York. Rebroadcast WICR, Indianapolis, July 28, 1988.

Johnson, Diane. "Hard Hit Women." Review of *How to Save Your Own Life* (and other novels). *New York Review of Books*, April 28, 1977, 6.

Johnson, Laurie. "Women's Sexuality Conference Ends in School 29." *New York Times*, June 11, 1973, 10.

Kahn, Tony. "Mommy and Daddy Are Fighting Again since Erica Jong Used Her Daughter's Name in a Children's Guide to Divorce." *People Weekly* (April 1984): 51–52.

Kaplan, Carey, and Ellen Cronan Rose. *The Canon and the Common Reader.* Knoxville: University of Tennessee Press, 1990.

Kapp, Isa. "And Erica." Review of *How to Save Your Own Life. Washington Post Book World*, March 20, 1977, 1, 4.

Kayle, Hilary S. "Booking Authors on the 'Today' Program: An Insider's Account." *Publisher's Weekly*, February 5, 1979, 57–58.

Kazin, Alfred. "The Writer as Sexual Show-off; or, Making Press Agents Unnecessary." *New York*, June 9, 1975, 36–40.

Keating, Peter. "Erica, or Little by Little." Review of *How to Save Your Own Life. Times Literary Supplement*, May 6, 1977, 545.

Kelly, Ann. "Mutual Attraction: Jonathan Swift and Popular Culture." Modern Language Association Convention, December 28, 1990.

Kemp, Peter. "Empty Vessels." Review of *Parachutes & Kisses. Times Literary Supplement*, November 16, 1984, 1302.

———. "Moll Flounders." Review of *Fanny* (and other novels). *Listener*, October 30, 1980, 588–89.

Kendall, Elaine. Review of *Parachutes & Kisses. Los Angeles Times Book Review*, November 11, 1984, 3.

———. *The Upper Hand.* Boston: Little Brown, 1965.

Kendrick, Walter. "Her Master's Voice." Review of *The Devil at Large: Erica Jong on Henry Miller. New York Times Book Review*, February 14, 1993, 10–11.

Kirsch, Robert. "The Poet Behind 'Fear of Flying.' " *Los Angeles Times*, August 5, 1975, D5.

Klein, Julia M. "Fanny." Review of *Fanny. New Republic*, September 20, 1980, 38–39.

Klemesrud, Judy. "Survey Finds Major Shifts in Attitudes of Women." *New York Times*, March 13, 1980, C1.

———. "That Suburban Matron, Erica Jong." *New York Times*, August 4, 1980, B6.

———. "A Surgeon and Author Explains His Chauvinism." *New York Times*, August 22, 1982, 60.

Korelitz, Jean Hanff. "How to Hit the Self-Destruct Button." Review of *Any Woman's Blues. Sunday Times Books* (London), August 5, 1990, 4.

Krupp, Charla, "Erica Jong's Solution to the Man Shortage." *Glamour* (October 1983): 83, 319.

Kuehl, Linda. Review of *How to Save Your Own Life. Saturday Review*, April 30, 1977, 27.

Larson, Janet. "Margaret Atwood and the Future of Prophecy." *Religion and Literature* 21:3 (Autumn 1989): 27–61.

Laughridge, Jamie. "Erica Jong: The Survivor." *Harper's Bazaar* (August 1984): 197, 249.

Leber, Michele. Review of *Parachutes & Kisses*. *Library Journal*, October 1, 1984, 1962.

Lee, Hermione, "Long Lost America." Review of *Parachutes & Kisses* (and other novels). *Observer Review*, October 28, 1984, 25.

———. *The Novels of Virginia Woolf*. London: Methuen, 1977.

———. *Philip Roth*. London: Methuen, 1982.

Lehmann-Haupt, Christopher. "Books of the Times." Review of *How to Save Your Own Life*. *New York Times*, March 11, 1977, C25.

———. "Nuances of Women's Liberation." Review of *Fear of Flying* (and one other book). *New York Times*, November 6, 1973, 35.

Leonard, John. "Bad-Boy Books." *Ms.* (January/February 1989): 124, 126.

———. Review of *How to Save Your Own Life*. *New York Times Book Review*, March 20, 1977, 2.

Lesser, Wendy. *His Other Half: Men Looking at Women through Art*. Cambridge: Harvard University Press, 1991.

Levine, Lawrence W. *Highbrow, Lowbrow: The Emergency of Cultural Hierarchy in America*. Cambridge: Harvard University Press, 1988.

Lewis, Peter. "Of Bonds and Bondage." Review of *Any Woman's Blues* (and other novels). *Stand Magazine* (Winter 1990): 74–83.

Lichtenstein, Grace. "The Daring New Woman of the 80's." Interview with Nancy Evans. *Glamour* (July 1981): 154–57.

———. "Fear of Landing." Review of *Parachutes & Kisses*. *Washington Post Book World*, October 21, 1984, 9.

———. *Machisma: Women and Daring*. New York: Doubleday, 1981.

Lovell, Terry. *Consuming Fiction*. London, Verso, 1987.

"The Loves of Isadora." *Time*, February 5, 1975, 69–70.

Luzzi, Michael. "Jong Sees Reversal in Divorce." *New York Times*, October 21, 1984, xxxiii, 21.

McDowell, Edwin. "Coaches Help Authors Talk Well to Sell Well." *New York Times*, March 2, 1988, A1, C20.

Mainland, Mary. "Feminist Myths Reconsidered." *America*, December 15, 1984, 396–99.

Malone, Michael. "The True Adventures of Shylock's Daughter." Review of *Serenissima*. *New York Times Book Review*, April 19, 1987, 12.

Mandrell, James. "Questions of Genre and Gender: Contemporary American Versions of the Feminine Picaresque." *Novel* 20:2 (Winter 1987): 149–70.

Mano, D. Keith. "The Authoress as Aphid." Review of *How to Save Your Own Life*. *National Review*, April 29, 1977, 498.

———. "Lib on the Rocks." *National Review*, March 15, 1974, 326–27.

Mars-Jones, Adam. "Fireworks at the Funeral." Review of *Einstein's Monsters* by Martin Amis. *Times Literary Supplement*, May 1, 1987, 457.

Martin, Judith. "The Pleasure of Her Company." Review of *Fanny*. *Washington Post Book World*, August 17, 1980, 4.

Maslin, Janet. "Isadora and Erica." Review of *How to Save Your Own Life*. *Newsweek*, March 28, 1977, 82–83.

Maxwell, William. Interview with David Stanton. *Poets & Writers* (May/June 1994): 36–47.

Mesic, Penelope. "Erica Jong: Flying Fearlessly." Review of *How to Save Your Own Life. Chicago Tribune Book World*, March 20, 1977, 1.

"Methinks the Lady Protests Too Much." (London) *Daily Mail*, April 11, 1974, 7.

Meyer, Ellen Hope. "The Aesthetics of Dear Diary." Review of *Fear of Flying* (and other novels). *Nation*, January 12, 1974, 55–56.

Middlebrook, Diane Wood. *Anne Sexton: A Biography*. Boston: Houghton Mifflin, 1991.

Miller, Henry, and Erica Jong. "Two Writers in Praise of Rabelais and Each Other." *New York Times*, September 7, 1974, 27.

Millet, Kate. *Sexual Politics*. Garden City, N.Y.: Doubleday, 1970.

Mishan, E. J. "Was the Women's Movement Really Necessary?" *Encounter* (January 1985): 7–10.

Mitgang, Herbert. "Books of the Times." Review of *Parachutes & Kisses. New York Times*, October 10, 1984, C23.

Montrose, David. "Imperfections of the Art and of the Life." Review of *Any Woman's Blues* (and other novels). *Times Literary Supplement*, August 17–23, 1990, 868.

Morris, Joan. *High Performance*. Host, Andre Previn, National Public Radio. WFYI, Indianapolis, August 24, 1988.

Morrison, Blake. "In Defense of Feminism." *Observer*, May 29, 1983, 27.

Morrow, Lance. "Oral History." Review of *How to Save Your Own Life. Time*, March 14, 1977, 74–75.

"NAL Aims Trade Paperback of 'Fanny' at a 'Middle Market' of Consumers." *Publisher's Weekly*, January 16, 1981, 43, 48.

Nelson, Cary. "Facts Have No Meaning: Writing Literary History in the Shadow of Poststructuralism." *College Literature* 20:2 (June 1993): 1–12.

Newcomb, John Timberman. "Canonical Ahistoricism vs. Histories of Canons: Towards Methodological Dissensus." *South Atlantic Review* 54:4 (November 1989): 3–20.

"New York: Day by Day." *New York Times*, February 28, 1983, B3.

"New York: Day by Day." *New York Times*, December 7, 1985, 30.

Nitzsche, Jane Chance. "'Isadora Icarus:' The Mythic Unity of Erica Jong's *Fear of Flying*." *Rice University Studies* 64:1 (Winter 1978): 89–100.

Norman, Marsha. Interview. *MacNeil/Lehrer Report*, PBS. WFYI, Indianapolis, June 10, 1988.

Novak, Ralph. Review of *Any Woman's Blues. People Weekly*, March 5, 1990, 26.

O'Brien, Sharon. "Becoming Noncanonical: The Case against Willa Cather." In *Reading in America*, ed. Cathy N. Davison, 240–58. Baltimore: Johns Hopkins University Press, 1989.

Ohmann, Richard. "The Shaping of a Canon: U.S. Fiction, 1960–1975." *Critical*

Inquiry 10:1 (1983): 199–223. Reprinted in *Politics of Letters*, 68–91. Middletown: Wesleyan University Press, 1987.

Onwurah, Chinyela. "Sixties and Seventies Lib Hasn't done Much for the Modern Ms." *Guardian*, January 7, 1985, 10.

"Pandora's Box." Montgomery College Channel 3/51, Baltimore, Md. March 17, 1993.

Parker, Rosie. Review of *Fear of Flying*. *Spare Rib*, no. 25 (1974): 41–42.

Patai, Daphne. "Surplus Visibility." Unpublished essay. 1991.

———. "The View from Elsewhere: Utopian Construction of Sexual Difference." In *"Turning the Century:" Feminist Theory in the 1990s*, ed. Glynis Carr, 132–50. Lewisburg: Bucknell University Press, 1992.

Pearlman, Mickey. "Belles Lettres Interview." *Belles Lettres* (May/June 1988): 9.

Pearlman, Mickey, and Katherine Usher Henderson. *Inter/View: Talks with America's Writing Women*. Lexington: Kentucky University Press, 1990.

Peer, Elizabeth. "Sex and the Woman Writer. *Newsweek*, May 5, 1975, 70–77.

Perloff, Marjorie. "The Joy of Jong." Review of *Loveroot* and *Here Comes and Other Poems*. *Washington Post Book World*. July 6, 1975, 1–2.

Phillips, Julia. *You'll Never Eat Lunch in This Town Again*. New York: Random House, 1991.

Phillips, William. "Further Notes toward a Definition of the Canon and the Curriculum." *Partisan Review* 56:2 (Spring 1989): 175–78.

Poirier, Richard. "Conservative Estimates." Review of *The Moronic Inferno: And Other Visits to America* by Martin Amis. *Times Literary Supplement*, July 1986, 785.

Polan, Dana. "The Spectacle of Intellect in a Media Age: Cultural Representations and the David Abraham, Paul de Man, and Victor Farías Cases." In *Intellectuals: Aesthetics, Politics, Academics*, ed. Bruce Robbins, 343–63. Minneapolis: University of Minnesota Press, 1990.

"Poll Finds New View of Women." *New York Times*, January 6, 1981, B12.

Prelutsky, Jack. "Kicking Jong Around." *Los Angeles Times*, May 25, 1975, (Calendar section) 75.

Pritchard, William M. "Novel Reports." Review of *Any Woman's Blues* (and other novels). *Hudson Review* 43 (Autumn 1990): 489–98.

Prose, Francine. "A Wing without a Prayer." Review of *Any Woman's Blues*. *Savvy Woman* (February 1990): 27, 95.

Pyrah, Gill. "Erica Tries a Parachute." (London) *Times*, November 2, 1984, 11.

Quinn, Sally. "Erica Jong: Learning to Cope with Her 'Fear of Flying.'" *Washington Post*, January 12, 1975, H1-2.

Radford, Jean. Review of *How to Save Your Own Life*. *Spare Rib* (June 1977): 45–46.

Radhakrishnan, R. "Toward an Effective Intellectual: Foucault or Gramsci?" In *Intellectuals: Aesthetics, Politics, Academics*, ed. Bruce Robbins, 57–99. Minneapolis: University of Minnesota Press, 1990.

Radway, Janice A. "The Book-of-the-Month Club and the General Reader: On the Uses of 'Serious' Fiction." *Critical Inquiry* 14:3 (1988): 517–38.

———. "Mail-Order Culture and Its Critics: The Book-of-the-Month Club, Commodification and Consumption, and the Problem of Cultural Authority." In *Cultural Studies*, ed. Lawrence Grossberg, Cary Nelson, and Paula A. Treichler, 512–30. New York: Routledge, 1992.

———. *Reading the Romance: Women, Patriarchy, and Popular Literature.* Chapel Hill: North Carolina University Press, 1984.

Raynaud, Philippe. "Feminism and the *Ancien Régime.*" *Partisan Review* (Fall 1991): 635–41.

Reardon, Joan. "*Fear of Flying:* Developing the Feminist Novel." *International Journal of Women's Studies* 1 (1978): 306–20.

Reuben, Elaine. "Fear of Flying." Review of *Fear of Flying. New Republic*, February 2, 1974, 27.

Review of *Parachutes & Kisses. Playboy* (December 1984): 33.

Review of *Serenissima. Time*, June 22, 1987, 74.

Review of *Serenissima. West Coast Review of Books*, no. 1 (1987): 21.

Rifkind, Donna. "Masochists in Love." Review of *Any Woman's Blues* (and other novels). *Wall Street Journal*, January 30, 1990, A16.

Rivers, Caryl. "E.R.A.'s Death and Fear of New Women." *New York Times*, August 29, 1982, 19.

Rodden, John. *The Politics of Literary Reputation: The Making and Claiming of St. George Orwell.* New York: Oxford University Press, 1989.

Rogers, Pat. "Blood, Milk, and Tears." Review of *Fanny. Times Literary Supplement*, October 24, 1980, 1190.

Roiphe, Katie. *The Morning After: Sex, Fear, and Feminism on Campus.* Boston: Little, Brown, 1993.

Rosen, Richard. "Heirs to Maxwell Perkins." *Horizon* (April 1981): 50–53.

Rosenfelt, Deborah Silverton. "Feminism, 'Postfeminism,' and Contemporary Women's Fiction." In *Tradition and the Talents of Women*, ed. Florence Howe, 268–91. Urbana: University of Illinois Press, 1991.

Rosenfelt, Deborah, and Judith Stacey. "Review Essay: Second Thoughts on the Second Wave." *Feminist Studies* 13:2 (Summer 1987): 341–61.

Ross, Andrew. "Defenders of the Faith and the New Class." In *Intellectuals: Aesthetics, Politics, Academics*, ed. Bruce Robbins, 101–32. Minneapolis: University of Minnesota Press, 1990.

———. *No Respect: Intellectuals and Popular Culture.* New York: Routledge, 1989.

Rubin, Merle. "Diving into the Shallows of Narcissism." Review of *Parachutes & Kisses. Christian Science Monitor*, October 24, 1984, 21–22.

Russ, Joanna. *How to Suppress Women's Writing.* Austin: University of Texas Press, 1983.

Ryan, Barbara. *Feminism and the Women's Movement: Dynamics of Change in Social Movement, Ideology and Activism.* New York: Routledge, 1992.

Sage, Lorna. "Fanny Jong." Review of *Fanny*. *Observer Review*, October 26, 1980, 29.

———. "Gobbling It All Up." Review of *How to Save Your Own Life* (and other novels). *Observer Review*, May 1, 1977, 24.

Schwartz, Lawrence H. *Creating Faulkner's Reputation: The Politics of Modern Literary Criticism*. Knoxville: University of Tennessee Press, 1988.

Schwartz, Lynne Sharon. Letter. *New York Times Book Review*, June 28, 1987, 36.

Scruton, Roger. "Bodily Tracts." *Times Literary Supplement*, July 23, 1982, 807.

———. "The Case against Feminism." *Observer*, May 22, 1983, 27.

See, Carolyn. "Where There's a Will, There's a Way for Jessica." Review of *Serenissima*. *Los Angeles Times Book Review*, May 18, 1987, 2.

Selden, Isobel. "Pleasures and Problems of Living Together." *Harper's Bazaar*, May 17, 1977, 116–17.

Shakespeare, Nicholas. "Lessing's Little Experiment, Fishnets, and Satirical Fantasies." Review of *Parachutes & Kisses* (and other novels). (London) *Times*, October 25, 1984, 16.

Shales, Tom "Erica Jong's 'Albatross.'" *Washington Post*, January 8, 1975, B2.

———. "Propriety vs. Censorship at the Smithsonian." *Washington Post*, November 23, 1974, B1–2.

———. "Smithsonian Institution: Nothing to Fear but 'Fear of Flying.' *Washington Post*, November 22, 1974, B1, B4.

Shapiro, Laura. "Isadora's Complaint." Review of *Parachutes & Kisses*. *Newsweek*, November 5, 1984, 88–89.

Shaw, Peter. "Feminist Literary Criticism: A Report from the Academy." *American Scholar* 57-4 (Autumn 1988): 495–513.

Shelton, Frank W. "The Image of the Rock and the Family in the Novels of Willa Cather." *Markham Review* 6 (Fall 1976): 9–14.

Showalter, Elaine. *Sister's Choice: Tradition and Change in American Women's Writing*. Oxford: Clarendon, 1991.

Shrimpton, Nicholas. "Womb's Eye." Review of *Mother's Helper* by Maureen Freely. *New Statesman*, October 26, 1979, 643.

Sigal, Clancy. "Jong's Ego Overwhelms Small, Sharp, Nasty Comedy." Review of *Parachutes & Kisses*. *Chicago Tribune Book World*, October 14, 1984, 39.

Sinclair, Andrew. "Fear of Falling in Love." Review of *Any Woman's Blues* (and other novels). *Times* (London), August 2, 1990, 20.

Smith, Barbara Herrnstein. *Contingencies of Value: Alternative Perspectives for Critical Theory*. Harvard University Press, 1988.

Spacks, Patricia Meyer. "The Difference It Makes." In *A Feminist Perspective in the Academy*, ed. Elizabeth Langland and Walter Gove, 7–24. Chicago: University of Chicago Press, 1981.

———. *The Female Imagination*. New York: Knopf, 1972.

———. "Fiction Chronicle." Review of *Fear of Flying* (and other novels). *Hudson Review* (Summer 1974): 283–95.

Spencer, Gary. "An Analysis of JAP-Baiting Humor on the College Campus." *Humor: International Journal of Humor Research* 2:4 (1989): 329–48.

Stanley, Alessandra. "Too Blue." Review of *Any Woman's Blues. Time*, February 5, 1990, 67–68.

Stein, Benjamin. "The Painful Acquisition of Self-Esteem." Review of *Fear of Flying. Wall Street Journal*, May 8, 1974, 20.

Steinem, Gloria, with Joanne Edgar and Mary Thom. *Post-ERA Politics: Losing a Battle but Winning the War? Ms.* (January 1983): 35–38.

Stokes, Terry. "In Freud's Old Backyard: *Fear of Flying.*" Review of *Fear of Flying. New York Times Book Review*, November 11, 1973, 40.

Suleiman, Susan Rubin. "(Re)Writing the Body: The Politics and Poetics of Female Eroticism." In *The Female Body in Western Culture: Contemporary Perspectives*, ed. Susan Rubin Suleiman, 7–29. Cambridge: Harvard University Press, 1985.

————. *Subversive Intent: Gender, Politics, and the Avant-Garde.* Cambridge: Harvard University Press, 1990.

Surette, Leon. "Creating the Canadian Canon." In *Canadian Canons: Essays in Literary Value*, ed. Robert Lecker, 17–29. Toronto: University of Toronto Press, 1991.

Sutherland, John. *Bestsellers: Popular Fiction of the 1970's.* London: Routledge, 1981.

Templin, Charlotte. "Sources for the 'Aging Midget-cum-Literary Critic' in Erica Jong's *How to Save Your Own Life.*" *Notes on Contemporary Literature* 21:1 (January 1991): 12.

Theroux, Paul. "Hapless Organ." Review of *Fear of Flying. New Statesman*, April 19, 1974, 554.

Thompson, Margaret Cezair. Review of *Any Woman's Blues. Elle* (January 1990): 69.

Todd, Janet. *The Sign of Angelica: Women, Writing, and Fiction, 1660-1800.* New York: Columbia University Press, 1989.

————. *Women Writers Talking.* New York: Holmes and Meier, 1983.

Tompkins, Jane. *Sensational Designs: The Cultural Work of American Fiction, 1790-1860.* New York: Oxford University Press, 1985.

Toth, Emily. "Dorothy Parker, Erica Jong, and the New Feminist Humor." *Regionalism and the Female Imagination* 3:2,3 (1977–1978): 70–85.

Tovey, Roberta. Review of *How to Save Your Own Life. New Republic*, March 19, 1977, 34–35.

"Trading Cards Introduced for the Young Girl." *New York Times*, February 5, 1980, 4B.

Treglown, Jeremy. "Zippy." Review of *How to Save Your Own Life* (and other novels). *New Statesman*, May 6, 1977, 612–13.

Tyrrell, R. Emmett, Jr. "Call It Women's Glib." *New York Times*, April 16, 1979, A17.

Updike, John. "Jong Love." Review of *Fear of Flying. New Yorker*, December 17, 1973, 149–51.

_____. *Picked-Up Pieces*. New York: Knopf, 1975.

Vidal, Gore. "From Outlaws to Intriguers." Review of *The Durrell-Miller Letters, 1935–1980*, ed. Ian S. MacNiven. *Times Literary Supplement*, September 9–15, 1988, 979.

Vincent, Sally. "Knee-Jerk Feminists." *Observer*, October 14, 1979, 64.

Wakefield, Dan. "A Novel Suggestion for TV." *New York Times Book Review*, January 19, 1975, 43.

Walker, Nancy A. *Feminist Alternatives: Irony and Fantasy in the Contemporary Novel by Women*. Jackson: University Press of Mississippi, 1990.

_____. *A Very Serious Thing: Women's Humor and American Culture*. Minneapolis: University of Minnesota Press, 1988.

Walker, Nancy A., and Zita Dresner, eds. *Redressing the Balance: American Women's Literary Humor from Colonial Times to the 1980's*. Jackson: University Press of Mississippi, 1988.

Warren, Joyce W. "Introduction." In *Ruth Hall and Other Writings* (Fanny Fern), ix–xxxix. New Brunswick: Rutgers University Press, 1986.

Waugh, Auberon. "How to Write a Sex Manual." Review of *How to Save Your Own Life*. *Evening Standard*, May 3, 1977, 20.

Weissman, Michaela. "The Rooms Where Writers Write." *New York Times*, January 22, 1981, C6.

Weissman, Stephen. "The Voltaire Project: A Collector's Obsession." *New York Times Book Review*, July 1, 1990, 23.

"What's Gone Wrong with the Women's Movement?" *Harper's Bazaar* (February 1976): 59, 141.

White, Hayden. "Historical Pluralism." *Critical Inquiry* 12:3 (1986): 480–93.

Widdowson, Peter. *Hardy in History: A Study in Literary Sociology*. London: Routledge, 1989.

Willis, Ellen. "The Feminist Papers: Betty Friedan's 'Second Stage': A Step Backward." *Nation*, November 14, 1981, 494–96.

Willis, Meredith Sue. "Yes to Family, No to Monogamy." Review of *In Every Woman's Life* by Alix Kates Shulman. *New York Times Book Review*, May 31, 1987, 56.

Wilson, Jane. "Erica Jong: Her Life Is an Open Book." *Los Angeles Times*, November 24, 1974, D1, D8–10.

Wolf, Naomi. *Fire with Fire: The New Female Power and How It Will Change the 21st Century*. New York: Random House, 1993.

Wood, Michael. "Flirting with Disintegration." Review of *Fear of Flying* (and other novels). *New York Review of Books*, March 21, 1974, 19–20.

Yglesias, Helen. "Odd Woman Out." Review of *Cat's Eye* by Margaret Atwood. *Women's Review of Books* (July 1989): 3–4.

Index

Abel, Elizabeth, 171
Abzug, Bella, 73, 128
Academic authorities, 167, 168, 185-86
  feminist, 168, 170-71, 173, 175, 177-80
Academic institutions, 10, 17
  and women, 8, 17
Academic reputation, 167, 169-75
Ackroyd, Peter, 93, 94, 96, 196(n29)
Adrian Goodlove (literary character), 26-27
Aesthetic value, 17, 18, 20-21, 66
Agnew, Spiro, 92
Aiken, Joan, 152, 157-58, 200(n26)
Algonquin Hotel, 72
Alternative press, 15, 21
Alther, Lisa, 3, 172
"Altitude Sickness" (anon.), 49
America, 136
American Bookseller's Association, 69
American Scholar, 17
American Spectator, 43, 106, 111, 112
American Stock Exchange, 30
Amiel, Barbara, 136
Amis, Kingsley, 50, 115
Amis, Martin, 50-51, 52, 192(n22)
Angelou, Maya, 128
Anthony, Susan B., dollar, 107
Antifeminists, 107, 132, 133-36
Antioch Review, 178
Anti-Semitism, 34, 35, 182, 184
Any Woman's Blues (Jong), 14, 151
  autobiographical assumption, 163, 164
  heroine (see Leila Sand)
  narrative structure, 158-59
  and popular culture, 159, 162
  reviews, 21, 63, 151, 152, 158-64, 169, 201(n32)
"Are Women's Novels Feminist Novels?" (Coward), 179
Aristotle, 9
"Art novel," 81
Arts and Humanities Citation Index, 170
Associated Press, 22

Atheism, 114
Atlantic, 111
At the Landing (Welty), 172
Atwood, Margaret, 5, 16, 87, 141, 164, 173, 180
Austen, Jane, 45
Autobiography, 86-87. See also Confessional novel
Avery, Evelyn Gross, 203(n6)
Awakening, The (Chopin), 6
"Awful Truth about Women's Lib, The" (Jong), 164

Bad writing, 46
Banned novels, 6
Barber, Benjamin R., 135, 136
Baumli, Francis, 203(n6)
Beautiful Women; Ugly Scenes (Bryan), 146
Beauvoir, Simone de, 39
Behn, Aphra, 1, 2
Belles Lettres, 87
Bellow, Saul, 87
Bennetts, Leslie, 164
Benokraitis, Nijole V., 132-33
Berger, Thomas, 52
Bergman, Ingmar, 78
Berlin, Irving, 81
Berman, Edgar, 134
Best-sellers, 66, 80, 81, 200(n18)
Bestsellers: Popular Fiction of the 1970's (Sutherland), 170
Bildungsroman, 59, 61, 63, 105, 167, 171-72
Binding, Paul, 156-57, 200(n23)
Birch, Helen, 161-62
Blakely, Mary Kay, 136
Bloom, Allan, 112, 114
Bolotin, Susan, 133
"Bookmark" (television program), 165
Book-of-the-Month Club, 63
Book reviewers, 10, 16, 19-20, 23, 28
  academic, 120-22, 152, 157
  and age, 41

Book reviewers, *continued*
American, 23, 78, 115, 137, 138, 151
British, 23, 38, 48–51, 75, 78, 91–97,
109, 115, 116–19, 137, 140, 146, 151–
52, 156–57, 161–63
conservative women, 40, 41, 42–43
feminist, 44, 57, 98–99, 124, 126, 153,
175–76, 186
French, 202(n4)
and gender, 23, 31, 33, 40–41, 46–54,
86, 95–96, 116, 144, 153, 163
high culture, 76, 80, 89, 90, 98, 102
interests and emotions, 31, 32, 33, 44–
45, 46, 90
novelists as, 28, 29, 31–32, 33, 90–91,
109, 146, 152, 157–58, 162
status of, 78–79, 97
See also Evaluative communities
Boulenger, Ghislaine, 60–61, 193(n32)
Bourdieu, Pierre, 54, 65, 75, 76, 80, 83, 96
Boyd, Nancy, 38
Brantlinger, Patrick, 77, 94
Braudy, Leo, 69, 183–84
*Bread and Circuses: Theories of Mass
Culture as Social Decay* (Brantlinger),
77
British cultural establishment, 92, 95,
122
British Press Awards, 50
British sensibility, 119, 170
Britt Goldstein (literary character), 100
Broner, E. M., 170, 171
Brontë, Anne, 2
Brown, Rita Mae, 172
Browning, Elizabeth Barrett, 2
Broyard, Anatole, 128
Bryan, C. D. B., 131, 139, 146, 199(n9)
Buchwald, Art, 127
Buckley, Jerome, 171
Buckley, William F., Jr., 30
Burckhardt, Jacob, 114
Burgess, Anthony, 81, 82, 92, 107, 109,
122–24, 140, 156, 157, 198(n14)
Butler, Robert J., 172, 174

Campbell, Mary, 22
Canada, 5
"Can a Million Americans Be Wrong?"
(Brown), 92
Candide (Voltaire), 38
Canfield Decision, The (Agnew), 92
Canon formation, 9–11, 13, 22. *See also*
Precanonical status
Cantwell, Mary, 180
Capote, Truman, 165

Carnival of the Animals, The (Saint
Saëns), 38
Catcher in the Rye, The (Salinger), 55
Cather, Willa, 7, 170
Cat's Eye (Atwood), 87, 141
CBS, Inc., 130
Censorship, 68
Centennial Review, 172
Chafe, William, 134
"Changing My Mind about Andrea
Dworkin" (Jong), 153–54
*Changing the Story: Feminist Fiction and
the Tradition* (Greene), 174
Charen, Mona, 136
Charney, Maurice, 172
Chicago Tribune, 16, 66, 67, 201(n32)
Chicago Tribune Book World, 85, 115,
144
Chopin, Kate, 6
Christian Science Monitor, 142
Cibber, Theophilus, 103
Civilization and Its Discontents (Freud),
119
Clapp, Suzannah, 157, 200(n24)
Clark, John R., 203(n6)
Class-based elite culture, 48
Cleland, John, 103, 105, 113, 119, 122
Coarseness, 2
Coates, Joseph, 201(n32)
Colander, Pat, 67
Cold War intellectuals, 7, 77
Cole, Diane, 155–56
Colette, 165
Collectivist ideology, 178
Collins, Jim, 65, 76, 77
Columbia Forum, 64, 177
Columbia Pictures (company), 67
Columbia University, 27
Comic mode, 38, 55
Commentary, 13, 42, 176
Commercialism, 48, 49
Commodification of art, 141
*Compleat Chauvinist, The: A Survival
Guide for the Bedeviled Male* (Ber-
man), 134
Confessional novel, 2, 3, 23, 37–38, 58,
86, 87, 89, 95
and gender, 87, 88, 95–96
Consciousness raising (CR), 58
Conservatives, 132. *See also* Cultural con-
servatives
Consuming Fiction (Lovell), 80
Consumption metaphors, 83, 186
Contemporary Literature, 175
Contingencies of Value: Alternative Per-

spectives for Critical Theory (Barbara Herrnstein Smith), 8
Cooke, Judy, 117–18, 126
Copland, Aaron, 22
Coward, Rosalind, 179
Coyne, Patricia S., 43
Crain, Jane Larkin, 42–43, 171, 176, 190(n12)
Creating Faulkner's Reputation: The Politics of Modern Literary Criticism (Schwartz), 7
Critics, 10, 37
    female, 40, 41, 42, 45, 46
    feminist, 6, 41
    male, 3, 6, 21, 33, 40–41, 46–54
    See also Book reviewers
Cultural authority, 10, 21, 66, 76, 102, 169
    and women, 77, 186
Cultural conservatives, 37, 38, 40, 41, 42–44, 47, 110, 116, 117
Cultural continuity, 114, 117
Cultural history, 11, 118
Cultural lag, 43
Cultural production, 65
Cultural values, 8, 45, 76
    and women, 187
Cunningham, Valentine, 152, 157, 200(n25)

Daily Mail (London), 34
Daley, Tammy K., 136
Darling, Lynn, 108
"Daughters" (Jong), 67
Davies, Bronwyn, 36
"Defenders of the Faith and the New Class" (Ross), 24
DeMott, Benjamin, 48, 63, 152, 160–61, 191(n19)
Denver Quarterly, 172
Derrida, Jacques, 9
Descartes, René, 10
Devil at Large, The: Erica Jong on Henry Miller (Jong), 5
Dialectic of Sex, The: The Case for Feminist Revolution (Firestone), 39
Diamond, Arlyn, 170
Diaries of Jane Somers, The (Lessing), 147
Diary of a Good Neighbor, The (Somers), 147
Didion, Joan, 3, 78
Dillon, Millicent, 41, 44, 45, 190(n14)
"Dirty Ladies, The: Earthy Writings of Contemporary American Women" (Broner), 170

Distinction: A Social Critique of the Judgement of Taste (Bourdieu), 53–54, 75, 83
"Distinguished women of letters" series, 62, 68
Doane, Janice, 51, 52
"Donahue" (television program), 153
Donne, John, 2, 10
"Dorothy Parker, Erica Jong, and the New Feminist Humor" (Toth), 170
Drabble, Margaret, 128, 173
Dresner, Zita, 174
Durrell, Lawrence, 52
Duval, Joanne, 125, 126
Dworkin, Andrea, 22, 33, 153–54, 179, 189(n3)
Dworkin, Susan, 125–26, 198(n16)

Edith Bunker Memorial Fund, 106
Editors, 27, 28, 127
Educational novel, 171
Ehrenreich, Barbara, 39, 46, 135, 138
Eighteenth century, 103, 104, 109, 110, 115, 116, 117, 121, 123, 124, 126
Eliot, George, 8, 10
Elle, 161
Encounter, 136
English women writers, 1, 2
Equality, 39, 135
Equal Rights Amendment (ERA), 30, 72, 73, 106, 107, 132, 135
Esquire, 50, 67
European tradition, 110
Evaluative communities, 36, 37, 142, 152–53
Evans, Stuart, 118
Evans, Timothy J., 49
Evening Standard (London), 95
Existential modernist, 7

Family relationships, 178
Fanny: Being the True History of the Adventures of Fanny Hackabout-Jones (Jong), 103–4, 105, 154, 155
    academic literary analysis, 104, 109, 120–22, 157, 171–72, 177–78
    characters, 103
    as feminist, 103, 105, 110, 111, 112, 114, 115–17, 118–19, 121, 125, 126, 172
    humor, 125
    language, 110, 111, 113, 121, 123–24
    literary allusions, 171–72
    mother-daughter relationship, 108

Fanny: Being the True History of the Adventures of Fanny Hackabout-Jones, continued
  as novel of ideas, 120, 126
  published excerpts, 104
  publisher, 104
  reception of, 105, 107, 109
  reviews, 4–5, 14, 15, 16, 21, 32, 107, 109–27
  as success, 127
Fanny Hill (Cleland), 103, 105, 113, 117, 119, 122
Farnol, Jeffrey, 118
Fast, Jonathan, 67, 130
Faulkner, William, 7
Feagin, Joe R., 132–33
Fear of Flying (Jong), 3, 4, 11, 21, 70, 91, 113, 146, 149–50, 182, 190(n11)
  allusions in, 53, 171, 173
  autobiographical elements in, 87
  as best-seller, 66, 81
  compared to *Fanny*, 104
  epigraphs, 53
  fan letters, 63
  as feminist, 38, 55–61, 63–64, 98, 102, 174
  fifteenth anniversary reprinting, 29, 63
  film script, 67
  galleys, 26, 27
  irony, 174
  Jong on, 81–82
  literary evaluation, 30, 170–71, 172, 174, 177
  literary reputation, 28, 30, 170
  in literature courses, 69
  paperback, 27, 29, 175
  plot, 26–27
  promotion of, 27, 29
  and reality, 46, 61
  review, most favorable, 54
  reviewers, 31, 40–51, 74
  reviews, 22, 26, 28, 29, 34–35, 37, 38, 41, 42–44, 45, 46, 47–57, 59–61, 74, 78, 79, 89, 94, 115, 191(n20)
  sales, 29, 84
  and sexual politics, 12, 40
  ten-year anniversary, 130
  typesetters, 26
  See also under Isadora Wing
Felski, Rita, 21, 58, 180
"Female Bloom," 57
Female body, 84, 126, 173
Female Body in Western Culture, The: Contemporary Perspectives (Suleiman), 173

Female bonding, 108
"Female Novel of Development and the Myth of Psyche, The" (Ferguson), 172
Feminism, 9, 29–30, 46
  acceptance of, 105–6, 107
  changes, 131–32, 133–34, 178–79
  cultural, 39, 108
  and Freudianism, 42
  high expectations of, 133
  journals, 15, 106
  and lesbianism, 133
  and media, 73–74
  middle-class, 178
  radical, 39, 41, 57–58, 107, 135
  success, 72–73
  survey, 72
  tensions in, 61, 107–8
  See also Antifeminists; Postfeminist age; *under* Jong, Erica
"Feminism, 'Postfeminism' and Contemporary Women's Fiction" (Rosenfelt), 133
Feminist Alternatives: Irony and Fantasy in the Contemporary Novel by Women (Walker), 168, 173, 174
Feminist authors, 78, 98, 163
Feminist criticism, 17, 21, 37, 45, 64, 98–99, 168, 170–71, 173, 174, 175, 177–80, 186
Feminist movement, 11, 30, 39, 40, 111–12
Feminist reviews, 21, 44, 57, 98–99. *See also* Book reviewers, feminist
Feminist scholars, 168, 170–71, 177–80
Feminist Studies, 164
Ferguson, Mary Anne, 171, 174
Fern, Fanny. *See* Willis, Sara Payson
Fielding, Henry, 105, 116, 117, 121, 163
Film industry, 10, 100–101
Firestone, Shulamith, 39
Fish, Stanley, 9, 20
Fisher, Craig, 100, 197(n35)
Fitzgerald, Karen, 200(n17)
"Flying from Work" (Diamond), 170
Follett, Ken, 183
Ford, Gerald, 68
Foundations, 10
Fox-Genovese, Elizabeth, 178
France, 6, 202(n4)
Franckling, Ken, 149
Freely, Maureen, 152, 156, 200(n22)
French, Marilyn, 128
Frenzy of Renown, The: Fame and Its History (Braudy), 69, 183
Freud, Sigmund, 50, 119

Freudianism, 42, 113
Friedan, Betty, 38–39, 73, 107
Friedman, Alan, 16, 107, 109, 120–21,
    198(n12)
Friendship, 100
*From Reverence to Rape: The Treatment
    of Women in the Movies* (Haskell), 59
Frontiers, 170
Fruits & Vegetables (Jong), 27
Frye, Northrup, 13
Fuchs, Marcia, 99, 197(n34)
Fundamentalist religion, 132

Gans, Herbert J., 23, 81
Gardner, Ralph, 105
Generic review, 156–57
Geng, Victoria, 38, 57
"Geraldo" (television program), 164
Getlin, Josh, 164
Gilbert, Sandra M., 177
Gilder, Joshua, 112–13, 116, 121, 197(n6)
Giovanni, Nikki, 68
Glamour, 127, 130, 164
Glasgow, Ellen, 5
Glendinning, Victoria, 148, 199(n12)
"Gobbling It All Up" (Sage), 94–95
Goldman, James, 16, 109, 115, 119,
    197(n8)
Gosling, Ray, 92
Gould, Becky, 70
Gould, Lois, 3, 45
Graeber, Laurel, 72
Gramsci, Antonio, 106
Grasso, Ella, 128
Green, Hannah, 175
Greene, Gayle, 174
Greer, Germaine, 30
Gribben, Alan, 38
Grossman, Anita Susan, 138, 140, 144
Gubar, Susan, 177
Guilt as aphrodisiac, 173
Gynecological novel, 53

Haley, Alex, 114
Half-Lives (Jong), 27
Hamlet (Shakespeare), 7
"Hapless Organ" (Theroux), 49
Happy ending, 81, 83
Hardy, Thomas, 7
Harper's, 13, 113
Harper's Bazaar, 73, 130
Harré, Rom, 36
Harwood, Ronald, 96, 197(n32)
Haskell, Molly, 59–60, 140, 192(n30)
Hawn, Goldie, 128

Hawthorne, Nathaniel, 32–33, 101
*Hearts of Men, The: American Dreams
    and the Flight from Commitment*
    (Ehrenreich), 135
Hegemony, 106–7, 123, 137
Helgesen, Sally, 110, 113–14, 116,
    197(n7)
Heller, Joseph, 127
Hellman, Lillian, 68
Henderson, Katherine Usher, 165
Heraclitus, 77
Here Comes and Other Poems (Jong), 71
Hess, Elizabeth, 39
Hess, Rudolf, 50
Hewlett, Sylvia Ann, 164
Hierarchies, 24
High culture, 46, 65, 74, 75–77, 81, 185
    simplicity versus complexity, 82
    and women, 80, 98
    See also under Book reviewers
Hirsh, Marianne, 171
History, 110, 114, 116, 197(n5)
Hite, Molly, 47
Hochman, Sandra, 45
Hodges, Devon, 51, 52
Hogarth, William, 103
Holley, Marietta, 38
Hollywood, 100–101
Holt, Rinehart and Winston, 27, 28
Holtzman, Elizabeth, 73
Homer, 7, 10
Hood, Ann, 201(n32)
Hoover, Julie, 14
Hopkins, Gerard Manley, 2
Horizon, 127
"How to Recognize a Poem When You See
    One" (Fish), 20
How to Save Your Own Life (Jong), 3–4,
    21, 81
    autobiographical assumption, 86, 88–
    90, 105
    cover, 75, 85
    excerpts published, 67
    lesbian episode, 96
    as popular culture, 77–78, 79, 82, 94
    reception of, 84, 130
    response to, 75, 77–78
    reviews, 4, 15, 22, 35, 74, 75, 78, 79, 82,
    84–100, 115
    sales, 95
    See also under Isadora Wing
How to Suppress Women's Writing (Russ),
    1
Huck Finn (Twain), 74
Hudson Review, 169

Hull, E. M., 93
Humanists, 45
Humor: International Journal of Humor Research, 35
Humorous raunchy novel, 145
Huyssen, Andreas, 79–80

Icarus myth, 171
Ice and Fire (Dworkin), 153
Individualism, 134, 178
In Every Woman's Life (Shulman), 148
Ingenue, 67
Institutional readers, 8, 12
Intellectuals, 7, 77, 141. See also High culture
Intercourse (Dworkin), 153
International Journal of Women's Studies, 171
International women's year (1978), 72–73
In the Lion's Den (Waugh), 95
Irigaray, Luce, 128
Irony, 173, 174
Irving, John, 52
Isabell, Sharon, 172
" 'Isadora-Icarus': The Mythic Unity of Erica Jong's Fear of Flying" (Nitzsche), 171
Isadora Wing (literary character), 12, 103, 104, 128, 142, 173
  and Any Woman's Blues, 158
  in Fear of Flying, 26, 45, 49, 50, 51, 56, 57, 59–60, 61, 113, 146, 160, 172
  in How to Save Your Own Life, 26, 84–85, 89, 90, 93, 94, 96, 99, 100, 130, 142
  in Parachutes & Kisses, 131, 138, 139, 140, 143, 144, 145, 146–47, 148, 149, 150
Is There a Text in This Class? The Authority of Interpretive Communities (Fish), 9
"Is There Life after Being a Good Girl?" (Jong), 164
"Is There Sexy after Forty?" (Jong), 164

Jackson, Marni, 159
Jacobs, Gloria, 39
Jacoby, Susan, 200(n21)
James, Clive, 16, 109, 118–19, 127, 198(n11)
Jane Eyre (Bronte), 2
Janeway, Elizabeth, 69, 175
Jewess stereotype, 131
Jewish American Princess (JAP), 35
Jewish writers, 48, 61

Johnson, Diane, 74, 84, 91, 128, 196(n24)
Jong, Erica, 34, 138–39, 153
  alter ego, 26
  art book, 197(n4)
  articles about, 66–67, 69–70, 92, 105, 108–9, 127–28, 129, 150–51, 164, 177, 183, 185
  articles about, in foreign press, 169–70
  articles by, 67, 153, 164–65, 202(n36)
  as celebrity, 66–74, 80, 101, 112, 127–28, 140–41, 166, 168, 180–81, 183, 187
  on celebrity status, 184, 185
  circus appearance, 72, 183
  college campus book tour, 104
  at Columbia University, 27
  criticism of, 2, 3–4, 6, 35, 36, 47, 48–49, 51, 61, 62, 69–70, 73–74, 75, 78, 96, 112, 113, 131, 142–43, 146, 150, 182, 203(n6)
  criticism of writing, 3, 11, 15, 20, 21, 28, 31, 47, 50, 65, 70, 71, 72, 78, 146, 147, 152, 182, 186, 203(n6)
  as "Daring Woman of the Eighties," 128
  daughter, 5, 108
  divorces, 129–30
  and feminism, 11–12, 16, 21, 37, 63, 72, 73, 74, 84, 95, 98, 113, 153, 164–65, 173, 178–79, 180, 182, 186, 187
  humor, 95, 170, 174
  husbands, 67, 108, 129
  literary commentary by, 5, 165
  literary influences on, 10, 63
  literary reputation, 7, 11, 16, 22, 24–25, 52–53, 64, 69, 74, 75, 101, 128, 140, 144, 153, 168, 177, 181, 185, 186–87
  literary reputation among academics, 167, 168, 169, 170–75, 176–80, 185, 186
  literary reputation as bifurcated, 168, 180–81
  media image, 168, 169, 181, 183
  novels, 3, 4, 9, 11, 12, 14, 15, 20, 23, 151, 152–53 (see also individual titles)
  novels, autobiographical elements in, 87, 88, 141
  novels, commercial success, 76, 78, 84, 129
  novels, cover blurbs for, 86
  novels, reception of, 65, 66, 75, 170, 182
  novels, responses to, 21–22, 25, 26, 28, 30, 54, 77
  novels, reviews of, 14, 15, 16, 19, 21–

22, 32, 33, 168, 176 (*see also under individual titles*)
poetry, 27, 63, 69, 91, 129, 130, 165, 174, 202(n3) (*see also individual titles*)
poetry, awards for, 175, 203(n7)
poetry, reviews of, 70-71
and popular culture, 77-78, 79, 82, 94, 131, 152, 153, 159, 162, 168-69, 170, 180
review, least favorite, 50
review, most hostile, 176, 203(n8)
scholarly articles about, 16, 168, 170-71, 175
television appearances, 67, 71-72, 78, 130, 153, 164, 165, 183, 193(n3)
tribute to Henry Miller, 29, 165
writing, 6, 9
as writing woman, 1, 4
Jong, Molly, 5
Jordan, Barbara, 73
Journal of the American Academy of Religion, 170
Journals, 10, 13-15, 177
Joyce, James, 53, 124

Kadushin, Charles, 14
Kaplan, Carey, 12
Kapp, Isa, 89, 196(n21)
Kazin, Alfred, 47-48, 53, 56, 191(n18)
Keating, Peter, 93, 94, 196(n28)
Kelly, Ann, 184
Kemp, Peter, 116, 139, 147, 197(n9)
Kendall, Elaine, 139, 141, 143-44, 198(n6)
Kendrick, Walter, 5-6
Kenner, Hugh, 10
Kern, John L., 109
"Kicking Jong Around" (Prelutsky), 70
Kinflicks (Alther), 3, 172
King, Billie Jean, 30
Kingston, Maxine Hong, 127
Kirsch, Robert, 71
Klein, Julia M., 124-25
Klemesrud, Judy, 108-9
Koedt, Anne, 40
Korelitz, Jean Hanff, 161, 162, 201(n33)
Koster, Elaine, 27, 29

Ladies' Home Journal, 67
Langland, Elizabeth, 172
Lasch, John Irving, 52
Laughridge, Jamie, 130
Lear, Norman, 106, 107

Lee, Hermione, 138, 140, 146-47, 199(n10), 200(n22)
Lehmann-Haupt, Christopher, 28, 88, 171, 191(n20), 195(n19)
Leila Sand (literary character), 158, 159, 160, 161, 162
Leonard, John, 55-56, 74, 90-91, 196(n23)
Lesbians, 96, 98, 99, 133, 165, 177
Lesser Life, A: The Myth of Women's Liberation in America (Hewlett), 164
Lessing, Doris, 12, 147, 173
Lewis, Peter, 152, 162-63, 202(n35)
Libraries, 10
Library Journal, 99
Lichtenstein, Grace, 127-28, 138, 146, 149-50, 199(n14)
Listener (London), 116, 157, 161
Literary critics. *See* Academic authorities; Book reviewers; Critics
Literary establishment, 168
Literary evaluation, 18, 20, 24, 66, 182. *See also* Evaluative communities; Literary value
Literary history, 9, 10, 13
Literary journalists, 13, 31, 128, 151
Literary reputation, 7-8, 10, 11, 13, 23, 25, 28, 30, 32
and media, 141, 151, 168, 182
See also under Jong, Erica
Literary value, 9, 13, 16-17, 18, 24, 25, 45, 48, 54, 62, 66, 111, 186
and academy, 167, 185
and gender, 66
Literature, 80
and academic authorities, 167
canons, 9-11, 13, 22 (*see also* Precanonical status)
and meaning, 8-9, 179
middlebrow, 82
popular, 25
social contexts, 7-8, 9, 10, 17-18, 19, 38, 46
value, 8, 15-16, 17, 18-19, 22, 104
and women, 161
See also High culture; Low culture; Mass culture; Popular culture; Reviewing process
"Literature and the New Bawd" (Dillon), 44
Live or Die (Sexton), 2
Locke, John, 103
London Review of Books, 151, 157
Longfellow, Henry Wadsworth, 32-33
Lord Byron (Thomson opera), 22

Los Angeles Times, 66, 67, 70, 71, 100,
143, 164
Los Angeles Times Book World, 70
Lovell, Terry, 80
Loveroot (Jong), 63, 69
Low culture, 65
as female, 77, 78, 79, 169
Lurie, Alison, 128

McGahern, John, 163
Machine Dreams (Phillips), 140, 147, 148
MacKinnon, Catherine, 179
Maclean's, 136, 154, 159
Mademoiselle, 66, 67, 72
Mailer, Norman, 47, 72, 87, 165, 183
Mainland, Mary, 136
Male-dominated society, 6, 8, 30, 41, 122,
180
Male impersonation, 117
Male impotence, 47
Male power, 90
Male subject, 66
Malone, Michael, 152, 155, 200(n19)
Mandrell, James, 172, 174
Mano, D. Keith, 3, 4, 35, 74, 86, 115,
195(nn15,16)
Marginalization, 179
Marriage, 42
"Marriage: Rational and Irrational"
(Jong), 67
Mars-Jones, Adam, 51, 52
Martin, Judith, 16, 109, 124, 198(n15)
Martin, Wendy, 81
Marxism, 113
Marymount College, 68
Masculine sexual norms, 84
Maslin, Janet, 89–90, 196(n22)
Mass culture, 65, 74, 75, 76, 77
Matriarchal power, 120
Maxwell, William, 88
Meaning, 8–9
Media, 7, 13, 69, 168, 169, 181
and social movements, 137
and women, 8, 182–83
See also under Literary reputation
Mediatization, 181, 182–83, 203(n9)
Megan's Book of Divorce (Jong), 129–30
Meir, Golda, 128
"Menstruation at Forty" (Sexton), 2
Merchant of Venice (Shakespeare), 154,
155
Mesic, Penelope, 84, 85–86, 195(n14)
Metaphor, 83, 89, 143
Meyer, Ellen Hope, 43–44, 45, 190(n13)
Middle class, 113, 178

Middlemarch (Eliot), 8
Millay, Edna St. Vincent, 38
Miller, Henry, 10, 22, 29, 52, 56, 62–63,
64, 67–68, 69, 165, 171, 175,
192(n26)
autobiographical aspects in writing, 87–
88
Millet, Kate, 33, 39
Mind/body dualism, 119
Minorities, invisibility of, 34
Mishan, E. J., 136
Misogyny, 52, 65, 141, 153, 168, 182, 184
"Missionary autobiographies," 43
Mitgang, Herbert, 131, 145, 199(n8)
Modernism, 79–80, 82
Modernists, 7, 10, 65
Modern Language Association (MLA), 62,
68–69, 153, 175, 178, 184
Montrose, David, 161
Moral Majority, 132
Morris, Joan, 81
Morrison, Blake, 136–37, 141
Morrison, Toni, 174, 180
Morrow, Lance, 74, 89, 196(n20)
Mother Goddess, 103
Motherhood, 4–5, 108, 116, 164–65
Ms., 125, 153, 165, 200(n17)
Murray, Margaret A., 103, 120
Mutter, Anne-Sophie, 22–23

Nabokov, Vladimir, 165
Narcissism, 46
Nation, 43, 44
National Advisory Committee for
Women, 105
National Book Award Committee, 165
National Book Critics Circle, 165
National Endowment for the Arts, 62
National Organization for Men, 134
National Organization for Women (NOW),
30, 31, 39, 165
Legal Defense and Education Fund, 106
National Review, 3, 43, 74, 86, 111, 136
National Women's Hall of Fame, 105–6
Nelson, Cary, 9
New American Library (NAL), 27, 104
Newcomb, John Timberman, 10
New Critics, 17
New Directions for Women, 15, 106, 125
New Literary History, 170
New Republic, 13, 14, 15, 61, 90, 124,
135, 136, 176
New Statesman (London), 23, 43, 50, 92,
117, 176
Newsweek, 66, 69, 89, 143

New Yorker, 13, 15, 28, 54
New York literary scene, 32
New York Review of Books, 13, 14, 16, 91, 118
New York State Department of Education, 106
New York Times, 28, 29, 31, 56, 88, 111, 127, 129, 145, 183
  best-seller list, 28
  "Style" section, 108
  survey of college students and women's movement, 72
  women featured in, 106
New York Times Book Review, 6, 13, 14, 16, 28, 78–79, 90, 120, 127, 128, 137, 141, 146, 148, 151, 155, 160
  Jong comments on, 32
  letters, 22
  readership, 14
  and women novelists, 148–49
New York Times Magazine, 133
Nietzsche, Friedrich, 77, 79
Nin, Anaïs, 68
99 Novels: The Best in English since 1939, A Personal Choice (Burgess), 81
Nitzsche, Jane Chance, 171, 174, 175
No Man's Land: The Place of the Woman Writer in the Twentieth Century (Gilbert and Gubar), 177
No Respect: Intellectuals and Popular Culture (Ross), 77, 92, 106
Norway, 6
Nostalgia and Sexual Difference: The Resistance to Contemporary Feminism (Doane and Hodges), 51
Notes for a New Culture: An Essay on Modernism (Ackroyd), 93
"Notes on Five Men" (Jong), 67
Novak, Ralph, 160, 201(n30)
Novel, 172, 174
Novel form, 80
Novelist-reviewer. *See* Book reviewers, novelists as
NOW. *See* National Organization for Women

Oates, Joyce Carol, 127, 141
O'Brien, Sharon, 7
Observer (London), 23, 50, 94, 97, 116, 136, 137, 141, 146, 151, 156
Ohmann, Richard, 13, 14, 15, 22, 23, 27, 78, 80, 81, 137, 151, 176, 177
Omni, 127
Onwurah, Chinyelu, 136
Ordinary Miracles (Jong), 129, 130

Orwell, George, 7, 101
Oxford University, 23

Paley, Grace, 128
Pan-textualists, 197(n5)
Parachutes & Kisses (Jong), 14, 21, 130
  as autobiographical, 131, 144
  epigraph, 129
  irony, 174
  literary allusions, 145, 148
  as popular culture, 131
  reviews, 131, 137–51, 199(n15)
  See also under Isadora Wing
Parker, Rozsika (Rosie), 60, 177, 192(n31)
Partisan Review, 9, 13
Patai, Daphne, 34
Patriarchal structures, 80, 186
Pearlman, Mickey, 87
PEN (writers' group), 72, 183
Penelope, Julia, 2
People, 15
People Weekly, 131, 159
Perelman, S. J., 145
Perloff, Marjorie, 70
Phillips, Jayne Anne, 140, 147, 148
Phillips, Julia, 67
Phillips, William, 9, 10
Picaresque, 172
Picked-Up Pieces (Updike), 64
Plath, Sylvia, 45, 50
Plato, 9
Playboy, 15, 63, 66, 67, 145, 185
"Pleasures and Problems of Living Together, The" (Selden), 67
Poets and Writers, Inc., 183
Pogrebin, Letty Cottin, 165
Poirier, Richard, 50
Polar, Dana, 182
Political consciousness of women, 58
Political correctness, 179
"Pollution of agency," 2, 3, 4
Pope, Alexander, 103, 116, 117
Popular culture, 48, 75, 79, 82, 131, 142, 152. *See also* Mass culture
Popular Culture and High Culture: An Analysis and Evaluation of Taste (Gans), 23
Popular reputation, 167
Portnoy's Complaint (Roth), 55, 140, 172–73
"Positioning: The Discursive Production of Selves" (Davies and Harré), 36–37
Postfeminist age, 131, 132–33, 137, 138, 139, 161, 164–65
Postmodernism, 24, 65, 76, 79–80, 169

Poststructural theory, 7, 18
Power, 8, 24, 30, 90, 120
Precanonical status, 63, 74, 78, 80, 174, 181
  preconditions for, 177
Prelutsky, Burt, 70
Presidential advisers on women's issues, 105
Princeton University, 107
Pritchard, William H., 169
Prolific writers, 141
Proper woman concept, 1, 4, 5
Prose, Francine, 152, 159, 201(n28)
Psychiatrists, 42
Public reputation, 167
Publishing industry, 8, 14
Pyrah, Gill, 150-51

"Questions of Genre and Gender: Contemporary American Versions of the Feminine Picaresque" (Mandrell), 172

Radford, Jean, 98-99, 197(n33)
Radhakrishnan, R., 107
Radway, Janice A., 18, 19, 66, 83
Readers, 18, 45
  evaluations of, 20, 83
  and gender, 66, 102, 112, 182, 197(n36)
  review, 14, 16
  and reviewers, 83, 84
  romance, 19
Readership study, 14
Reading the Romance: Women, Patriarchy, and Popular Romance (Radway), 19, 83
Reardon, Joan, 171, 174, 175, 176
Redford, Robert, 164
Redressing the Balance: American Women's Literary Humor from Colonial Times to the 1980's (Walker and Dresner), 174
Regionalism and the Female Imagination (journal), 170
Re-Making Love: The Feminization of Sex (Ehrenreich et al.), 39
Republicans, 132
Reputation, 167, 202(n1). See also Literary reputation
Rest Is Done with Mirrors, The (See), 165
Reuben, Elaine, 61, 193(n33)
"Revenge Symposium" (Esquire), 50
Reviewing process, 13-20, 22
  gender bias, 15
Reviewing the Reviews: A Woman's Place

on the Book Page (Cooter et al.), 15, 33
Review of Contemporary Literature, 175
Rice University, 69
Rich, Adrienne, 33
Rifkind, Donna, 159, 201(n29)
Riggs, Bobby, 30
Rivers, Caryl, 135
Robinson, Jill, 128
Robinson, Marilynne, 180
Rocky Mountain Review, 170
Rodden, John, 101, 167
Rogers, Carl R., 48
Rogers, Pat, 107, 109, 110, 121-22, 198(n13)
Roiphe, Anne Richardson, 45
Roiphe, Katie, 179
Roman à clef, 144
Romance novel, 93
Romance readers, 19
Romantic fantasies, 142
Room of One's Own, A (Woolf), 3
Roots (Haley), 114
Rose, Ellen Cronan, 12
Rosenfelt, Deborah (Silverton), 132, 133, 164
Ross, Andrew, 24, 77, 92, 106
Roth, Philip, 140, 172
Rubin, Merle, 139, 141, 142-43, 144, 198(n5)
Rubyfruit Jungle (Brown), 172
Russ, Joanna, 1-2, 3, 5, 173
Russia, 138, 139, 143, 145
Ruth Hall (Willis), 6
Ryan, Barbara, 132, 134

Sabin, Albert, 127
Sage, Lorna, 94-95, 97, 116-17, 196(n30)
Saint-Saëns, Camille, 38
Salmagundi, 170
Sappho, 7
Sarachild, Kathie, 39
Sarton, May, 128
"Sass," 160
Saturday Review, 13, 15, 122
Savvy Woman, 159
Sawyer, Forrest, 130
Scapegoating, 182, 184
Schaeffer, Susan Fromberg, 87
Schwartz, Lawrence H., 7
Schwartz, Lynne Sharon, 148
Scruton, Roger, 53, 136
Seaman, Barbara, 40
Season of Youth (Buckley), 171
Second Stage, The (Friedan), 107

Second Wave Feminism, 132
See, Carolyn, 152, 165, 200(n21)
Self-help, 158
Self-indulgence, 46, 116, 117, 139, 147,
    148, 160, 168, 169
Self-irony, 173
Self-promotion, 47
*Sensational Designs: The Cultural Work
    of American Fiction, 1790-1860*
    (Tompkins), 18, 32
Serenissima: A Novel of Venice (Jong), 14,
    21, 151
  dialogue, 158
  language, 157
  literary allusions, 155
  plot, 154
  reviews, 151, 152, 153, 154-58
  sales, 200(nn18,27)
Settle, Mary Lee, 127
Sex, 94, 119, 143, 161
  and age, 131, 142
  eighteenth-century attitude, 104
  female expression of, 9, 20, 25, 46, 53,
    140, 149, 161, 185
  heterosexual, 179
  male expression of, 52, 119, 140
  pornographic, 126
Sex discrimination, 133
Sex equality, 132, 133
Sexton, Anne, 2, 50
Sexual explicitness, 20, 40, 46, 52, 109,
    127, 140, 148, 156
Sexual fantasies, 58-59, 60, 68, 119, 171
Sexual Fiction (Charnel), 172
Sexual impropriety, 1
Sexual intimidation, 4
Sexuality, 3, 6, 25, 31, 40, 47, 116, 119,
    122, 127, 131, 178, 185, 187
  of women writers, 35-36
Sexual liberation, 39
"Sexual poetics," 173
Sexual politics, 12, 40, 108, 115, 132, 133,
    178
Sexual Politics (Millet), 39
Sexual promiscuity, 49
Sexual relationships, 39, 40
Sexual revolution, 39-40
Shaftesbury, Anthony Ashley Cooper, 103
Shakespeare, Nicholas, 147-48
Shakespeare, William, 10, 141, 154
Shapiro, Laura, 143
Shaw, Peter, 17, 18
Sheehy, Gail, 106
Shelton, Frank W., 170

Showalter, Elaine, 2, 64, 177
Shulman, Alix Kates, 40, 45, 148
Sigal, Clancy, 131, 139, 140, 144-45, 199(n7)
*Sign of Angelica, The: Women, Writing,
    and Fiction, 1660-1800* (Todd), 1
Siller, Sidney, 134
Sills, Beverly, 128
Simon, Neil, 127
Simpson, Louis, 2
Sinclair, Andrew, 152, 162, 202(n34)
Sixteenth century, 154
Sixty Minutes (television program), 67-68
Smeal, Eleanor, 73, 165
Smith, Barbara Herrnstein, 8, 16, 18, 45,
    62, 97, 98, 167
Smith, Carol, 64, 177
Smithsonian Institution, 62, 68
Smollett, Tobias, 121
Snyder, Tom, 67
Social change, 30-31, 51
Social equality, 39
Solipsism, 40, 44, 46, 57
Somers, Jane, 147
South Atlantic Review, 10
Spacks, Patricia Meyer, 45-46, 191(n17)
Spare Rib, 15, 24, 60, 98, 176, 177
Spectator (London), 93, 95
Spencer, Gary, 35
Stacey, Judith, 132, 164
Stand Magazine, 162
Stanley, Alessandra, 159
Status quo, 30, 43
Stein, Benjamin, 56-57, 192(n27)
Steinem, Gloria, 73, 164
Stephens, Eleanor, 177
Storey, David, 78
Styron, William, 127
*Subversive Intent: Gender, Politics, and
    the Avant Garde* (Suleiman), 173
Such Good Friends (Gould), 3
Suleiman, Susan Rubin, 173, 174
Sunday Times (London), 92, 96, 147, 162
"Supersister" trading cards, 106
Surplus visibility, 34-35
Sutherland, John, 170
Swift, Jonathan, 103, 116, 125, 184

Taste, 24, 54, 75, 76, 118
  hierarchies, 83
Tenant of Wildfell Hall, The (Brontë), 2
Theroux, Paul, 49-50, 51, 53, 115, 171,
    176, 192(n21)
Thomas, Margaret Darlene, 156, 200(n27)
Thompson, Margaret Cezair, 161
Thomson, Virgil, 22

Threepenny Review, 44
Time, 70, 74, 89, 159
Times (London), 147, 150, 162
Times Literary Supplement (TLS) (London), 23, 49, 51, 53, 93, 121, 127, 137, 141, 147, 151, 157, 161
Todd, Janet, 1, 91, 128
Tom Jones (Fielding), 105, 124
Tompkins, Jane, 18–19, 32, 101
Toth, Emily, 170, 176
Tovey, Roberta, 90
Traditional values, 132, 134
Treglown, Jeremy, 92–93, 196(n27)
Twain, Mark, 38, 141
Twentieth Century Literature, 69, 175
Twice-Told Tales (Hawthorne), 32
Tyrrell, R. Emmett, Jr., 106, 111–12

Ullmann, Liv, 67
Ulysses (Joyce), 124
Uncommon Cultures: Popular Culture and Post-Modernism (Collins), 65
United Press International (UPI), 149
University of California, Los Angeles (UCLA), 69
University of Chicago, 68
University of Michigan, 30
University of Wisconsin, 69
University professors, 10, 12, 14, 24, 31
Updike, John, 10, 22, 28, 29, 54–56, 62–63, 64, 74, 140, 160, 192(n24)
USA Today, 153, 155
U.S. News and World Report, 136
Utilitarian realm, 18

Vacuum cleaner art, 143
Value. *See* Literary value; *under* Literature
Vanity Fair, 164
Vassar College, 68
Venice (Italy), 154
Very Serious Thing, A: Women's Humor and American Culture (Walker), 174
Vidal, Gore, 47, 52, 169
Vietnam syndrome, 132
Village Voice, 176
Village Voice Literary Supplement, 59
Vogue, 67, 104, 136, 164, 185
Voltaire, François, 38
Von Karajan, Herbert, 22
Voyage In, The: Female Fictions of Development (Abel et al.), 171–72
Vulgarity, 46, 47, 48, 49, 50, 51, 89, 146, 173
    and mass culture, 77

Walker, Nancy A., 168, 173–74
Wallace, Mike, 67–68
Wall Street, 30
Wall Street Journal, 56, 144, 159
Walters, Barbara, 67
War and Peace (Tolstoy), 7
Washington Post, 16, 68, 89, 108, 124, 149, 176, 201(n32)
Washington Post Book World, 157
Waugh, Auberon, 95–96, 196(n31)
Weissman, Stephen, 38
Weldon, Fay, 156, 180
Welty, Eudora, 172
White, Hayden, 110
White, Patrick, 78
Whores, 1
Wife of Bath, 54, 63
Williams, Raymond, 163
Willis, Ellen, 107
Willis, Sara Payson, 6
Wilson, Meredith Sue, 148
Witchcraft, 103, 120
Witches, 1, 108, 111, 118
Witches (Jong), 197(n4)
WNET, 164
Wolf, Naomi, 179
Woman as subject, 9
Womanhood, 135
"Woman Writer as American Picaro, The: Open Journeying in Erica Jong's *Fear of Flying*" (Butler), 172
Women in politics, 106
Women in Publishing (British group), 15, 33
Women's liberation debate (Cambridge Union), 30
Women's movement, 31, 43, 46, 73, 95, 136
    branches, 38–39
    success, 73, 84
    survey, 72
    See also Feminism; Feminist movement
Women's Review of Books, 141
Women's sexuality conference, 31
Women's sexual role, 9
Women's studies, 72, 107
Women writers, 1, 2, 80, 87, 101–2, 148, 153, 187. *See also* Feminist authors; Writing women
Women Writers Talking (Todd), 128
Woolf, Virginia, 3
"Writer as Sexual Show-Off, The: Or, Making Press Agents Unnecessary" (Kazin), 47
Writers, known and celebrity, 166, 183
Writer's Digest, 109, 127

Writers Guild, 33
Writers Talk to Ralph Gardner (Gardner), 105
"Writer Who 'Flew' to Sexy Fame Talks about Being a Woman" (Jong), 67
Writing woman, 1
  and book review space, 15
  criticisms of, 2-3, 5, 6, 19
  and low culture, 65, 66
  nineteenth century, 6

twentieth century, 7, 11, 12
Wyse, Lois, 137

Yale University, 107
Yankelovich, Daniel, 106
Yesterday's Lesson (Isabell), 172
Yglesias, Helen, 141

"Ziplash: A Sexual Libertine Recant" (Jong), 165
"Zipless fuck," 57, 59, 165, 203(n6)